28

Social History of Canada

Michael Bliss, general editor

T. Phillips Thompson (1843-1933), a journalist and author, was one of the leading spokesmen of the Canadian labor and socialist movements for over three decades.

Jay Atherton is chief archivist in the Public Records Division of the Public Archives of Canada.

1886 witnessed the height of a period of violent industrial strife in North America. In that year the eight-hour day movement culminated in Chicago's notorious Haymarket Riot. Both the Trades and Labor Congress of Canada and the American Federation of Labor became firmly established and held their first annual meetings; the Knights of Labor were at their peak. Unemployment, worker dislocation, and social unrest were focusing public attention on the abuses of the emerging industrial system. Those with power – the big business monopolies – were exploiting those without, and the various levels of government seemed unable or unwilling to intervene. It was all too evident that wealth and progress were for the few, and poverty and alienation were for the many. What were the causes of this inequality, and how could the balance be restored? This was the 'Labor Question' that engaged the imagination of so many writers in the 1880s, men such as Henry George, Laurence Gronlund, Edward Bellamy – and T. Phillips Thompson. Thompson was one of the leading spokesmen of the Canadian labor and socialist movements for over three decades. This book presents a distillation of his thought in a constructive critique of the American political and economic system. Time has proved Thompson a prophet: much of what he advocated in *The Politics of Labor* has come to pass in the years since 1886.

APPENDIXES

1/FOUR ARTICLES WRITTEN FOR 'THE PALLADIUM
  OF LABOR'
2/THE LABOR REFORM SONGSTER

The politics of labor

T. PHILLIPS THOMPSON

WITH AN INTRODUCTION BY JAY ATHERTON

UNIVERSITY OF TORONTO PRESS
Toronto and Buffalo

University of Toronto Press 1975
Toronto and Buffalo
Printed in Canada

Library of Congress Cataloging in Publication Data

Thompson, Thomas Phillips
    The politics of labor

    (The Social History of Canada; 28 ISSN 0085-6207)
    Reprint of the 1887 ed. published by Belford, Clark, New York;
    with new introd. and appendixes.
    Includes bibliographical references.
    Appendixes (p.   ): 1. Four articles written for the Palladium of
    Labor. 2. The labor reform songster.
    1. Socialism. I. Title.   II. Series.
    HX86.T44 1975   330.9'73'08   75-9924
    ISBN 0-8020-2192-1
    ISBN 0-8020-6270-9 pbk

Social History of Canada 28

This book has been published with the help of a grant from the
Canada Council.

The Politics of Labor was originally published in New York and
Chicago in 1887 by Belford, Clarke & Co., Publishers. The four
'Enjolras' articles reprinted as Appendix 1 were originally published in *The Palladium of Labor* (Toronto) on 22 December
1883, 3 January 1885, 17 October 1885, and 26 December
1885 respectively. *The Labor Reform Songster*, reprinted as
Appendix 2, was originally published in Philadelphia in 1892 by
the Journal of the Knights of Labor Print.

Contents

An introduction

BY JAY ATHERTON

Monopoly, of itself, while an injustice and a wrong to the community by enriching a few individuals at the expense of the whole,
would not necessarily produce the extreme deprivation and suffering
to which large classes are now subject. It is monopoly in the broad
sense of the word, combined with absolute and unrestricted competition among the wage-earners, which causes the result. Monopoly
above and competition below are the upper and nether millstones
between which the toiler is crushed.[1]

THE WORDS ARE THOSE of a Canadian describing the American
labor situation. They were written in 1886, at the height of a period
of violent industrial strife in North America. That year the eight-
hour-day movement culminated in Chicago's notorious Haymarket
Riot. Both the Trades and Labor Congress of Canada and the American Federation of Labor became firmly established and held their
first annual meetings. The Knights of Labor were at their peak.
Unemployment, worker dislocation, and social unrest, resulting from
the business depression that lasted from the Panic of 1873 to the
close of the century, were focusing public attention on the abuses of
the emerging industrial system.[2] Those with power – the big business monopolies – were exploiting those without. Government
seemed unable and unwilling to intervene, often preferring to take
refuge in the commission of enquiry. (The year 1886 also saw the
appointment by the Macdonald government in Ottawa of the Royal
Commission on the Relations of Capital and Labor. It was the eighth
federal commission of enquiry since the beginning of the decade to
investigate questions related to labor.[3]) The all too evident result was
wealth and progress for a few, but poverty and alienation for many
others.

What were the causes of this inequality, and how could the balance be restored? This was 'the Labor Question' that engaged the
imagination of a number of writers in the 1880s, 'propagandists who
hoped to alter conditions by rousing the conscience of the nation.'[4]
Henry George was one such journalist who had searched for a solution, a panacea, for the troubles. He found it in the familiar concept
of land reform. George's *Progress and Poverty* (1880) was an immediate sensation in Britain, the United States, and Canada. For many
who read it, land monopoly stood revealed as the prime cause and
land reform the sole remedy for society's ills.[5] In 1884 another

journalist, Laurence Gronlund, published a diluted Marxist critique of industrial capitalism, under the title *The Cooperative Commonwealth*.[6] Four years later the most famous work of all appeared. Edward Bellamy's *Looking Backward* depicted the gradual evolution of a socialist utopia, devoid of industrial strife, with equality and happiness for all. It quickly became the most popular utopian novel ever written in America.[7] Phillips Thompson's contribution to this debate, *The Politics of Labor*, appeared in 1887. A constructive minor critique of the American political-economic system, it combined the essential elements found in all three, especially Henry George and Edward Bellamy.

Thomas Phillips Thompson was born in 1843 in Newcastle-on-Tyne, England.[8] His family was Quaker in religious persuasion, which probably accounts for the strong social conscience, interest in social justice, and belief in universal brotherhood that characterized much of his writing. Emigrating to Canada in 1857, the Thompsons took up residence briefly in Belleville, then moved on to Lindsay and, later, St Catharines, where young Phillips studied law and was admitted to practice. Finding the life of a lawyer filled with frustrations and unacceptable compromises, he abandoned it for a career in journalism (a course of action also followed a decade later by both Laurence Gronlund and Edward Bellamy[9]). Thompson's first position was with the St Catharines *Post* during the middle 1860s. While with the *Post* he covered the Fenian Raids of 1866 and wrote his first separately published work – a pamphlet entitled *The Future Government of Canada*, in which he refuted Thomas D'Arcy McGee's proposal for a monarchical form of government and advocated in its place a 'British American Independent Republic.'[10] Already, at the age of twenty-three, Thompson was exhibiting republican sympathies and a somewhat radical independence of spirit.

In 1867 Thompson moved to Toronto and a position as a police reporter for the *Daily Telegraph*. The activities of the police court in the growing metropolis provided ample material for his impish sense of humor, which he was able to use to even greater advantage following his switch (around 1870) to the Toronto *Mail*. While he was with the *Mail* Thompson began producing a weekly column of political commentary under the pseudonym 'Jimuel Briggs, D.B., of Coboconk

University.' Light, irreverent pieces of satiric nonsense, filled with puns and humorous asides, the columns (in the form of letters from an imaginary Toronto correspondent of the equally imaginary 'Coboconk *Irradiator*') flowed easily from his pen. Thompson gained a fair amount of fame and popularity through the Jimuel Briggs personality, even delivering a few public lectures in that guise.[11]

In January 1874, Thompson left the *Mail* to join forces with a local publisher, Henry E. Smallpiece, in the founding of *The National*, an unofficial, 'independent' spokesman for the principles of the Canada First Movement.[12] Gradually, however, the paper's editorial position on social issues swung away from Canada First. Disenchantment increased to the point of a formally announced break in July 1875. Thereafter *The National* exhibited growing critical interest in immigration and labor questions, at one point advocating abolition of Canadian government immigration offices in Britain and Europe. The cause of this change may be surmised easily, for the middle 1870s were years of widespread economic depression. The poverty and inequality that Thompson saw around him must have pricked his social conscience and activated a swing to the left – a not uncommon phenomenon in the later years of the decade.[13] For either editorial or financial reasons, Thompson and Smallpiece relinquished their ownership and control of *The National* in September 1875. Shortly thereafter the journal merged with another and for all practical purposes temporarily ceased to exist. Early the following year Thompson moved to Boston to join the staff of the *Traveller*. In addition to becoming its literary editor and assistant editor, over the next three years he wrote for a number of other North American journals, including *American Punch*, the Boston *Courier*, and *The National*, which began appearing again in its old format and vigor in July 1878. Prior to its becoming thoroughly embroiled in the Canadian election campaign of 1878 on behalf of Sir John A. Macdonald's national policy, *The National* managed to print a number of columns from the Boston *Traveller* on socialism and reform topics, probably written by Thompson.[14]

Returning to Toronto in 1879, Thompson obtained a post on the editorial staff of the *Mail* and, the following year, a similar position with *The Globe*.[15] The latter in 1881 dispatched him to Ireland as a special correspondent to cover Charles Stuart Parnell's land campaign. His thirty letters from Ireland, which appeared in *The Globe* regularly throughout November and December and were reprinted together as a special supplement in January 1882, attracted considerable attention. While in Ireland, Thompson met another, rather better known, newspaper correspondent – Henry George. Whether or not Thompson had read *Progress and Poverty* by this time is unclear. However, there is no doubt that George's personality and ideas created a lasting impression on him.[16]

In November 1883, Thompson joined the staff of *The Toronto News*, under its new proprietor and editor, Edmund E. Sheppard. Energetic, intelligent, and independent of spirit, Sheppard was, in the words of a journalist who worked with him a decade after Thompson, 'the most picturesque figure in the Canadian literary and journalistic Bohemia' of the 1880s. Although born in Canada, he had had some education in the eastern United States and had worked as a cowboy and stagecoach driver in the southwest.[17] 'A natural rebel against all conventions,' Sheppard turned the *News* into a popular spokesman for progressive reform. The journal's platform included such planks as 'national independence,' universal manhood suffrage, the election of the governor general, provincial lieutenant governors, and all local officials, legislation to 'make the existence of a permanent office-holding class impossible,' and the issuing of all paper money by the federal government instead of by the banks.[18] The *News* also supported the Knights of Labor, then reaching their zenith. However, Thompson's association with the Knights was not limited to his employment with the *News*. Coincidentally with his move to that journal, he began producing articles for the Knights' chief Canadian organ, *The Palladium of Labor*, published weekly in Hamilton from December 1883 until early 1887. Thompson wrote a front-page column for the *Palladium*, over the *nom de plume* 'Enjolras,' in which he vigorously held forth on the various questions of concern to labor reformers. The Knights advocated a scheme of producer and consumer co-operatives to supplant the wage system, peaceful agitation and arbitration rather than strikes in labor disputes, land reform, nationalization of public utilities (beginning with the railroads), and a number of other reforms. Thompson especially sympathized with their search for a more equitable and moral system to replace capitalism. He also agreed with their belief in the necessity of educating the working classes, to prepare them for the millenium.[19] Joining Local Assembly 7814 when it was formed in

Toronto in July 1886, Thompson was chosen its delegate to the
convention of the Canadian Trades and Labor Congress in September. At that meeting he spoke in favor of a compulsory arbitration
resolution, moved a resolution demanding legislation to forbid the
establishment of private police forces, and supported a motion calling for the abolition of the Senate.[20]

A philosophy closely related to that of the Knights of Labor was
theosophism, with its mystic conception of universal brotherhood
and belief in the necessity of slow, inevitable progress. In fact, the
two movements were related, religious mysticism having played an
important role in the evolution of the principles of the Knights.[21]
The influence of theosophism on Thompson himself was no less
significant, for its precepts contained the roots of his socialism. 'The
one essential truth which all Theosophists must accept,' he wrote in
1903, 'is the principle of human brotherhood.' In addition, they
subscribed to the Buddhist principle of karma, 'in other words of
cause and effect.'[22] Permanent reforms could not be achieved
through mere political change alone; the actual ideals and standards
of society would have to be altered as well, something which could
be accomplished only gradually over a considerable period of time
through education. The theosophist, therefore, shunned the idea of
radical, rapid change, believing rather

in the continuity of development, and that every act or aspiration
for the upbuilding of individual character or the betterment of society has its sure, inevitable result in exact proportion to the impetus
put forth. He of all men ought logically to be a Socialist and to bring
to the [Socialist] movement the steadying, staying power of a deep-rooted conviction, and firm self-purpose, which looks far beyond
mere temporary triumphs or spasmodic enthusiasms, and knows no
doubt or depression fully realizing that under the great law of Karma
society like the individual attains precisely that development for
which it fits itself.[23]

Thompson expressed his evolving socialism during the middle
eighties in his 'Enjolras' articles, a number of public lectures, and a
book.[24] *The Politics of Labor* was published in 1887, thanks largely
to the efforts of Henry George, who, in addition to reading Thompson's draft over for him, found him a publisher in New York.[25] Many
of the ideas in the book appeared again the next year between the

covers of Edward Bellamy's immensely successful *Looking Backward*. Evidently, contemporary currents of thought (especially theosophism) were strong enough to produce like results in the work of
two similar commentators writing at about the same time, although
we have no evidence that they had actually met. In fact, neither
book was particularly original. Each was a restatement of elements
of popular reformist ideology.[26]

In December 1890, Thompson became editor of *The Labor Advocate*, a new journal issued in the interests of the Toronto laboring
classes by the Grip Publishing Company. Under his editorship the
Advocate vigorously supported a number of local reforms, especially
public ownership of the Toronto street railway franchise. Unfortunately, the paper was not a financial success, with the result that it
ceased publication in October 1891, barely ten months after its
founding.[27] Meanwhile, Thompson had become an ardent exponent
of Edward Bellamy's 'Nationalism,' taking an active role in the activities of the Toronto Nationalist Association in the early nineties and
serving as its president for the 1893-4 term. His name appeared
several times in the columns of Bellamy's journal *The New Nation.*[28]

Thompson was becoming more widely known in the Toronto
labor community. A certain amount of local publicity had attended
the publication of *The Politics of Labor* in 1887, his editorship of
The Labor Advocate, and the appearance in 1892 of his *Labor Reform Songster* – a collection of inspirational songs for the working-
man, published by the Knights of Labor and reprinted as Appendix
2 to this volume.[29] His activities in the local Nationalist and Single
Tax associations increased his prominence. Also in 1892 he ran (unsuccessfully) as a Labor Reform candidate in a provincial by-election
in Toronto (a feat which he repeated early the next year), and
participated actively in a 'Conference on Social Problems' in December. In his two election campaigns he espoused the nationalization of
industries, land reform, and adoption of the initiative and referen-
dum. At the conference he supported the concept of co-operation
and delivered a lecture on the sources of and remedy for unemployment.[30] He gained further notoriety early in 1895 when he participated in a controversial debate with another Toronto labor spokesman, Alfred Jury, before the Political Science Association at the
University of Toronto. The immediate cause of the controversy was
the action of the University Council in denying to the Association

the use of the Student's Union Hall for the debate. As the incident occurred during a time of student unrest, however, it was viewed and treated as a part of that unrest.[31]

During the later nineties Thompson seems to have acquired the necessities of life by undertaking various writing assignments for departments in the provincial government. From about 1895 to 1905 he served as one of the writers for the legislature and performed a number of literary and clerical tasks (such as writing the annual reports) for the Bureau of Mines, the Colonization and Forestry Department, and the Bureau of Industries.[32] He also continued to produce items for labor and trade journals and to speak out on labor reform whenever the occasion presented itself.

By 1900 Thompson had gained sufficient reputation as a writer and spokesman for the Toronto labor movement that the federal government appointed him Toronto correspondent of the *Labour Gazette*, which was to be published monthly by the new Department of Labour in Ottawa.[33] During his period in that capacity, Thompson established himself as one of the more able correspondents.and a valuable asset to the Department of Labour. (In 1904, the deputy minister of labour, W.L. Mackenzie King, told the minister, Sir William Mulock, that Thompson 'does his work carefully, and in fact in better form than any [other] correspondent we have.'[34]) He lasted until the defeat of the Laurier administration late in 1911, after which he retired to Oakville. During the first decade of the century, in addition to his part-time work for the Department of Labour, Thompson undertook writing projects for the provincial government, wrote for mining and textile trade journals, and contributed frequent articles to the labor and socialist press. His columns appeared regularly in the Vancouver *Western Clarion* during 1903 and the Toronto *Toiler* in 1904.[35] In 1902 he became secretary and organizer of the Ontario Socialist League. For several years in succession (1904-6) he contested unsuccessfully a seat on the Toronto Board of Education, as a Socialist party candidate.[36]

At the time of his retirement to Oakville in 1912, Thompson was sixty-eight years of age. As a class-conscious socialist, he continued to speak out on issues where he considered injustices had been perpetrated or condoned. As a theosophist, he remained a strong, vocal supporter of the concepts of universal brotherhood and continuity of development. During World War I he assumed an anti-Imperialist, isolationist, pacifist stance, expressed in frequent letters to the editor.[37] Despite blindness which hampered him during the last ten years of his life, he continued to lash out whenever he felt required to do so. Death came, following a stroke, in May 1933. He was then in his ninetieth year.

Thompson developed his ideas for *The Politics of Labor* in his 'Enjolras' articles, four of which are printed as Appendix 1 of this volume. In fact, most of his concepts and phraseology had already appeared in *The Palladium of Labor* before he decided late in 1885 to write the book.[38] The one interesting variation between the two versions is their different literary styles: the vigorous, sarcastic militancy of 'Enjolras' contrasts sharply with the comparatively turgid, serious prose found in the book. The ideas are the same, but the language is not, presumably because Thompson was writing in the one case anonymously for the laboring class and, in the other case, under his own name for a more sophisticated reader.

Thompson's objective was to solve 'the labor question' and thereby ameliorate the social ills that were evident in industrial society. 'The labor question' for Thompson was 'simply the question as to whether America shall in the future be a free democratic land, with equal rights and opportunities, as far as may be, for every citizen – or a country where the many are ruled, as in Europe, by the privileged few.'[39] Since all the evidence seemed to point to the second alternative rather than the first, one had to locate the primary cause of the problem. This Thompson found and expressed in his 'upper and nether millstone' concept, first stated in *The Palladium of Labor* in 1884: 'monopoly is the upper and competition the nether millstone between which Labor is crushed and ground.'[40] Monopoly not only decreased the working man's pay; it also lessened his purchasing power by forcing prices up. And the most insidious and oppressive form of monopoly was that of private land ownership: 'Labor pays in increased rents, increased prices, and diminished wages the tribute imposed years before by those who "made money" from the augmented value of land.'[41] This burden existed because three things were regarded as commodities, 'to be traded and trafficked in,' that should not be so categorized, namely land, money, and labor.[42] The three products of this injustice were, of course, rent, usury, and profit, each of which deprived some men of the full value of their labor and gave to others value not justly earned. In this argument, Thompson shows clearly the influence of Henry George. The concept of capitalists living off the toil of others was central to most labor commentaries of the day.[43]

The problem thus defined, what was the solution? For Thompson it lay not in revolution, but in evolution. 'A work of such magnitude,' he wrote, 'is not to be accomplished by any one man or any generation of men. It must essentially be a work of slow and gradual accomplishment' — 'a slow, a very slow, toilsome, uphill process.'[44] However, he was steadfast in his optimism as to the final, inevitable result. 'Fortunately for the future of the race human nature is progressive and susceptible of improvement. Had it been otherwise we should never have risen above barbarism.'[45] Here we see evidence of the Darwinian threads of late nineteenth-century thought, as well as the influence of theosophism. Similarly optimistic currents came to Thompson through American Fourierism and early Marxist socialism, the most recent example having been Laurence Gronlund's *Co-operative Commonwealth* published in 1884. A product of the early transition in the socialist movement from utopianism to class struggle, Gronlund's work was intended 'to demonstrate that society was moving inevitably toward socialism, and that each individual was consciously or unconsciously contributing his mite toward the ultimate consummation.'[46]

According to Thompson, the solution of the problem would require a change in the character of government and in the attitude of the laboring classes toward government:

We have to create a revolution in public opinion before we can hope to revolutionize the system. — We have to change not only men's formally expressed beliefs, but their aspirations and desires — to eradicate this deep-rooted selfishness begotten of competition and to instill in its place a love for humanity and a strong sense of justice.[47]

Thompson disputed the traditional political economy of competition, urging in its place a 'new political economy' based on co-operation. 'The wrong aims of the present political economy,' he said in 1884, 'should be abandoned, and the role of legislation should be that of "the greatest good to the greatest number." '[48] Society had outgrown the Jeffersonian, 'laissez-faire' philosophy of government.

The collectivist tendency, he wrote, 'breaks down the old mediaeval idea of government as a power aloof from and above the people, paving the way for the acceptance of the new radical idea, that government should be nothing more than a committee delegated by the people to attend to their business with as little unnecessary ceremonial or formality as may be.'[49] The solution, therefore, lay in 'the extension of the powers and functions of government to include the organization of industry.'[50] Such an action would be a natural outgrowth of the existing 'one-sided socialism'[51] and the increasing rationalization of industry caused by the growth of monopolies: 'The organization of modern commerce and industry is so complete, and the different departments so dependent on each other, that every fresh extension of the sphere of government control would suggest and justify a further inclusion of some similar or closely allied industry.'[52] (This is a similar argument to that at the core of Edward Bellamy's *Looking Backward*, that the tendency toward industrial monopoly simply facilitated the nationalization of industries.) Such a change could only be accomplished through labor solidarity, for

the solidarity of labor means the annihilation of capitalism. When all who toil are practically unanimous in demanding the social reorganization of industry, and the recognition of labor-value as the only right to subsistence, the day of those who claim the lion's share of production, as possessors merely, will be over.[53]

The result would be the solution of all other social problems:

Labor, in working out its own emancipation, will regenerate the world. In solving the labor problem, the other vexed questions which have so long pressed for solution will be settled. All the various forms of social and moral evil which afflict humanity are traceable to caste-rule and the spoliation of the laboring class. War, intemperance, prostitution, and crime are due either to the greed begotten of capitalism, the selfishness, arrogance, and luxury of the moneyed and influential class, or the abject necessity, ignorance, and debasement of the disinherited. With social and political equality established, and every man and woman secured in the enjoyment of the full earnings of their labor, the motives which prompt and the conditions which foster these evils would largely cease.[54]

How successful was *The Politics of Labor*? It seems to have received many notices in the press, especially in labor journals, but sales were small. (The publisher warned Thompson about this shortly after the book's appearance.[55]) In other words, it had no popular impact, and, thus judged, was a failure. However, the Toronto *Mail* literary critic thought that the work was 'deserving of a careful perusal, as the effort of a man evidently in dead earnest to find a solution for one of the great questions of the day.'[56] The reviewer in *The Globe* found it 'interesting and valuable' and pointed to the fact that Thompson, unlike many other writers on the labor question, looked at the subject from a laboring class viewpoint.[57] Hector Charlesworth later referred to it as 'a very able book'; and Mackenzie King in 1900 found Thompson's statements 'rather true' though 'sometimes general and of a socialistic flavour . . .'[58]

The influences on Thompson when he wrote *The Politics of Labor* in the winter of 1885-6 were primarily American. In fact, the book is devoted to a discussion of the American economic and political system and is aimed at the American reader. However, it does have interest for students of Canadian social and labor history during the decade of the 1880s. In addition to the obvious fact that the book was written by a Canadian, one should bear in mind that the mechanisms of industrial life in the United States extended into Canada. That is, the industrial system that Thompson described was (and still is) *North* American. Thompson himself wrote in an 'Enjolras' article in 1884 that he was using 'the term "American" in its broad continental sense as including Canadians.'[59] In the 1880s, this was a fairly revolutionary concept, really understood only by the laboring classes. Michael Katz has demonstrated that the 'tramping artisans' described by Eric Hobsbawm as a significant factor in nineteenth-century British society were an equally important North American phenomenon.[60] In an age when neither government controlled migration across the Canadian-American boundary, there was a considerable infusion into Canada of American laborers, bringing with them the current popular American political mythology. One result was the development of republican sympathies as a vital element in labor's protest. Another was the tendency of Canadian workers to look for protection from the various abuses of industrial capitalism (such as the importation of alien 'scab' laborers) in alliance with organized American workers.[61]

In two respects Thompson was prophetic. First, he was clearly in advance of laboring class opinions as to the advantages or disadvantages of the capitalistic system and its socialist alternatives. As professors Craig and Bliss have observed, most Canadian workers in the eighties accepted the conventional wisdom of the National Policy. They did not seriously question the industrial system itself. Such questioning came later in Canada than it did in the United States, largely because industrialization started later and developed more slowly in this country.[62] In addition, Thompson's prophecy of how the capitalist system of the gilded age would gradually change to a socialist one has partially been borne out by subsequent events. With the development of the welfare state in Canada much of what he advocated has transpired.

NOTES

1 T. Phillips Thompson, *The Politics of Labor* (New York 1887) 21-2
2 'Many of the characteristic features of an industrial society [came] into existence, one might say, at one great bound, in the decade of the 1880s.' P.B. Waite, 'Sir Oliver Mowat's Canada: Reflections on an Un-Victorian Society,' in Donald Swainson, ed., *Sir Oliver Mowat's Ontario* (Toronto 1972) 14. On the industrial growth of the 1880s in America see Philip S. Foner, *History of the Labor Movement in the United States* (New York, 1955) II 12-14. Robert H. Wiebe, *The Search for Order, 1877-1920* (New York 1967), gives an excellent summary of the 'strange assortment of symptoms that appeared rather abruptly during the mid-eighties' (p 44). Not to be neglected also is the chapter on 'The Labor Troubles of 1886-87' in Douglas R. Kennedy's published thesis *The Knights of Labor in Canada* (London, Ontario 1956) 57-76, and Fred Landon, 'The Canadian Scene, 1880-1890,' Canadian Historical Association *Annual Report* (1942) 8-11. For a summary of the political attitudes of Canadian labor during the decade see Bernard Ostry, 'Conservatives, Liberals, and Labour in the 1880's,' *Canadian Journal of Economics and Political Science* XXVII (May 1961) 141-61.
3 Russell G. Hann, Gregory S. Kealey, Linda Kealey, and Peter Warrian, *Primary Sources in Canadian Working Class History, 1860-1930* (Kitchener 1973) 153-4

4 Robert H. Bremner, *From the Depths: The Discovery of Poverty in the United States* (New York 1956) 84

5 Henry George, *Progress and Poverty* (London 1943), Everyman's Library edition. A shorter statement of George's economic theories may be found in his *The Irish Land Question: What it Involves, and How Alone It Can Be Settled; An Appeal to the Land Leagues* (New York 1881). The best biography of Henry George is by Charles Albro Barker, *Henry George* (New York, 1955).

6 Laurence Gronlund, *The Cooperative Commonwealth*, edited by Stow Persons (Cambridge, Mass. 1965) ix-xii

7 Edward Bellamy, *Looking Backward, 2000-1887* (New York 1951). This is the Modern Library edition, which contains an informative introduction by Robert L. Shurter. See also Sylvia Bowman, *The Year 2000; A Critical Biography of Edward Bellamy* (New York 1958).

8 The basic facts about Thompson's career have been taken from a brief biographical article in Henry J. Morgan, ed., *The Canadian Men and Women of the Time* (Toronto 1912) 1097-8; obituaries in the Toronto *Globe, Toronto Daily Star*, and London *Free Press* of 22 May 1933; and the annual editions of the *Toronto City Directory*.

9 Persons, introduction to Gronlund, *The Cooperative Commonwealth* x; Bowman, *The Year 2000* 37-8

10 T. Phillips Thompson, *The Future Government of Canada* (St Catharines 1864)

11 *The National* (Toronto), 19 November 1874, advertised the fact that 'Jimuel Briggs, D.B., the Canadian Humorist, is prepared to make arrangements for the delivery of his entertaining lecture "Experiences of a Bohemian",' which had been 'delivered with great éclat in Toronto . . .'

12 Thompson's departure from *The Mail* was indicated in his last 'Jimuel Briggs' column for that journal, which informed the reader that Briggs had received an appointment as an emigration agent (*Mail*, 17 January 1874). 'A Tribute to Jimuel Briggs' appeared in the form of a letter to the editor of the *Mail* (21 January 1874) from 'The Undersigned' – obviously Thompson.

The platform of the National Association, as printed frequently in *The National*, included: consolidation of the Empire, with Canada having a voice in the negotiation of treaties affecting her interests; closer trade relations with the British West Indies, with a view to

some ultimate political connection; the imposition of protective
tariffs to encourage native industries; an improved militia under the
command of trained Canadian officers; the removal of property
qualifications for members of the House of Commons; the reorganization of the Senate, its members to be chosen by the provinces;
compulsory voting and extension of the franchise; the encouragement of immigration and granting of free homesteads in the public
domain; and 'the pure and economical administration of public
affairs.' *The National* is available on microfilm in the Ontario
Provincial Archives.

13 On the growth of the American socialist movement in the late 1870s
    see Ira Kipnis, *The American Socialist Movement, 1887-1912* (New
    York 1952) 9-11.

14 See the article, 'A Thing Misnamed "Socialism" ' in *The National*, 11
    July 1878. The new *National* was published by Henry Smallpiece
    and edited by A.W. Wright.

15 *Grip* (Toronto) 18 December 1880

16 *The Globe*, Extra, 'The Condition of Ireland,' January 1882, page 8,
    letter XXIX; *Grip*, 29 October 1881, 31 December 1881, 21 January
    1882. On George's tour of the British Isles (November 1881 to Octo-
    ber 1882) see Barker, *Henry George*, chapter 12, pp 341-77. For evi-
    dence of George's influence on Thompson see the latter's articles
    over the pen-name 'Enjolras' in *The Palladium of Labor* (Hamilton),
    11 October 1884, 13 December 1884, 2 May 1885, 9 May 1885, and
    7 August 1886, and the letters from George to Thompson in the
    Phillips Thompson Papers (Public Archives of Canada).

17 Hector Charlesworth, *Candid Chronicles* (Toronto 1925) 72-3

18 *The Toronto News*, 20 December 1883. The first issue of the *News*
    under its new editorship was that of 26 November 1883.

19 Kennedy, *Knights of Labor in Canada* 47-8; Victor Oscar Chan,
    'Canadian Knights of Labor With Special Reference to the 1880's,'
    University of Rochester Canadian Studies Series, No. 17 (Rochester,
    N.Y., ca, 1956; on microcard; originally an MA thesis at McGill
    University 1949); Peter B. Waite, *Canada, 1874-1896; Arduous Des-
    tiny* (Toronto 1971) 178-9. The identification of Thompson as the
    author of the 'Enjolras' articles is based on a comparison of the writ-
    ing style, concepts, and expressions appearing in those articles with
    those in contemporary lectures and other written work by Thomp-
    son (especially *The Politics of Labor*).

20 'The best way to reform the Senate,' he said, 'was to reform it out of existence.' Trades and Labor Congress of Canada, *Proceedings* (1886) 9, 30-1, 35, 40

21 The interconnection between the Knights of Labor and theosophism, and their influences on the reformist philosophies of the 1880s, is best described by Robert H. Wiebe, *The Search for Order*, chapter 3. Kennedy also points out that Uriah Stephens, the founder of the order, was a Quaker who had been educated for the Baptist ministry: 'This religious mysticism largely shaped the principles of the Knights of Labor . . .' Kennedy, *Knights of Labor in Canada* 2

22 'Socialism and Philosophy,' letter to the editor of *The Western Socialist* (Vancouver), 24 April 1903. The work 'karma' is Sanskrit and means 'deed' or 'action.' 'As applied to the action of a conscious being, it is the doctrine that every deed, good or bad, receives due retribution.' *Encyclopaedia Britannica*, 14th edition XIII 283

23 *Western Socialist*, 24 April 1903. For a description of the influence on North American thought of the Darwinian concepts of sequence and consecutive change see Ray Ginger, *Altgeld's America, 1890-1905: The Lincoln Ideal Versus Changing Realities* (Chicago 1965), chapter 14, pp 331-52.

24 Reports of public lectures by Thompson appear in *The Palladium of Labor*, 7 June 1884, 15 February 1885, 26 December 1885, and 7 December 1886.

25 Phillips Thompson Papers, Henry George to Thompson, 6 August 1886

26 'Edward Bellamy . . . was not an original thinker but only a populariser of other men's ideas.' G.D.H. Cole, *Socialist Thought: Marxism and Anarchism, 1850-1890* (London 1954) 361

27 *The Labor Advocate* is available on microfilm in the Library of the Department of Labour, Ottawa.

28 *The New Nation*, 1 August 1891, 28 May 1892, 18 June 1892, 1 October 1892, 22 October 1892, 17 December 1892, 28 January 1893. Documentation on Thompson's activities with the Toronto Nationalist Association is also found in *The Labor Advocate* from its first issue on 5 December 1890 through to what was almost its last, 25 September 1891. Concerning the relationship between theosophism and the nationalist movement spawned by *Looking Backward* see Bowman, *The Year 2000* 119-20.

29 Phillips Thompson, *The Labor Reform Songster* (Philadelphia 1892)

30 On his two election campaigns see *The Globe*, 23 April 1892, 27
    April 1892, and 29 November 1892. The 'Conference on Social
    Problems' was fully covered in *The Globe* of 12 December 1892.
31 *The Toronto Mail* 10, 19, 23, 26, and 28 January 1895. 'Report of
    the Commissioners on the Discipline and Other Matters in the Uni-
    versity of Toronto,' Ontario, *Sessional Papers*, 1896, No. 38, pp
    12-17, 23-6.
32 See the 'Public Accounts for the Province of Ontario' in Ontario,
    Sessional Papers (usually no. 1) for the years 1896 to 1906.
33 On the circumstances surrounding his appointment (by Sir William
    Mulock) see R. MacGregor Dawson, *William Lyon Mackenzie King:
    A Political Biography* I (Toronto 1958) 102, and J.J. Atherton, 'The
    Department of Labour and Industrial Relations, 1900-1911,' MA
    thesis, Carleton University 1972) 95-6.
34 Mackenzie King Papers (Public Archives of Canada), vol. 3, pp 3398-
    3402, King to Sir William Mulock, 5 October 1904.
35 Both journals are available on microfilm in the Library of the De-
    partment of Labour, Ottawa.
36 The list of candidates for the Board of Education in the civic elec-
    tion of January 1895 includes the names of James Simpson, report-
    er, Harry E. Smallpiece, reporter, and Phillips Thompson, journalist
    (*Toronto Daily Star*, 28 December 1904). Both Simpson, a future
    (1906-8) vice-president of the Trades and Labor Congress, and
    Thompson were the candidates of the Ontario Socialist party. A
    copy of the 'Manifesto of Local Toronto, Ontario Socialist Party' for
    that election may be found in the Phillips Thompson Papers.
37 See, for example, *The Globe* of 6 May 1915, 14 January 1916, 30
    June 1916, 27 July 1916, and 29 March 1918.
38 Phillips Thompson Papers, Henry George to Thompson, 4 November
    1885
39 *The Politics of Labor* (hereafter cited as *'Politics'*) 5
40 *The Palladium of Labor* (hereafter cited as *'Palladium'*), 11 October
    1884
41 *Politics* 35
42 Ibid. 40
43 See the 'Enjolras' article of 22 December 1883, reprinted below in
    Appendix 1. For a summary of Henry George's argument, see his
    The Irish Land Question 59.
44 *Politics* 19, 20

45 *Palladium*, 23 February 1884

46 Stow Persons, introduction to Gronlund, *Cooperative Commonwealth* xii. Charles Fourier (1772-1837) was an imaginative French
   social reformer who advocated a utopian society based on producers'
   co-operatives. American Fourierism 'rested on a conception of universal history as the progressive emancipation of the human emotions
   or passions.' Ibid. viii

47 *Palladium*, 17 October 1885. This article is reprinted in its entirety
   below in Appendix 1.

48 Lecture to the Toronto Secular Society, 25 May 1884, reported in
   the *Palladium*, 7 June 1884

49 *Politics* 96. For a description of the legislative processes in Thompson's imagined ideal society, see his 'Enjolras' article of 26 December
   1885, below in Appendix 1.

50 *Palladium*, 3 January 1885. Also reprinted below in Appendix 1.

51 *Politics* 85

52 Ibid. 123

53 Ibid. 175

54 Ibid. 193

55 Phillips Thompson Papers, R.J. Belford to Thompson, 17 November
   [1887]

56 *Toronto Mail*, 2 November 1887

57 *The Globe*, 29 October 1887

58 Hector Charlesworth, *More Candid Chronicles* (Toronto 1928) 72;
   Mackenzie King Papers, Family Papers V, King to John King, 6
   August 1900

59 *Palladium*, 30 August 1884

60 Eric Hobsbawm, *Labouring Men; Studies in the History of Labour*
   (London 1964) 34-63; Michael Katz, 'The People of a Canadian
   City,' *The Canadian Historical Review* LIII (December 1972) 405

61 Russell G. Hann, Gregory S. Kealey, Linda Kealey, and Peter Warrian, introduction to *Primary Sources in Canadian Working Class
   History, 1860-1930* (Kitchener 1973) 11-12

62 Gerald M. Craig, *The United States and Canada* (Cambridge, Mass.
   1968) 165; Michael Bliss, 'Canadianizing American Business: the
   Roots of the Branch Plant,' in Ian Lumsden, ed., *Close the 49th
   Parallel, etc.: The Americanization of Canada* (Toronto 1970) 40

The social history of Canada

MICHAEL BLISS, GENERAL EDITOR

CONTENTS.

I dreamed in a dream, I saw a city invincible to the attacks of the whole
　　of the rest of the earth,
I dreamed that was the new City of Friends,
Nothing was greater there than the quality of robust love—it led the
　　rest,
It was seen every hour in the actions of the men of that city,
And in all their looks and words.

WALT. WHITMAN.

THE POLITICS OF LABOR.

CHAPTER I.

INTRODUCTORY.

For what avail the plough or sail,
Or land or life, if freedom fail ?

EMERSON.

"THE Labor question," as it is called for want of a better
name, is simply the question as to whether America shall in
the future be a free democratic land, with equal rights and
opportunities, as far as may be, for every citizen—or a country
where the many are ruled, as in Europe, by the privileged
few. It is no new question, but a new phase of a very old
one. The rights of Labor are the rights of Man. Within
the last generation a danger to American liberty has manifested itself in the power of wealth concentrated in the hands
of a few, and the disposition to use that power oppressively
and arbitrarily for the further aggrandizement of its possessors
and the virtual enslavement of the mass. Apart from this
conscious voluntary action on the part of the great money and
railroad kings, the natural result of the increase of population
under our existing social system is to intensify the pressure of
competition, to make opportunities less equal, and to widen
the chasm between rich and poor.

America is no longer the land of promise for the down-
trodden of the Old World. The old-time boast that certain prosperity and success awaited every honest, industrious, and thrifty man who, dissatisfied with the cramping and

hopeless conditions of European life, made his home upon our shores, has been sadly falsified by the experience of recent years. We have become habituated to the idea of a chronic pauperism—a permanently outcast class, once imagined to be an impossibility on the free soil of America. And, which is perhaps the most ominous sign of all, there has been a gradual degeneracy of public opinion, partly owing to European influences, partly to the social changes which are taking place; so that these things are not regarded as utterly antagonistic to the spirit of democratic institutions and inconsistent with and in the end fatal to liberty itself.

Because this danger comes from a new direction, because it is closely associated with undertakings such as the great railway and telegraph enterprises and the development of our manufactures and commerce, which have built up the material prosperity of the country as a whole, the public have been blind to its real significance. Under the influence of democratic traditions and the memories of the revolutionary struggle, the vigilance of those who jealously sought to guard American liberty from assault was directed without rather than within. Monarchy, aristocracy, the influence of foreign gold, the intrigues of European statesmen, jealous of the phenomenal growth of the giant republic, have been not unnatural objects of suspicion, while the process of sapping free institutions by striking at their tap-root—the independence and selfhood of the citizen—was going on rapidly without objection or protest save from an uninfluential few. Economic formulas and political rules of action inherited from an age the requirements of which were widely different from those of our time, are largely responsible for this slowness to recognize industrial evils as coming within the sphere of legislative amelioration. The maxim that "the best government is that which governs least" was excellent when population was sparse and scattered, when land was to be had for the asking, and men's wants were simple and for the most part supplied by themselves or their immediate neighbors. It is a misleading anachronism in these days of steam and electricity, of complicated and clashing interests, of vast wealth and abject poverty, of giant corporations and swollen city populations, dependent for their very existence on the working of the social mechanism of exchange and transportation. The framers of the American constitution were wise in their day. It is no discredit to their memory to say that they were not omnis. cient, and that by no possible exercise of human sagacity could they have foreseen the revolution in industry and commerce which has since taken place, or provided against the social abuses and dangers accompanying it. Fidelity to their teaching and example demands not the blind perpetuation of an outgrown system because they adopted it as best suited to the needs of their time, but rather that the questions of to-day should be dealt with in their spirit—resolutely faced and grappled with as they would have faced and grappled with them.

When Oliver Cromwell was at the height of his power as Protector of the Commonwealth of England, an anonymous pamphlet appeared under the title of "Killing no Murder" which struck terror even into that strong sagacious soul by its menacing invective. "Shall we, " asked the writer, " who would not suffer the lion to invade us, tamely stand and be devoured by the wolf?"

That is the question which now confronts the people of the American continent. Will the nation that defied kingly tyranny and overthrew the slaveholding aristocracy, tamely submit to see their institutions perverted, their blood-bought freedom destroyed, and a system of the meanest and most hateful class-supremacy established upon its ruins?

To all human appearance we are on the verge of a great crisis. Political freedom cannot long co-exist with industrial serfdom. The new wine of Democracy cannot be put into the old bottles of social inequality and caste privilege without disaster.

The industrial revolution has already begun. Though the issues as yet are far from being clearly defined, or the lines which will finally divide the contestants in the coming struggle

drawn with any degree of precision, Labor has had its Bleeding Kansas and its Harper's Ferry many times over in the
armed conflicts between the desperate and starving working-
men and the mercenary cohorts of capitalism, which are now of
such frequent recurrence that they attract but little attention.
It has its Lloyd Garrisons and Wendell Phillipses of the press
and platform, whose pleading for justice and exposition of
right, however forcibly and eloquently urged, are as contemptu-
ously pooh-poohed by the sleek and shallow optimists, and
the wealthy and well-to-do classes who create public opinion,
as were the protests of their predecessors against chattel
slavery. And latterly the question has taken on a new phase
by the appearance, in the forum of public discussion, of a
numerous and influential class of professed sympathizers with
Labor, who preach compromise and conciliation—who propose
palliatives, mutual concessions, and the alleviation of the
symptoms of the social malady. Actuated no doubt by the best
motives, but ludicrously ignorant of the real causes of poverty
and suffering among the wage-workers, they propound such
maxims as " Labor and Capital allies, not enemies," " Property has its duties as well as its rights, " and urge employers
to treat their working-people justly, to refrain from taking
advantage of the iron law of competition, to keep up the rate
of wages and " make work " in slack times rather than discharge their employés—advice as utterly futile, even though
it were followed, to permanently abate the evils of a bad
system, as the kindly treatment of slaves by many of their
masters was to justify negro slavery.

The very form in which these conciliatory teachings are
epitomized shows how far we have unconsciously drifted from
genuine Democracy. " Capital "—property is spoken of as a
distinct force and factor in social organization—a sort of distinct estate of the realm as they would say in England, with
a status of its own apart from the great body of the commonwealth. Dead, inert matter, supposed to endow its owner
with other rights, duties, and prerogatives than those attaching
to him as a man and a citizen !

Change the phrase and the undemocratic character of the assumption that property or capital, as such, ought to be regarded as a distinct interest apart from, if not superior to, labor will be at once apparent. "Rank has its duties as well as its rights." "Aristocracy and labor allies, not enemies." The complete incongruity of the idea with the fundamental principles of Democracy strikes one at the first glance. Such an utterance would excite the strongest opposition as a reactionary sentiment entirely at variance with the spirit of free institutions. Yet what is "capital," when the word is used in the sense above implied, but the aristocracy of money?

No! Property has neither rights nor duties! Labor and capital are not and ought not to be "allies"; because capital is merely the thing created by labor; the instrument which should be under its control, not the force to direct it.

It is necessary, in order to have a clear understanding of the proper relations between labor and capital, to discriminate between capital as an instrument and capitalism as a force. Many of the arguments by which the existing industrial system is supported are simply a play upon words, "capital" being used in a double sense. Primarily it signifies those accumulations of the product of labor used for further production. Factory buildings, machinery, iron ore, raw cotton, seed wheat, threshing machines, these are all forms of capital as well as the money in the bank which the employer draws to pay his workingmen their wages. No one doubts the value or, practically speaking, the necessity of capital, in these and like forms, to industrial progress. But "capital," as the term is ordinarily used in politico-economical discussion, implies a great deal more than this. When men speak of the rights of capital, the conflict between capital and labor, etc., they refer to the power which the possession or control of capital gives to a small minority of the community of regulating how much labor shall receive of what it produces—to the special interest of the accumulator of labor products in the result of further productive industry. They quibble on the word capital, sometimes using it in the material and strictly correct sense when they wish to prove how helpless labor is without it, and on the admitted necessity of capital as an instrument and a creation, basing their argument for the necessity of capital as a controlling force and a creator.

Capital, properly so called, is a beneficent auxiliary to Labor in the work of production. Capitalism, or the control by means, firstly, of monopolizing resources and, secondly, of competition among workers, which the possessors of capital exercise over the distribution of products and the general regulation of industry, is a wrong, a usurpation, and a growing menace to popular freedom.

Labor is just as much interested in the maintenance of capitalism, that is to say, the supremacy of capital, as the slave was in the perpetuation of the slave power.

A large class of superficial observers, who, as long as it was possible, ignored the prevalent feeling of dissatisfaction among the working people, now seek to belittle it. They do not believe that any crisis is approaching—that the deep-seated unrest of those upon whom the competitive system presses hardly has any special significance. " It has always been so," they tell us. " It is the old story—as old as human society itself. It is natural that as America takes on more and more the condition of older countries, the volume of poverty should increase and its cry be more loudly raised. But there is no reason to suppose that the labor movement will lead to any other result than the chronic agitations among the working classes of the Old World. All old countries have their periods of social disquietude and upheaval. We must expect these phenomena, but they do not necessarily imply an industrial revolution."

The study of history is frequently misleading. Those who attempt to " unlock the future's portal with the past's blood-rusted key," and to reason by analogies drawn from history, are apt to leave out of account the factors of the problem which are of later growth, to overlook the changed conditions which render the parallel incomplete and deceptive. The result of the present agitation cannot be inferred from the familiar examples of the uprisings headed by Jack Cade and Wat Tyler, the peasants' war in Germany, the Jacquerie, or the French Revolution. The book-learned ignorance of those who have read a great deal more than they have thought, which assumes that, because in the past labor agitations and popular upheavals have not secured any permanent, satisfactory adjustment of the question, no such adjustment is possible, loses sight of three important respects in which modern and especially American social unrest is unlike all historical examples.

1. The discontent of our day is an educated discontent. Owing to universal free education, the American working-man has at all events the rudiments of a common-school education. He reads the newspaper even if he reads nothing else, and brings a shrewd, keen-witted intelligence to bear upon every fact or opinion which has any direct relation to his position and livelihood. The wonderful enterprise and ever-broadening scope of the modern press enlarge the circle of his ideas and sympathies. He learns something of the great truth of the mutual dependence on each other of the different forms of industry and the workings of the mechanism of exchange and transit. He begins to understand that the "Labor question" is not simply a difference between himself and his employer as to the amount which he ought to receive as wages, but that there are a hundred other considerations entering into the subject, apart from his employer's ability or willingness to comply with his demands or his own power to enforce them by combination. If he be an intelligent, thoughtful man he is able to trace the various causes of social and industrial evils, to know the why and the wherefore of the growing inequalities which exist. He knows how he is robbed and by whom. The coal-miners of western Pennsylvania, for instance, receive wages according to a sliding-scale based upon the selling price of the coal at Pittsburg. Every miner consequently studies the market reports and watches intently the fluctuations of price, not only at the trade center, but at remoter points, as the barometer which indicates the rise or fall of his scanty wages. This is a training in itself more valuable than the theoretical teaching of half a

dozen professors of political economy. He understands **how** his position is affected by the relation between demand **and** supply. He knows almost to a cent just what proportion **of** the price paid by the consumer comes to him as wages **and** what goes into the pockets of mine operators, railroad companies, and wholesale and retail dealers, and can trace the effect of rings and deals among these classes upon prices and wages. The cotton operative in Fall River or Lowell, who can hardly keep body and soul together on the miserable pittance received in that highly-protected, but most wretchedly paid, of American industries ; the street-railway conductor whose exhausting hours allow him barely time for the animal requirements of food and sleep ; though they are robbed are no longer robbed in the dark. The profits and the dividends of the wealthy corporations employing them are published in the newspapers. The wage-workers know that the reason why they are poor is because so large a share of their earnings goes to make others rich. The saving, industrious mechanic who has, by dint of hard toil and frugality, scraped together a few hundred dollars in the hope of becoming his own landlord, and finds that owing to the high price at which land is held the purchase is not within his means, sees the speculator grow prosperous by the system that keeps him poor. He reads year after year of the increase of rents, and is made familiar with the growth of what is really a landed aristocracy—a class of enormously wealthy idlers whose resources are wrung from industry in the shape of a continuously increasing burden on the occupants of land. The American press gives a degree of publicity to the actions of prominent men, the doings of important corporations and syndicates, and the movements which influence legislation unknown in any other country. When a man becomes either sufficiently wealthy or sufficiently prominent in political or business affairs to attract general interest, his every movement is scrutinized by the watchful eye of the reporter or special correspondent, "set in a notebook, learned and conned by rote," and blazoned forth in the newspaper. If a millionaire makes a large investment, gives a banquet, puts up a new mansion, or takes a journey, the insatiable public demand full particulars, and his purposes are everywhere canvassed and criticized. If a syndicate or capitalist enters the stock market, buys a mine or a cattle ranch, corners pork or petroleum, or makes a political deal at Washington or Albany, the remorseless interviewer discloses the whole transaction. No important move in political, financial, or social affairs can now be made without becoming known to a nation of newspaper readers. Matters which in Europe would be done in a corner and never become known beyond a select circle, are the common topics of the readers of our one-cent journals. The tendency of this publicity is to throw light on the methods by which industry is defrauded, to educate the mass in a knowledge of the causes of poverty, and to suggest to thinking minds the adequate remedies.

How different was the condition in this respect of the European artisan or peasant, whose blind and desperate struggles against oppression are referred to as prototypes of the modern labor movement! Ignorant and untutored, his knowledge of the world was narrowed to his immediate surroundings; whatever in the way of instruction he received inculcated content with his lot and submission to his superiors. Inequality of conditions he accepted as a matter of course—a feature of a divinely ordained system under which kings and lords, priests and landowners, were born to rule and to enjoy the good things of life, while he was born to toil and endure "in that station of life to which it had pleased God to call him," as the Episcopal catechism has it. To him it seemed perfectly natural that society should be divided into classes and grades, and that the higher class should have a profusion of comforts and luxuries without anxiety or labor. He took his place uncomplainingly as an inferior. It was not inequality which he resented, but absolute privation. If the great truth that all men have equal rights dawned at intervals upon some bolder and more enlightened minds, it was but the dire physical necessities of the mass which gave their teachings a temporary acceptance.

It was the cravings of hunger and the passion for revenge of men driven mad by oppression which steeled their hearts and nerved their arms; not the clear, intelligent perception of the causes of their misery.

2. The American working-class possess political power, and are coming to the determination to use it in their own interests. The means of an ample and absolute redress of every wrong is within their own hands. That they have not hitherto availed themselves of it to any extent is due to a variety of causes. Among the principal may be enumerated the strength of old party associations and lines of cleavage based upon past issues, the force of the *laissez faire* tradition, difference of opinion as to the course to be pursued, dependence upon political nostrums, palliatives, and trivial concessions by politicians to " capture the labor vote," and bribery and intimidation exercised by employers. The old school of Democracy were apt to look upon the ballot as an end rather than a means, to imagine that all the social problems, if not solved, were placed in the way of solution by manhood suffrage. We are only just beginning to realize that the franchise is, after all, merely an instrument and not intrinsically a cure-all. Unless it be used honestly and intelligently its mere possession is not only no benefit but a positive detriment; as it enables corrupt and self-seeking rulers to do in the name of the people actions which an irresponsible non-elective government might shrink from.

Labor is just awakening to a dim consciousness of its political strength. Hitherto, like a shorn and blinded Samson, it has ground in the prison-house of partyism, the mock and sport of its despoilers. The time approaches when the aroused giant will put forth his long wasted energies and level to the dust the strongholds of oppression.

3. Never before in the world's history was there any parallel to the thoroughness of organization which now obtains among the laboring classes of America. The idea of the solidarity of Labor has taken firm root. The old trade unions, admirable in their way as a step in advance, and temporarily useful

as a defence against acts of oppression on the part of individual employers, though powerless to deal with the deep-
seated and widespread causes of social disquiet, are rapidly
being superseded by or merged into more comprehensive
organizations—the order of the Knights of Labor, trades
federations, central labor unions, and similar bodies. Their
design is to weld labor into a compact mass, and to confront
capitalism with the locked shields and levelled lances of a
Pyrrhic phalanx instead of leaving the isolated bodies to be
beaten in detail.

Based on the principle that " an injury to one is the concern of all," this newer form of labor organization seeks to
deal with the concentrated and organized power of capitalism
by uniting those whose common interests and common rights
are menaced by its encroachments. They are looking more
and more to the ultimate causes of the subjection of labor, and
less to the relations between the working-man and his immediate employer, which were all that the old trade unions
took account of. The leaders and the more intelligent members
of these bodies see very clearly that reformatory measures, to
be effective, must be co-extensive with the wide-reaching
agencies and influences which operate adversely to Labor.
Realizing that the great productive, commercial, financial, and
transportation interests are firmly linked and interlaced together in a vast and complicated network closely allied with
the controlling influences in politics, they understand that
the struggles of small and isolated bands of workers against
special local grievances are as futile as the resistance of a
tribe of Indians to the advancing outposts of settlement. In
either case a temporary victory may be won. But just as
surely as the onward march of civilization, the immense
slowly moving force behind the pioneer and the squatter, in
the end drives out and exterminates the savage, so the capitalistic system, despite an occasional repulse at the immediate
point of contact, ultimately hems round, outflanks, and by indirect and almost imperceptible advances weakens the power
of resistance of the worker, and finally crushes him down to a
lower standard of living.

The organization of labor on a large scale for protective purposes is the natural result of its more perfect organization industrially. When men of the same trade are massed together by the thousand; when single establishments have an army of employés under a minute and thorough system of discipline and organization, the circumstances are obviously more favorable to combination among working-men for their own interests than when shops and factories were small and widely scattered. The common interest is much more apparent; the opportunities for intimate acquaintance, for interchange of opinions, for frequent gathering and discussion are far greater. The whole matter is infinitely simplified. Combination among capitalists tends to abolish the last lingering belief that labor and capitalism have interests in common. When competition between employers had full swing there was a certain foundation for this idea. Whatever the points of disagreement between employers and men, each shop or factory, considered as a unit, had an *esprit de corps*. When one was trying to undersell the other or turn out goods more quickly to meet the demand, the spirit of rivalry between one set of employés and the other naturally militated to some extent against union among laborers. There was of course the ever-present discontent with an arrangement under which capital drew the lion's share of the product, but the community of interest, as against the competing establishments, was a powerful counteracting influence. The employer's ever-ready argument, " How can I raise wages or shorten hours without placing myself at a disadvantage ? " was much more plausible and effective than it is at present, when " combination, not competition" is the watchword among employers. Manufacturers combine to fix selling prices and limit production. Mining operators secure themselves against competition by regulating the output and the price. The great railroad interests, by means of pooling arrangements, amalgamations, and leases, are continually being concentrated in fewer hands. Everywhere the working-man sees going on around him the same process not merely of accumulating wealth, but the welding together, as with links of steel, of the forces of capital under the mastery of which the industrial system becomes an enormous machine. The organization and concentration of capitalism thus gives the impulse, sets the example, and removes the obstacles to organization and concentration of labor.

These considerations ought to convince every thoughtful student of the problem, that the labor question, as it now presents itself, has so little in common with past phases of popular discontent or outbreak, which may seem to present a superficial resemblance to it in some particulars, that history affords no clue to the probable issue.

We are living in a transition period. The influences above enumerated as placing American working-men in a specially favorable position for securing their rights, have only begun to operate in the direction of social reconstruction—in some of their phases they have been distinctly antagonistic. "Knowledge comes, but wisdom lingers." Education, for instance, while immensely increasing the power of the working-class for effective combination, if perverted by the inculcation of the untruths and half-truths of bourgeois political economy, is a hindrance rather than a help. Political power, if misdirected to the furtherance of the ends of partisans who are the tools of capitalism, is worse than wasted; because, in the first place, it lends the authority of the popular vote to the usurpations of monopoly; and secondly, because by raising false cries and rallying the people into opposing parties divided on trivial or extinct issues, it diverts their attention from questions of paramount importance. The comparison between the position of the American laborer as affected by education, the ballot, and organization, and that of the toilers elsewhere and in other times, refers to the possibilities suggested by the possession of these powers—not to the slight and temporary ameliorations of his condition hitherto secured by their means.

To direct these forces aright—to secure unity of aim and harmony in methods among all who realize the supreme urgency of the labor problem—to indoctrinate the masses with large and comprehensive views of the causes of industrial

2

evils and their remedies—to substitute for a blind unreasoning sense of personal wrong and the desire for individual advancement the loftier conception of a system based on justice
and equal rights to all—to arouse the deadened intellects and
the torpid consciences of the comfortable class, drugged by
the sophistries of a misleading political economy, appealing
to their selfish interests—to regenerate the whole tone and
temper of public opinion and bring it to bear upon the forces
of capitalism in their thousandfold ramifications through every
fiber of national life, to the end " that government of the
people, by the people, and for the people may not perish from
the earth "—such is the task which confronts the Labor Reformers of America—such the object towards which the present writer hopes, in however small a degree, to contribute.

Hitherto, from causes to which reference has been made, the
labor struggle presents to the merely superficial observer
a spectacle of wasted opportunities and unused powers—of
heroism and endurance misdirected—of lavish expenditure
for temporary and trivial objects—of energy and self-sacrifice
squandered in attempts to gain insignificant ameliorations—of
isolated advances at some few points, followed by gradual re-
treat all along the line before the power of concentrated and
organized wealth.   What has been gained thus far is almost
altogether in the way of preparation.   In so far as the efforts
hitherto made have been educational in their result, so far as
they have effected the disciplining of the hosts of labor, so
far as they have had a tendency to dissipate the prejudices
and antagonisms of party, creed, and nationality which have
stood in the way of union, they have been invaluable as a
preliminary training for the final encounter on a broader scale.
Whatever of apparent failure and defeat has attended the agitation was inevitable in view of the very nature of the conflict, the obstacles to be encountered, and the forces ranged
on the side of capitalism.   If much has been learned, more
has to be unlearned.   Old and deeply-rooted ideas of government and social organization are to be overthrown.   Prejudices tenaciously adhered to must be removed.   False notions

as to the relations between labor and capitalism, the functions of the state and the rights of property, which have become part of the mental constitution of the race, have to be eradicated. And differences of opinion and antagonistic methods of action among those who are honestly striving according to their lights for the improvement of social conditions are to be reconciled, and whole-heartedness of purpose and steadiness of aim substituted for intermittent and badly directed enthusiasm.

A work of such magnitude is not to be accomplished by any one man or any generation of men. It must essentially be a work of slow and gradual accomplishment. It cannot be brought about by any ready-made scheme for the reconstruction of society to be suddenly imposed upon men whose feelings, wishes, and ideals are not in harmony with it. Instead of dogmatizing as to the ultimate form of social re-adjustment, the immediate thing to be done is to procure the acceptance of the principles which must underlie effective reform, and to indicate the general direction in which lies the path of progress; to educate the people up to a consciousness of their true interest and a knowledge of the powers within their grasp; to accept every plan which seems to have in it the promise of substantial good tentatively, and nothing as a finality.

Thought crystallizes slowly on great issues. In occupying ourselves too exclusively with ideals of the social regeneration of the future, it is possible to overlook the immediate practical issues which may be the stepping-stones to broader and more comprehensive reforms. Every Labor Reformer should be willing to aid in any movement which seems to be in the general line of advancement, whether it is exactly in accord with his pet theories or not. If it succeeds and the results prove favorable, he will have reason to change his opinion. If, on the contrary, it proves impracticable or does not work beneficially, the experiment removes another stumbling-block and simplifies the problem. For instance, the failure of the so-called protective tariff

to protect labor plainly shows that not in that direction
must the remedy for industrial evils be looked for. Had the
experiment not been tried the labor movement might now be
taking the form of an agitation for tariff protection. No
great invention ever attained perfection at one bound. The
history of all social or political systems is that of a series of
experiments now in this direction, now in that. Here evolution, there revolution, schemes for more perfect working
brought to failure one after the other, until a partial success
is obtained; then another re-adjustment of conditions followed
by a break-down from a defect in the mechanism. Then more
amendments, more experiments, until, little by little, the
system approaches perfection. A slow, a very slow, toilsome,
uphill process. Is there cause for discouragement in the prospect? Is not this the mode by which anything of great and
permanent value of man's invention has been produced?
How many hundred trials and experiments, how many apparent failures, how many improvements and alterations by
one inventor after another were necessary before the steam-
engine arrived at its present stage of perfection? Think you
a perfect social state is easier to create than a perfect steam-
engine?

"It is with true opinions courageously uttered," said
Goethe, "as with pawns first advanced on the chess-board,
they may be beaten, but they have inaugurated a game which
must be won."

CHAPTER II.

THE UPPER AND THE NETHER MILLSTONE.

> See yonder poor o'erlabored wight,
> So abject, mean, and vile,
> Who begs a brother of the earth
> To give him leave to toil;
> And see his lordly fellow-worm
> The poor petition spurn,
> Unmindful though a weeping wife
> And helpless offspring mourn.
>   BURNS.

ONE of the most formidable difficulties, in the way of clearness of thought, on the labor question, is the lack of appropriate terms in the English language to express the ideas suggested by new social and industrial developments. Reference has already been made to the double sense in which the word " capital " is customarily employed, and the confusion arising from the use of the same term to express the accumulated wealth used in production, and the powers, interests, and privileges claimed by its possessors. A like difficulty confronts us when we seek to characterize by a word or phrase the existing system, so as to convey at once the idea of the monopoly of resources by the few, and competition among the many for the means of livelihood. There is no word in the language which will answer. There is none even approaching the meaning sought to be expressed, and the writer has either to resort to a clumsy periphrasis, lacking in point and unavailable for frequent repetition, or to confine himself to vague generalities of expression, such as " the existing industrial system," which call up no clear and tangible idea of its salient features. The word " monopoly " has of late been much in vogue, having been wrenched from its original meaning—that of a privilege granted to a single individual—in order to fill a gap in the language. But to speak of the monopoly system only conveys half the idea. Monopoly, of itself, while an injustice and a wrong to the community by enriching a few individuals at the expense of the whole, would not necessarily produce the extreme deprivation and suffering to which large classes are now subject. It is monopoly in the broad sense of the word, combined with absolute and unrestricted competition among the wage-earners, which causes this result. Monopoly above and competition below are the upper and nether millstones between which the toiler is crushed.

That the social crime which condemns so large a proportion of the community to perpetual poverty should be—like Duncan's murder—"a deed without a name" is very significant of the slight concern taken by the literary and educated classes in the social problem. Political economy pretends to have spoken the last word as regards the relations between labor and capitalism, yet its exponents have not even invented a term which in any way describes this process of grinding or crushing between the opposing forces of monopoly and competition. Probably the French word "exploitation" is the nearest approach to the crystallization of the idea in a single expression; but it is used in too vague and general a sense to be available in any discussion requiring precision of statement.

This lack of adequate phraselogy in which to set forth the evils of the existing system has given an immense advantage to its upholders. They are able to use language in a misleading way, to play upon words and to twist ambiguous phrases so as to bear the significance required by their arguments. If it be urged, for instance, that "capital" is antagonistic to labor, straightway the hired apologist for capitalism proceeds to point out that but for capital—the accumulated product of labor—the toiler would be reduced to starvation, and to draw the inference that labor, in quarrelling with capital, is arraying itself against its best friend. The fallacy which underlies this intellectual thimblerigging is unperceived by many. Those who do perceive that there is a flaw in the reasoning somewhere are perhaps unable to meet it with logical argument by showing the distinction between capital as a factor in production and capitalism as a controlling force. In like manner, where the evils of the competitive system are dwelt upon, the advocates of capitalism assume that competition exists in full force between capitalists as well as between laborers, and ignore all other aspects of the problem than the relations between the worker and his employer. They leave out of the account altogether the pressure of the upper millstone.

Obviously it is not only the amount of wages which have to be considered, but the purchasing power of those wages. While competition lessens the pay received by labor, monopoly not merely decreases it to a still further extent, but lessens its purchasing power as well. It oppresses the worker in countless ways both directly and indirectly. In the larger centres, land monopoly taxes him enormously over and above the value of the house accommodation he obtains. The price of his fuel is enhanced by a coal ring; a series of extortionate and conscienceless middlemen, also stand between him and the Western farmer—railroad kings, elevator men, and produce-exchange gamblers put up the price of bread by their exactions, and oppress producer and consumer alike. On numberless articles of manufacture he is taxed far above their value by rings and combinations. But the pressure upon him as a purchaser and consumer does not stop here. Every class with whom he has business relations shifts its burdens imposed by monopoly onto his shoulders. The storekeeper includes rent, light, fuel, and personal outlay, all enhanced by monopoly, among the expenses to be met by his business, and fixes the prices of his goods accordingly. The fees of the professional classes are regulated on the same principle. All burdens imposed on society in general by the landowner and bondholder, the railroad monopolist and stock exchange sharper, the coal-mining syndicates and manufacturing rings, ultimately fall upon productive industry. Every dollar of the fortunes " made " but not earned, is finally paid by labor, simply because there is no other source from which it can possibly be paid. But because the robbery is indirect, because the monopolists' first victim recoups himself from those with whom he has dealings, and the loss is passed on down the line until it finally falls upon the producer, men have been for long unable to trace the connection between the wealth of the millionaire and the poverty of the toiling masses; to see that the one is the cause of the other. It is not so long since even those who had a heartfelt sympathy with the poor contented themselves with moralizing over the apparent injustice of a system under which some were superfluously wealthy, and others miserably poor. Thanks to the spread of enlightenment, we now know that a real injustice is involved, inasmuch as the poverty of the many is caused by the unearned, and therefore stolen, wealth of the few.

The same process of shifting the burdens of monopoly down to the worker decreases the amount of wages as well as lessens their purchasing power. In so far as these burdens fall in the first instance upon the employer, he reckons them as part of the expenses of his business, which must be met out of its returns. Heavy ground-rents, increased prices of raw material, usury, extortionate freights, and the like must be provided for by lessening other expenses or increasing the gross receipts, and mean either decreased wages to employees or increased prices to the public—perhaps partly the one and partly the other, according to the condition of the labor market. In either case the result as regards the working-class as a whole is practically the same. The tax imposed by monopoly is paid by the earnings of industry. Where else could the money come from to pay it?

Of all forms of monopoly, the most oppressive and the most insidious is that of private land-ownership. The most oppressive, because its exactions are vastly greater than those of all other forms combined, and because they constantly increase in a ratio proportioned to the necessities of the landless class —the most insidious, because unlike others of recent growth, it is so deeply rooted in and firmly intwined with our institutions, ideas, and economic system, that its injustice is not

generally recognized, and because the interests of the idlers
whom it enriches by the labor of others are falsely identified with those of a large and most important class of actual
producers, wrongfully supposed to be concerned in its preservation. The great truth that the land belongs of right to the
whole community, and that any claim on the part of an individual to more than a right of occupancy or cultivation on
paying into the public treasury its yearly value is a robbery,
has been so fully and clearly set forth by Henry George in
words which have commanded the respectful attention of a
class hitherto little disposed to attach importance to the utterances of Labor Reformers, that an elaborate presentation of
this phase of the subject might seem superfluous. But the
scope of this volume requires a thorough investigation of all
those influences which combine to depress the condition of
labor before the direction in which a remedy is to be looked
for can intelligently be considered. In the case of so prominent and widespread a cause of social disarrangement, something more than a mere reference is clearly called for, even
though no new light be thrown on the subject.

In a new land, such as America, where a single generation
witnesses the growth of crowded cities and populous states
out of the sparsely settled wilderness, it is much more easy
to trace the workings of an unjust social system than in old
countries where institutions have been crystallized for centuries, so that in the eyes of many they seem part of the eternal order of things. But the insidious indirectness of the
process and the lapse of time between the beginning and the
culmination, brief though it is as compared with the slower
operation of the same causes in Europe, have hitherto prevented a general recognition of the evil effects of land monopoly. If these effects, instead of being at first imperceptible, then slightly experienced, and so gradually and slowly
growing with the growth of the community, were suddenly
to be produced by a direct, concrete, overt act on the part of
the exploiting class, every one would understand the essential
injustice of the system.

Let us adopt a familiar form of illustration to make this clear. That clearness rather than originality is the object in view must be my apology for its triteness.

Here is an uninhabited island in the Pacific Ocean. Uninhabited, but fertile; overgrown with luxuriant and spreading vegetation, swarming with game, and abounding in everything required for the support of man. One day a ship is stranded on the neighboring coral reefs, the breakers dash her in pieces, and the crew plunge wildly for the shore. Some are drowned, some meet their death by being thrown against the jagged rocks; and of the whole number a dozen manage to reach the shore in safety, but breathless and exhausted by their struggle for life. As soon as they have recovered sufficiently to realize their situation, they take the necessary measures for providing for the immediate future. Some of the ship's stores, some fragments of the wreck, are cast ashore. They manufacture rude implements of agriculture. They put up temporary houses. They gather fruit and dig roots, and set about cultivating the soil in primitive fashion. The island is amply large enough to support ten times their number, but our sailors have been brought up with orthodox ideas of political economy and cannot reconcile themselves to the " communistic " notion of holding the land in common, so it is duly divided up among them. Each man surrounds his patch with a rude fence, or blazes the trees as a line of demarcation, and the little community starts according to the most approved principles of modern civilization.

So matters go on for a year or so. A rude plenty prevails in the colony. There is enough and to spare for all, and the worst evils of civilization are unknown. But one morning there is great excitement. A boat appears in the offing. Slowly it nears the shore. The mariners run down to the beach. The keel grates on the sand, and a few haggard, emaciated men step with difficulty ashore. They are the survivors of a boat-load who put off from a sinking vessel a week before in the hope of reaching land. Their comrades have all perished of starvation, and they are themselves at the last gasp.

Their immediate necessities are supplied and in a few days the new-comers regain their strength. So far provisions and shelter have been given them and no questions asked; but after awhile the old settlers give unmistakable hints that their visitors have outstayed their welcome. Finally, one of them speaks out.

"Say, boys; don't you think you ought to shift for yourselves now? 'He that won't work neither shall he eat,' as the Book says."

"Just so," says one of the later arrivals. "We were just thinking that we ought to scratch for our own living from this out. To-morrow we intend to put up a cabin on the bluff over there and go to work."

"Well, if that ain't cool!" ejaculates one of the early settlers. "That's my land! You can't build on my land!"

"Your land, eh? It does not seem to be in use by anybody; but if you have pre-empted it we won't quarrel about it. There's another location where the land shelves up from the beach, just past that rocky point there, will do us about as well."

"Hold on though—that's my lot!" observes another of the first inhabitants.

"Well, we wont dispute your claim. It's altogether likely we can find some other place to suit us. Anyhow we'll look around to-morrow for a location, and we won't ask you to do anything more for us."

The old settlers look at each other in amaze at the ignorance or audacity of the new arrivals. Finally, one of them explains.

"You seem to be under a strange misapprehension. You can't settle *anywhere* upon our island. You have no right here at all. We as first comers have taken possession, and the land is regularly divided amongst us. We have an indefeasible title to it. Go off and find an island for yourselves."

"But," says one of the new-comers, "we have as much right here as you. This island is large enough to support a hundred people. You have more land than you can possibly need,

You have, it is true, divided it up; but that is about all you have done. It is nearly all in a state of nature; let us have at least a few acres."

" If, " replies the spokesman of the land-grabbers, " you had studied even the rudiments of political economy, you would know that neither your necessities nor our superfluities have anything to do with the question. But you are no doubt socialists or anarchists, upon whom the principles of that sublime science would make no impression ; so we will not argue the matter further than to observe that we have not merely an unimpeachable title, but the necessary force to maintain it. We are two to one. We own this island and mean to keep it for ourselves. There lies your boat, under the circumstances we will not charge you for wharfage—Go ! "

" But where—where ? We are a hundred leagues from anywhere, with neither chart nor compass nor provisions. It would be sailing to certain death ! "

Meanwhile, one of the property-owners has been struck by a brilliant idea. He mentions it to the rest. They confer awhile, and the spokesman, advancing to the little group who are mournfully preparing for their departure, addresses them as follows :

" As you don't seem to like the idea of leaving, we will allow you to stay here on certain conditions. You must dig our ground. You must sow and harvest our crops. You must put us up better houses than we at present occupy, cut us down fuel in the bush, catch us fish and game, in fact do all the hard, rough work that we have hitherto been obliged to do for ourselves. And you must acknowledge us as your natural superiors and always speak and act respectfully towards us, no matter how much we may abuse you. In return for which we will permit you to live here, and so long as you raise plenty of food for us we will allow you enough to live on ; but if you are lazy and do not produce sufficient to feed both us and yourselves, of course you must starve ; for, ' He that will not work neither shall he eat, you know."

" Pretty hard terms ! " says one of the unfortunates.

"Hard? Hard! Why, man, we don't ask you to accept them. We believe in perfect freedom of contract. Those are our terms—if you don't like them you can go anywhere else."

Of course there was practically only one alternative; so the second shipwrecked crew became the slaves of those who by accident had arrived a year or two before them, and raised their corn, chopped their wood, and caught their fish, while the proprietors of the soil loafed about in the shade of the palm trees in all the dignity of land-ownership.

Did land monopoly in the outset assume this crude phase, its hardships would be obvious to all. Nobody could deny the injustice of a positive hard-and-fast law by which an individual or a society should take advantage of the necessities of those whom accident placed in their power, and enslave them as the condition of permitting them to exist. But because these cruel results are of slow and gradual development, and are the outcome of social conditions instead of direct personal action, the abuses of the system have not been recognized by the mass.

The parallel is in no single respect overdrawn. The condition of the man without resources except his labor of muscle or brain, in a settled and organized community, is practically that of the shipwrecked sailor driven to choose between slavery and death. That he inhabits a crowded continent instead of an almost unpeopled island makes no appreciable difference. So long as all the resources of life for hundreds of miles around him are held in the clutch of monopoly, he is as completely cut off from availing himself of natural rights and opportunities as though surrounded by a waste of waters.

But the illustration, though sufficiently apt as regards the working of monopoly alone, falls short of the reality resulting from *monopoly with competition.* Under this double pressure the man without resources sometimes has not even the alternative of wage-slavery. When the struggle for leave to work becomes intense, owing to the increase in the number

of would-be toilers without the means of self-employment,
some are denied the privilege upon any terms, because those
who control the avenues of labor have no use for their services. They become outcasts and vagrants, seek by crime the
bread denied to honest labor, eke out a miserable existence on
the alms of the charitable, or die of slow starvation, while all
around them is abundance, and the lives of their fellows are
made a burden by hard monotonous overwork.

In addition to the gradual development of the evils of land
monopoly, the comparatively wide distribution of the unearned
increment during its earlier stages is another cause why its
injustice is not generally realized. While land is rising in
value, a great many people are making money and many more
mistakenly think they are, while the pressure upon the landless class is only beginning to be slightly felt. As a matter
of fact it is only those who hold land to sell or rent who are
benefited by any increase in land values. Those who
simply occupy land for their individual use, for cultivation,
residence, or business purposes, are in no degree advantaged by the rise. A man who has bought a house and lot
in a growing town, for instance, for one thousand dollars,
feels greatly elated when he learns that owing to the increase
of population it has doubled its value. He fancies himself a
thousand dollars richer than when he made the purchase. In
one sense he is. He can sell out for a thousand dollars more
than he paid. But if he means to continue a resident he
must purchase or rent at the increased value, so that his
unearned increment is no benefit. True, he may, by watch-
ing his chances and exercising his judgment, invest his money
to better advantage. But for the purposes of the present argument we are not considering those changes of a speculative
character made by owners of real estate, but the effect of a
rise in value upon those who hold property for other than
speculative purposes. Clearly the man who lives in a thousand dollar house and means to continue living in the same
locality is really no richer for any purpose except that of
speculation because after the lapse of some years, the house

meantime having grown visibly out of repair from age, the property is said to be worth two, five, or ten thousand dollars. Neither is the manufacturer or store-keeper, as a manufacturer or storekeeper, any the better off by reason of a similar rise in value of the land on which his place of business stands. He can sell out for more, that is all; but to continue his calling he would have to pay a price either in the form of purchase money or rent equivalent to his gain apart from the chances of a lucky speculation in exchanging a more for a less costly site. Nevertheless the adventitious increase in value deceives many people into supposing that they are really wealthier because the property which they hold and have all along held for a particular purpose, independent of its selling price, is nominally held at a higher figure. So far as the real value of the property for trade, occupation or ersidence is concerned they are in precisely the same condition as before the rise. And the change which enriches the land speculator or the individual property-owner who takes advantage of the unearned increment to realize upon his land lays a heavy and always increasing burden upon the laboring class as a whole.

Let us suppose that John Wilson, a blacksmith, settles in the small village of Boomington, which seems to afford a good opening for one of his craft. Land is still cheap though considerably advanced beyond farm prices, owing to the prospects of the community ; and John thinks himself fortunate in being able to secure a good-sized lot on the straggling main street for $100. He builds a shop and small house adjoining, and being an industrious and sober mechanic, soon finds himself in a fair way of business. The calculations of the villagers as to their future were well-founded. The place, owing to its natural advantages as a business center, rapidly increases in population. Shops and stores are springing up in all directions. One day John Wilson is confronted by a demand for taxes greatly in excess of the amount he had previously paid. He looks over the paper in surprise. " Why, you have valued my place at two thousand dollars. All I paid for the lot was $100 : and the buildings ain't worth more than $500.

" Ah, but you know we've had a re-valuation. Your property is worth every cent of $2000. You wouldn't take that
much for it, you know."

"Come to think of it, I guess I would'nt," says John to
himself ; and he pays his taxes with a reluctant grunt, chuck-
ling inwardly, however, at his good fortune in having "made "
at least fourteen hundred on land the value of which grew
whether he was sleeping or working, in addition to the snug
little sum saved from the proceeds of his honest toil. But
though his position as a land-owner is indisputably bettered
by the growth of the place, as a blacksmith he is no better
off than before. Increased population has brought increased
business, it is true ; but it has also brought increased competition. At first he had no competitors—now there are
half a dozen ; and though work is perhaps somewhat more
plentiful, prices are decidedly lower, and, as we have just
seen, his taxes are higher. Nevertheless John is vastly pleased
with his foresight in the choice of a location, because he
knows that whatever may become of his business, he has in
his land an investment of steadily increasing value.

Time goes on, and despite some fluctuations, Boomington
continues its growth. The village has become a city. Property
on the main street is too valuable for business purposes to be
occupied as dwellings, and John Wilson is finally tempted to
sell the portion of his lot on which his cottage stands for
several thousand dollars. With a shrewd eye to the future, he
buys a residence in the suburbs with a large area of vacant
land adjoining. The blacksmith business is no better than
before, but John has now become a capitalist. He has several
journeymen in place of the solitary apprentice of old. But
his interest in his trade is not the same. The profits he can
make as a blacksmith are a small matter compared with the
prospects of realizing a competence from the increase in the
value of his land. The old blacksmith shop has a strangely
incongruous aspect amid its surroundings of handsome stores
and palatial blocks of business offices, and so one day John
Wilson lays down his hammer and throws off his leather

apron forever. He has sold out the site to an enterprising merchant at a handsome figure. He can now take life easy. He is a "self-made man," and is never tired of boasting that he made every cent of his money by his honest industry. John has no sort of toleration for the complaints of labor. Talk to him of the uncertainty of employment and the pressure of competition; tell him that the tendency of land monopoly is to make the rich richer and the poor poorer, and he will reply—"All nonsense, sir. The whole trouble comes from the teaching of agitators and demagogues. Why, look at me! I came here thirty years ago, with hardly a cent to my name, worked hard, grew up with the place, and to-day, sir, I'm worth thirty to forty thousand dollars. Any working-man who is sober and industrious can do the same."

A short time since, Mr. Wilson received a visit from Tom Judson, son of an old friend and former shop-mate. The young fellow had taken to his father's trade, and learning of Wilson's prosperity had concluded that Boomington ought to be a good place in which to settle. He had a few hundred dollars, and furnished by his father with a note of introduction to his old friend, came to ask his advice and assistance.

"Ah—um" said Wilson. "Glad to do anything I can. But things are very different now, you know. Any number of good hands looking for work. You might get a job at Coulter's place, perhaps, at nine dollars a week or so."

"But I thought of starting on my own account. I have a few hundred dollars, and if I could buy a shop—"

"Buy a shop in Boomington for a few hundred dollars! You must be crazy. It would cost a great deal more than that to buy the land. You might perhaps rent a place. But it's no use to start a one-horse establishment in these days of competition. Like everything else it requires capital. You'd better not risk your money in starting on your own account, but look out for a job. Are you married?

"Yes. I want to start housekeeping right away. I thought perhaps I could get a lot cheap, and then get a small house put up on time."

3

" Well, that is perhaps the best thing you can do; but of course if you expect to buy cheap you will have to go some distance out. I think I have just the lot that will suit you for $500. It will be two or three miles from your work, but the street cars are handy. I did intend holding it for a further rise, but seeing you are Tom Judson's son I don't mind letting you have it for that, and its a bargain I assure you. If you have steady work and are saving and economical, you ought to be able to pay for the house in four or five years."

Now the difference between the positions and opportunities of John Wilson and Tom Judson at the outset of their careers is due to land monopoly. The wealth of the former, though partly the earnings of his calling, was mainly the result of his power as a land-owner to levy a tax on future industry. His enrichment involved the poverty of future generations of laborers by making the conditions of existence for them less endurable and diminishing their prospects of success in life. But the connection is lost sight of owing to the fact that the processes are not simultaneous—that the pressure is not felt in its intensity in the earlier stages of the development—and that when it does begin to be felt the victims themselves, owing to the complications of the system, may be in turn reaping or hoping to reap compensating advantages, at the expense of their successors. Tom Judson, for instance, while forced to recognize the, to him, melancholy fact that " things have changed " since the day that John Wilson came to Boomington with no more money than he had, and was able to become his own landlord and employer, does not clearly trace the connection between that change and the accumulation of wealth in the hands of Wilson and others through the ownership of land. And supposing he does see it, he is now himself a landowner. He may fairly hope before he dies to see the value of his five hundred dollar lot at least doubled or quadrupled by the further expansion of Boomington, and his supposed self-interest inclines him to believe that private land-ownership is rather a good thing. He overlooks altogether the tax he pays to monopoly. His small but obvious and tangible interest as a landowner looms larger in his eyes than the detriment he suffers from the subtle, indirect, atmospheric pressure, so to speak, which crushes him as a worker and a consumer.

Considering, then, that land monopoly in the earlier stages of a community's growth appears to be benefiting a great many people without injuring any one, and that the real advantage is so widely distributed as to be shared by many laborers to an extent which often more than counterbalances the injury they sustain, and in many other cases appears to do so, it is not to be wondered at that the people have been slow to realize this great cause of industrial evils.

But before long there comes a time in the history of all populous centers when the immense majority of the people are deprived of all compensating advantages, either real or apparent; when land has reached such a price as to be entirely beyond the reach of the wage-earner, and the results of monopoly and competition are felt to their full extent. Labor pays in increased rents, increased prices, and diminished wages the tribute imposed years before by those who "made money" from the augmented value of the land.

In all great cities rents are enormously high, and by the operation of land monopoly and competition are steadily growing higher. In *Harper's Magazine* for November, 1882, there appeared an article by Junius Henri Browne on the subject of living in New York, setting forth in very strong terms the discomforts and exactions to which even the comparatively well-to-do classes were subject. The following is an extract :—

" There is no prospect, in fact, of desirable flats—that is, apartments of any size, convenient, light, and airy—being other than expensive in this city. It is twelve years since the first apartment houses were built; hundreds of them of divers grades have been put up all over town; but those capable of accommodating a small family, with an elevator and pleasant, well-ventilated rooms, cannot be had for less than from $1,500

to $2,000. There are flats in poor quarters that rent for from
$600 to $800, but they usually have dark chambers, they are
ill-arranged, and are seldom really wholesome. As a generali-
zation, it may be said, that reasonable apartments are not good,
and that good apartments are not reasonable. The fond antici-
pations cherished eight or ten years ago, that a nice healthful
apartment might be procured for from $500 to $600 annually,
have long been dispelled. They who have no more than that
to spend for a house, so-called, are obliged to put up with sun-
dry discomforts, and to jeopard their health more or less by
sleeping in dark, close chambers. It would seem as if economy
of any kind were impracticable in this the costliest of capitals.
The mere decencies of life are well-nigh beyond the reach of
men dependent on salaries or ordinary incomes. The average
earnings here of men even of education and taste are not, it
is alleged, in excess of $1,500 to $1,600, and as the majority of
them have families (the unwritten law of Manhattan demands
that no couple, unless financially independent, shall have more
than two children), they are forced into a ceaseless contest
for self-sustainment. They toil through life, endure vexation,
disappointment, tribulation, pain, and quit the world leaving
no provision for their families, but generally in debt. Comparatively few men who can command credit, die, it is said,
with all their liabilities discharged."

If such is the condition of "men of education and taste,"
those who can earn no more than $1,500 or $1,600—what of
the poor man, of the average mechanic or laborer, whose entire
yearly earnings out of which he must feed, clothe, and educate
his family, may not amount to the six or eight hundred necessary to procure even "flats in poor quarters," ill-arranged, dark,
and unwholesome? Frequently the nature of their employment is such that they are obliged to live near their work.
They have not the time necessary for a journey to and from
the city every day. Consequently they are compelled to herd
together in squalid and filthy tenements, amid such surroundings of moral and physical pollution as render it almost impossible for them, even if they manage to preserve their own re-

spectability, to bring their children up in the ways of decency. In these abodes of destitution and wretchedness, where honest poverty and shameless degradation are thrust into close asso_ ciation, every influence tends to drag the self-respecting, cleanly, and industrious poor down to the level of the weltering mass of depravity which closes around them. In the fetid and reeking slums of great cities there is contamination in the very air. The privacy of home life is impossible. The throng of human beings who swarm and huddle in the crowded tenements can know nothing of the joys of a free and wholesome natural life, such as brings its compensations to the lot of rural poverty. Deprived of the sunshine and the fresh air, hemmed in between walls which exclude the light of Heaven, and robbed even of that limited and circumscribed share in the earth which gives the occupant of a hovel or a shanty a temporary footroom, at least, upon the soil, the denizens of the city slums are in reality poorer than the wretchedest peasantry in Europe. The latter, at any rate, have elbow-room and fresh air. If their toil is hard and their lives monotonous, they know something of the freshness and freedom of nature. To the poor dweller in the purlieus of great cities, monopoly denies even the prayer of Ajax—" Let us perish in the face of day." He is poisoned and stifled in the gloom.

Since the condition of the poor has become a prominent subject of discussion, the attempt has been made by leading political economists and statisticians to answer the indictment framed by Labor Reformers against the competition-monopoly system, by the assertion that the rate of wages has increased. At the meeting of the British Association at Montreal, in 1884, Edward Atkinson of Boston undertook to show that poverty was not increasing with the expansion of industry ; contending that during the previous 40 years, wages had been largely increased and the hours of labor shortened. Even were these statements justified by a wider range of observation than that upon which Mr. Atkinson appears to have based his conclusions, they would not disprove the contention that the monopoly of resources and competition between

workers exercise an increasingly depressing influence upon
the condition of labor. Political economists of the Atkinson
and Giffen stamp invariably fall into the error previously
noted, of narrowing the labor question down to the relations
between the working-man and his employer. This, as has been
shown, is a very superficial view. Obviously, any calculation
based on the wages paid at particular periods leaves out of
account altogether the condition of the unemployed. The
gist of the Labor Reform contention is, that owing to the augmented pressure of competition and the limitation imposed to
self-employment by monopoly, there is a large class of people,
greatest always where population is most dense, who are only
able to obtain work intermittently. The first annual report
of the United States Labor Bureau, issued in the spring of
1886, stated that out of the total number of industrial
establishments, such as factories, mines, etc., existing in the
country, about five per cent. were absolutely idle during 1885,
and perhaps five per cent. more, idle a part of the time ; making
7½ and cent. a just estimate of the whole number idle, or
equivalent to idle, during the year. On this basis, the Bureau
obtains a total of 998,839 wage-workers unemployed during
1885. But obviously this falls short of the reality. It only
gives the number of the unemployed for whose employment
there is provision in connection with existing establishments,
and takes no account of the class outside of this who are not
attached to any special form of industry. Never until very
recently in the history of this continent was there this large
unemployed or half-employed class, crowded out of the
avenues of labor by the pressure of population, excluded
from access to the untilled acreage by the operation of
monopoly, and falling into habits of permanent idleness.

Obviously, no mere increase in wages to those fortunate
enough to obtain steady employment can compensate those
who are out of work, any more than they can indemnify even
those who are sure of continuous employment, for the lack of
comfortable homes. Even though the increase were sufficient to
make up for the additional outlay in rent, what money con-

sideration would be adequate to atone for the change for the worse in the home surroundings of the working-class, consequent upon the increase of land values and the growing density of population. There are, it is true, many wage-workers who own their homes, but the proportion of those who are thus fortunate is steadily decreasing. In any manufacturing center it will be found on inquiry that the working-men who pay no direct tribute to the land monopolist are in nearly all cases the older residents, who have acquired their homesteads under more favorable conditions than now prevail— that comparatively few of the new generation are in a position to become their own landlords. The typical American laborer of the cities is no longer an independent self-owning citizen, with a fixed place and stake in the community, but a proletarian, without the local attachment and deep rootage in the soil which develops the virtues of citizenship; compelled by the fluctuations of industry and the chances of competition to frequent changes of residence. He does not first choose a home and then seek work, but is compelled to follow work wherever he can find it, and then look for a place to eat, sleep, and bestow his belongings. His interests as a man and a citizen are subordinated to the needs of the toiler.

If these alterations for the worse in the lot of labor were due to any inevitable cause, were there, for instance, such a " pressure of population on the means of subsistence " that it was but reasonable and just that each should be content with diminished comfort and freedom, they might well be borne without complaint. But the thing that adds bitterness to these evils is the thought now beginning to be firmly grasped by the disinherited masses, that the process of exploitation which robs them, adds enormously to the wealth of the few. That within the past two generations there has sprung up in America a millionaire class simultaneously with the growth of a proletariat is seen to be something more than a coincidence. It is perceived that under the regime of monopoly the economic forces carry out to a literal fulfillment the text, "For whosoever hath, to him shall be given, and

whosoever hath not, from him shall be taken even that which
he seemeth to have." The "seeming" increase in wages is
no real increase, because their power of purchasing, not merely
cotton, sugar and coal, but the comfort, manliness and independence of the recipient, diminishes, to enrich the monopolist.

Rent, usury, and profit are the three heads of the modern
Cerberus of capitalism which devour the toiler; three forms
of one and the same essential injustice, of regarding as commodities—as something to be traded and trafficked in, and
made to pay tribute to idlers and schemers—things which
should not be placed in that category.

Land ought not to be a commodity, because like air and
water it is necessary to human existence; and all men have by
birthright equal rights to its use.

Money should not be a commodity, because it is used for the
exchange of other commodities, and when it is made an article
of trade, the laborer is taxed to pay the dealer in money a
profit under the name of interest for which he receives no
value.

Labor should not be a commodity, because it is human life.
The difference between the slaveholder, who robs the slave
of his whole time, and the capitalist, who robs the wage-serf
of a portion of his time, during which he works for his employer's "profit," is obviously one only of degree.

The commodity-theory in regard to land, money, and labor
is diametrically opposed to the idea that every man has a
right to the full value of his labor, and no man the right to
receive value for which he does not labor, which appeals to
every man's natural sense of right and justice. It converts
the natural resources of the soil and the mechanism adopted
to facilitate exchange into the means of extorting from labor
a continually increasing proportion of its product.

The exaction of usury is an essential feature of the present
industrial organization. So long as capital remains in private
hands, and is regarded as a means of personal enrichment
rather than a power to be used for the benefit of the whole
community, the advocates of interest as a natural and legit-

imate payment for an advantage received occupy an impregnable logical position. The declamations of the Greenbackers against usury, while they do not propose to disturb the other features of capitalism, are inconsistent, and show a want of exact thought. To admit that capital should be under the absolute control of private individuals, for the purpose of realizing a gain additional to and irrespective of the value of their labor of superintendence and organization, justifies the entire system of usury.

A man invests let us say $ 100,000 in a commercial or manufacturing enterprise, out of which he clears $ 10,000 a year after all expenses are paid. This is called by the misleading and inaccurate term, "profit." Analyzed, it comprises two elements—labor value, the legitimate return for the skill and labor expended, and usury on the sum invested. Yet because these two components are lumped together and called " profit," the essentially unjust nature of the transaction passes unrecognized by many who consider themselves the uncompromising opponents of usury. Four thousand dollars of the employer's " profit," let us suppose, is a fair equivalent for his personal labor of supervision and technical knowledge ; the remaining $ 6000 is interest on his investment. Now, supposing that instead of going into business on his own account, he had lent his $ 100,000 capital to another man, who agreed to pay him six per cent. interest upon it. In this case, the " profit " is lessened by the elimination of a part at least of the usury element. But practically it makes no sort of difference to the laborer whether his employer receives the whole $ 10,000 profit, as being a capitalist as well as an organizer of labor, or whether these functions are divided and one man receives $ 6000 as usury, pure and simple, and another receives $ 4000 as profit. In either case there is just so much withdrawn from the product of labor, and handed over to one who has not earned it. The wrong and the injustice is in no way lessened by the fact that the capitalist-employer has earned a portion of his total receipts, and that the usury is merged in the amount reckoned as profit. During the greenback agita-

tion the "bloated bondholder" was the object of much
vigorous denunciation by men who had a, clear perception of
the iniquity of the system by which the mere possession of
wealth enables its owner to live without exertion by taxing
the labor of others. But they failed to see that the personal
ownership of capital to be used without control for the
benefit of the individual logically justifies usury in all its
forms. Morally there is no difference between the investment of capital by the owner, in a business subject to his own
direction, in the expectation of gaining a profit comprising
usury *plus* wages of superintendence, and his investing it
in bonds, stocks, or mortgages for usury alone. Once admit
the right of capital as such to bring in a yearly return to the
individual, additional to the worth of his personal services in
connection with its management, and the whole case of the
orthodox political economist as regards the interest question is
conceded. To reverse the old legal maxim, "What a man
does by himself he can do through another." If it is right
and just for the capitalist-employer to take the products of
labor for the use of the means of employment and the tools
of trade, it is equally right and just for the capitalist who is
not an employer to delegate to another the same power.

The weakness of the position of the Greenbackers is the result of a want of clearness of thought. They have wasted
their strength in fighting certain phases of usury which were
mere incidents of the capitalistic system, and which can in no
way be overthrown while the system itself endures. They
have, however, done much to educate the public as to the evils
of usury, and to prepare the way for more comprehensive
measures than they had in view.

Although, while the individual power of the capitalist to
control production and exchange continues to be recognized,
no possible change in the currency system would of itself
destroy usury, yet the present gold basis system greatly in-
tensifies its evils, by making money artificially scarce and dear.
The inadequacy of the currency to the legitimate demands of
industry and commerce necessarily enables the usurer to

increase the tax levied upon production for the use of the medium of exchange. Money is called the tool of trade, and just as an artificial scarcity of axes, spades, and hammers would enable those who were in a position to monopolize the supply to charge exorbitant prices for their use, so the requirement of a gold basis in the face of a continually expanding commerce and a steadily decreasing gold supply, forces up the price of money—which is equivalent to forcing down the price of labor.

According to the United States census reports the increase in the gross value of manufactured products during the period of thirty years between 1850 and 1880 was 426 per cent.; the increase in their net value, 325 per cent.; the increase in capital invested, 423 per cent.; and in wages paid, 300 per cent. Compare this wonderful expansion with the diminished gold production as shown by the reports of the director of the mint, and the very slight and gradual increase in the aggregate yield of gold and silver.

In 1857 the yield of gold in the United States was valued at $55,000,000 ; in 1860 it was $46,000,000 ; in 1870, $50,000,000 ; in 1880, $36,000,000, and in 1884 only $30,800,000. Taking the aggregate of gold and silver, the production was $46,150,000 in 1860 ; $66,000,000 in 1870 ; $75,200,000 in 1880 ; and $79,600,000 in 1884. Had the opponents of silver coinage been able to restrict the currency to a monometallic basis, the increasing disproportion to business needs of the gold supply, which it must be remembered is drawn upon for a hundred mechanical and artistic uses in addition to that of coinage, would have resulted in widespread and intensified industrial depression. Every form of industry and trade would have been crippled, while the dealers in money would have reaped a similar harvest from the scarcity of the commodity to that which has fallen to the lot of the money monopolists in England, where the monometallic system prevails.

The manner in which those who control the currency profit during times of general industrial depression is shown by the following, which appeared in the Toronto *Week*, the organ of Professor Goldwin Smith, on the 11th of March, 1886.

" Considering the depression of trade, the dividends paid by the great British Joint-Stock banks are remarkable. The Bank of Ireland, with a capital of $15,000,000 and a reserve of almost $6,000,000, paid its stockholders 12 per cent. last year, while the Bank of Belfast excelled this, its dividend being 20 per cent.; and the prosperity of the Irish banks seems more remarkable when we remember the stories of depression, failure of crops, and agrarian troubles which come from the Emerald Isle.   The Bank of Sydney, New South Wales, delights the fortunate holders of its stock with a clear dividend of 25 per cent., and the Bank of Australasia pays 16 on a capital of $5,000,000.   The Lancashire County Bank gave its lucky stock owners 25.   The largest dividend declared by any Bank in Great Britain in 1885 was 33⅓, and the concern that paid it was the Whitehaven Joint-Stock Bank, a close corporation institution in London, the majority of its stock being held by the Duke of Westminster. The Scottish banks are very prosperous too.   The Royal Bank of Scotland—the second oldest in Great Britain, for it was established in 1695 —with a capital of £4,500,000, paid a dividend of 14 per cent., while the Commercial Bank, with a capital of £5,000,000, declared the same amount. The Clydesdale Bank, the next richest bank in Scotland, earned 12 per cent. on £5,000,000. These results are brought about by the shrewdest management and a thorough understanding of the business in hand ; but besides this, there is a cause as yet but little appreciated—the enhancement of the value of money, the commodity dealt in by banks, as compared with all other commodities.   While property of all other sorts has depreciated in value by 20 or 25 per cent. during the past five years, the value of money has remained stationary, to the porportionate advantage of all owners of money."

" Considering the depression of trade, the dividends paid by the great British joint-stock banks are remarkable " ! This is putting the cart before the horse with a vengeance.   It would be just about as logical to say that " considering the losses sustained by householders by robbery, the amount of plunder secured by burglars is remarkable."   As the concluding sentences of the quotation, in singular contrast to the absurdity of its opening remark, clearly show, the depression of trade is the effect of the artificial enhancement in the value of money resulting from the gold basis system.

All money ought to be issued by the government directly, without the intervention of corporations, not in the form of promises to pay, but as absolute money receivable as legal tender for all purposes, including all taxes and debts due the government. The delusive and fraudulent gold basis and all pretense of intrinsic value or redeemability, should be abandoned. Its volume should be regulated by the demands of commerce. Flippant and shallow sneerers at the fiat money principle have ridiculed the idea of a scientific and systematized supply of money proportioned to the actual needs of production and exchange in place of the present plan of artificial restriction, according to the opportunities for individual profit, as a chimerical and unattainable project. But in this age of statistics and elaborate commercial calculations,when the details of every important branch of industry and business are so closely estimated, why should it be considered impossible to arrive at an approximate conclusion, based on the returns of material wealth, production, trade, and transportation, as to the amount of money needed to keep the wheels of industry in motion ? The volume of the currency required surely has some ascertainable ratio proportioned to the work to be done, to the number of persons to be employed, and the quantity of the product to be distributed. Given the statistics of these factors, and surely the boasted economic science is competent to answer the problem of how much of the medium of exchange is needed to prevent undue friction and keep the machinery of trade moving.

The dangers of inflation are always held up as a bugbear, in connection with the proposal to dispense with a metallic basis. But, as has been abundantly shown by experience, these dangers are not averted by a "redeemable" currency. The worst evil of undue expansion under the fiat money system would be that the puchasing power of money would decrease all round. The dollar would not buy as much as if the currency were fairly adequate to the needs of trade and no more. This would be an evil, and one to be carefully guarded against in fixing the amount to be issued ; but a very slight one indeed as compared with the evils of the too great expansion of a redeemable currency followed by a forced contraction, when, as in the case of the resumption of specie payments after the war, the creditor class realized enormous sums from the payment in gold or its equivalent of debts contracted during the inflation period.

The advocates of a gold standard urge that the worth of the dollar is determined by the actual value of gold as an article of commerce. In other words, that the conception of a dollar is that of a certain fixed amount of the precious metal; the only thing which imparts value to the paper dollar being the knowledge that behind it there is this metallic value. As a matter of fact, the supposed gold basis is about the last thing that any one thinks of in the everyday transactions of business.

"Lend me a dollar." "I made five dollars this morning." "I'll bet you twenty dollars." Who, in using or hearing these similar customary expressions, ever gives a thought to the gold coin or its equivalent in bullion which is supposed to be the only real dollar, of which the paper currency is merely the representative? The idea called up by these phrases is that of the purchasing power of the sum named; or, if it take a more concrete form, that of the familiar crisp or tattered greenback. The real "dollar" is not the gold or the paper, but a conception of value in labor or its products. No absolute permanently fixed standard of value can be secured under any conceivable system. Value is not determinable with the same definiteness and precision as weight or bulk or distance, and least of all can it be fixed by adopting as the standard of measurement a commodity which of itself fluctuates in value as the supply becomes scarce or plentiful. Obviously, when any article which has in itself value is fixed upon as the standard, its supposed unchangeableness can only be maintained by artificial fluctuations in the value of other articles which become relatively high in proportion to its plentifulness, and are said to fall in value, when it becomes scarce. This is illustrated by the article above quoted from the *Week*. If other property has "depreciated in value by 20 or 25 per cent. during the past five years," it is not because it is really any the less valuable, but simply because gold is scarcer and from its position as the regulator of all other values, relatively more valuable.

Were the gold basis a genuine thing, did the actual gold coinage bear the proportion to the total volume of money in circulation which it should do to justify the theories of the metallic currency advocates, the consequences of this fluctuation would be much more severely felt than they are at present. As it is, the value of money is steadied, as it were, and the rise or fall of prices lessened by the comparatively large volume of paper in circulation in proportion to that of gold. A currency without intrinsic value is better adapted to the presentation of the ideal standard of purchasing power signified by the " dollar " than one the commodity-value of which is subjected to continual fluctuations, calculated to raise or depress its relative worth as compared with the products, the value of which is subjected to its measurement.

Most writers upon this question confuse the subject by introducing a host of historical details as to the origin and functions of money, with the object of showing that in the earlier ages the idea of intrinsic value was inseparable from money. They trace the beginning of the monetary system from the use of cattle and cowries, by pastoral and barbarous peoples, as a means of superseding barter, to the general adoption, as civilization progressed, of a gold and silver coinage ; and infer that, because the various commodities used from time to time as money possessed an inherent value, therefore it is an essential quality and characteristic of money. This is altogether a misleading argument ; in the ruder stages of social development it was necessary that the medium of exchange should possess intrinsic value. When commerce was of an intermittent and transitory character, society insecure and government unstable, nothing else than a commodity would answer the purposes of money. Paper money is only possible in connection with a thoroughly established commercial system, with all the modern agencies and appliances, and with the guarantee of a settled government. At a time when business transactions were few and of the simplest kind, the mechanism of exchange unknown, and the vicissitudes of war or social disturbance always imminent, no man would

part with his property in the way of trade except in return
for some object prized and sought after on its own account—
something having an actual value irrespective of political dis-
turbances and interferences with the primitive system of traffic.
Paper money is the product of a high stage of enlightenment,
incompatible altogether with the ideas and wants of barbarism or semi-civilization. That at first it should be based on coin,
and brought into use as an ingenious means of supplementing
a defective supply of the precious metals was a necessary
phase of the process of evolution, by which the barbaric idea
of intrinsic value as a requisite of money is being slowly
eliminated.

But to go back to first principles, as the orthodox political
economists are so fond of doing. The essential feature of a
circulating medium is the general agreement to accept it as
an equivalent and measure of the value of goods sold or
services rendered; its intrinsic value or otherwise is merely an
incident. This agreement, at first a matter of individual compact, then a general understanding, the outgrowth of custom,
and finally ratified and expressed by law, rendering a particular
coinage or currency a legal tender, is the real money basis.

There is no appreciable intrinsic value in a postage stamp.
Yet every man who is in the habit of writing letters will
readily accept stamps at their face value to an amount limited
by his probable requirements within a short period. That
he may not care to accept a larger quantity is due to the fact
that the kind of service they will procure is restricted to a
single function. That he is willing to accept any, is due to the
absolute guarantee of the State that the stamp will procure
the single kind of service specified. If the government has the
power to impart an exchangeable value to a square inch of
paper, by guaranteeing the performance of a certain valuable
service for the possessor, so that, though its purchasing power
is legally restricted to one direction, stamps readily pass current as small change, how can it be doubted that if the government were to make paper money as legal tender for all transactions, including all taxes and debts due to itself, it would

answer all the purpose of a national currency irrespective of
any specie basis? Much stress has been laid upon the supposed
fact that such a currency would not be available for foreign
trade, or exchangeable with the gold-based currencies of Europe except at a heavy loss. It might not be so great a misfortune from the standpoint of labor as it doubtless appears
to the bourgeois mind, if the foreign trade, which on our side
principally consists of the importation of luxuries which could
either be very advantageously dispensed with or manufactured at home, were considerably curtailed; nor yet if the
annual rush of wealthy Americans to Europe, to waste in dis-
sipation and extravagance the means extorted from labor, were
also checked, by reason of the inconvertibility of fiat money
into gold excepting at a heavy discount. The foreign-trade
bugbear may have its terrors for the profit-mongering, specu-
lating class; for those whose profits or pleasures or both depend
on the commercial relations of this country with Europe. It
has none for the toiler who only sees in the restriction of im-
portations and foreign travel the stimulus to increased production and expenditure at home. But it is not probable that
the discount upon an American irredeemable currency would
be as heavy as is anticipated. Our debts to Europe are paid
neither in gold nor in paper, but in exports; and so long as the
foreigner's demand for our wheat, corn, cattle, sugar, cotton,
and other staples of production was maintained, and America
held its position as an exporting nation, the money which was
available for their purchase would maintain even its exchang-
able value abroad.

It is true that the history of finance records very many instances of depreciated paper currencies. But the reason can
always be traced to some other adequate cause than the inherent unsoundness of the theory of fiat money—generally to
a complication of causes, any one of which would be sufficient
to result in depreciation. Either the currency assumes to be
a promise to pay gold, which is notoriously impossible of fulfillment, or the government issuing it is unstable and liable to
be overthrown, or the country is backward and unproductive

owing to wars, revolutions, and the unprogressive character of
the people. When a government refuses to accept its own
currency in payment of customs duties, as did the United States
during the war of the rebellion, the necessity of obtaining
gold to meet them, as a matter of course depreciates the paper.
To quote the examples of Hayti or the insecure and chronically
disturbed South American States, or to instance the Confed-
erate money, the value of which was contingent upon the success of a rebellion, or the French assignats issued by a revolutionary government, not as money, but as bonds secured by
land, itself of depreciated and uncertain value, in condemnation of the principle of fiat money, is a flagrant perversion of
the truth. Governments in desperate straits have frequently
resorted to the expedient of issuing paper promises to pay gold,
and the ruin and disturbance which have resulted from the
absence of every condition and element which all advocates
of absolute money recognize as essential to the system, are
most unfairly charged against it by the advocates of metallic
currency.

Not the least of the advantages of an irredeemable paper currency over an issue based upon gold would be that in case of
undue inflation, instead of having to resort to a spasmodic contraction, such as caused such widespread calamity at the time
of the resumption of specie payments after the war, it would
merely be necessary to wait until the growth of population and
the increasing demands of a rapidly expanding commerce and
industry restored the equilibrium. A currency scientifically
proportioned to the demands of trade would right itself, should
it be issued in too ample a volume, without causing injustice
to any class ; an inflated specie-based currency, on the other
hand, enriches the gold monopolist at the expense of the producer during the period of contraction. It lends itself to the
exactions of the usurer, and enables the capitalist-employer to
depress wages, by the artificial restrictions it imposes on production, and the consequent increase of competition among
laborers.

That plenty of money will not of itself set the wheels of industry in motion, is perhaps a truism ; but certainly an undue scarcity of the currency will check production, where other circumstances are favorable to its expansion. Money is the life-blood of industry, and though its free circulation may not by itself either cause or evidence perfect health, yet perfect health is impossible without it.

CHAPTER III.

THE NEW POLITICAL ECONOMY.

> What constitutes a state ?
> Not high-raised battlement or labored mound,
>   Thick wall or moated gate ;
> Not cities proud, with spires and turrets crowned,
>   Not bays and broad-armed ports
> Where, laughing at the storm, rich navies ride;
>   Not starred and spangled courts
> Where low-browed baseness wafts perfume to pride.
>   No ! Men, high-minded men,
> With powers as far above dull brutes endued
>   In forest, brake, or den,
> As these excel cold rocks and brambles rude.
>   Men who their duties know,
> Know too their rights and knowing dare maintain,
>   Prevent the long-aimed blow,
> And crush the tyrant while they rend the chain—
>   These constitute a state.
>   SIR WILLIAM JONES.

Political economy needs to be re-written from the stand-point of the Sermon on the Mount and the Declaration of Independence. Hitherto it has concerned itself only with the production of wealth and the promotion of the material interests of the nation in bulk. According to its teaching, national prosperity has been reckoned by the aggregate of production and accumulation—the increase of exports and imports—the volume of capital invested and business transacted. It takes no account of equity in distribution—the degree of comfort and independence of the masses of the people. Labor in its eyes is simply a " commodity "—raw material to be used up

in the production of wealth, and the cheapness of which, like
the cheapness of coal, cotton, iron ore, or other forms of raw
material, is to be viewed as an advantage rather than a detriment, because it tends to cheapen production, and so to increase the total amount of national wealth at the year's end.
With the rights of the laborer as a man, with his status as a
citizen, it has no concern. It has invented the lie upon which
the whole industrial and competitive system is based, that instead of labor being primarily entitled as of right to the product of human exertion exercised upon natural resources, the
prior claim rests with those who permit access to those resources and supply the tools. It has justified the assumption
by capitalism of the power to control and fix the remuneration of labor, retaining the whole surplus as profit. It has
inverted the natural order of things, and, instead of regarding
capital, or the proceeds of previous labor, as a mere subsidiary
aid to further production in the hands of labor, regards it as
the prime mover and directing force.

It may be urged here that political economy in this only
recognizes established conditions; that, as a matter of fact,
capitalism does control and fix the remuneration of labor, and
consequently political economy is not to blame for its teachings in regard to the working of the system. But political
economy does more than this. Its doctrines furnish the apol-
ogists for capitalism with a store-house of argument, to show
that the existing system is just, natural, and inevitable. Its
teachers are, for the most part, the tenacious and uncompromising upholders of the usurpation by which the rights of man
are subordinated to the interests of property. It has laid
down the dictum, that society has no right to interfere,
through its agent the government, so as to ensure a fair distribution of wealth; but that the economic laws of competition
and supply-and-demand must have free course and be glori-
fied, as securing by their unrestricted operation a more desirable and satisfactory result than could otherwise be obtained.

The orthodox political economy is more than an exposition
of the manner in which—certain conditions being granted—

certain natural laws will operate. It starts by assuming that
the conditions are not only actual, but intrinsically beneficent
and permanent, and finds in the existence of the laws which
it discovers a reason why their operations should not be interfered with. It is the bulwark and buttress of the system
of monopoly and competition. As the pen of the historian
has been employed to blacken and degrade the reputation of
the Gracchi, Jack Cade, Wat Tyler and others, who have incurred the deadly hate of the powerful and wealthy by their
support of the rights of the people, so the ingenuity of the
political economist has been devoted to combining economic
truths and half-truths, right reasonings from wrong premises,
and false deductions from axiomatic principles, into a compact system of doctrine, by which public opinion has been
misled into imagining that existing evils were irremediable.
Thus, injustice and oppression have been sanctioned in the
name of science.

Labor Reformers have been accused of ignoring demonstrated scientific truths, and flying in the face of eternal and
immutable natural laws, when they have proposed to remedy
industrial abuses by legislation. Supposed scientific truths
and irreversible natural laws have so frequently, in the history
of the world, been quoted by the venal or short-sighted de-
fenders of systems, which all now admit to have been opposed
to the best interests of society, that the reproach has lost
much of its force. Those who remember how the name of
science was invoked in favor of negro slavery and against
the higher education of women—how every successive stage
of human progress has been retarded by the opposition offered on the ground that the proposed reform ran counter to
immutable laws, will not be disposed to admit the finality of the
current dogmas of political economy.

There are truths embodied in the doctrines of the political
economists which we should as little think of denying as the
laws of gravitation or the motion of the earth round the sun.
But the inferences which are drawn from these truths are
often false, and their relations to the questions between

producer and consumer, capitalist and laborer, mis-stated.
For instance, it is obviously true that the price of a commodity is regulated by supply and demand, and that if labor be
treated as a commodity its price will also be fixed by the
same inexorable law. To infer from this, that existing industrial relations are necessarily permanent, is to ignore the possibility which exists of changing, not the law, but the conditions under which the law operates. Society, while recognizing to the full the immutability of the law of supply and
demand, may neutralize its effect either by regulating the
supply so as to bring it down to the level of the demand, or
by taking labor altogether out of the category of commodities.

In other departments than political economy, natural laws
are studied as much in order to interpose an artificial check
to their operations, as to allow them unrestricted scope. It
is a natural law that a certain degree of cold will destroy life.
We provide against it by thick clothing and warm houses.
Under the laws of electricity, lightning will fire buildings,
and kill or injure the occupants. We do not deny or ignore
that law when we adopt the artificial protection of a lightning
conductor. We simply change the conditions under which it
operates. Floods and storms, pestilence and earthquakes, endanger the safety of life and property. Instead of submitting
to their effects, in the spirit of a blind fatalism, science en-
deavors to study the natural laws which govern them, and the
methods of their operation, so as to anticipate and counteract them by artificial means. Modern research and progress,
the improvements and inventions of which we boast, the appliances and methods by which the conditions of civilized life
are rendered possible, represent a continual struggle to overcome natural obstacles, and to interfere with the workings of
natural law. In the realm of political economy alone do we
find the exception. Only in that department of science which
deals with the economic forces regulating production and
distribution, is the existence of a law of nature regarded as an
imperative reason for holding all attempts to narrow the scope

of its working, or interpose artificial means to prevent its evil results, as unscientific, irrational, and foredoomed to failure. To find a parallel to the fanaticism which looks complacently upon the degradation and wretchedness of the victims of industrial competition, because their condition is brought about by unchangeable natural laws, we must look back to the ages of superstition and ignorance, when the ravages of pestilence were regarded as proofs of the Divine wrath, any attempt to arrest which would be equally impious and futile.

The new political economy must be based upon the liberty and brotherhood of man, and the equal right of all to natural resources and opportunities. It must not only expound the natural laws which govern the distribution of wealth, but where those laws are found to operate unjustly, it must point out how the evil effects are to be counteracted. Instead of regarding the aggregate volume of wealth as the test of national greatness and welfare, it must concern itself with the condition of the individual citizen. Its highest ideal must be the greatest possible good to the greatest possible number, and its constant aim to secure to each and all the just value of their services to the community. Labor, and labor alone, either of hand or brain, should be regarded as entitling any to share the product which only labor can create. Land must be held as the common heritage to which all have an equal natural right, and which none can therefore be permitted to use without paying into the common fund the value of its usufruct, and capital, simply as the tool auxiliary to labor, and subservient to the will of its creator.

Adam Smith, the father of political economy, has stated in plain terms the axiomatic truth, that labor is the creator of all wealth. In the fifth chapter of his " Wealth of Nations " we read :—

" The real price of everything, what everything really costs to the man who wants to acquire it, is the toil and trouble of acquiring it. What everything is really worth to the man who has acquired it, and who wants to dispose of it, or exchange it for something else, is the toil and trouble which it can save to himself, and which it can impose upon other people. What is bought with money, or with goods, is purchased by labor as much as what we acquire by the toil of our own body. That money or those goods, indeed, save us this toil. They contain the value of a certain quantity of labor which we exchange for what is supposed at the time to contain the value of an equal quantity. Labor was the first price, the original purchase-money, that was paid for all things. It was not by gold or silver, but by labor that all the wealth of the world was originally purchased, and its value to those who possess it, and who want to exchange it for some new productions, is precisely equal to the quantity of labor which it can enable them to purchase or command."

The broad principle thus enunciated strikes at the root of the entire system of capitalism. If all value is based upon labor alone, it follows that the only honest title which any man can hold to wealth created by others is by giving an equivalent in his own labor for what he receives. If he does not do this, if he depends simply on his parchment or paper monopoly "right" to the soil, to exact a personal tribute for the use of the land to which all have an equal right; if, by usury or profits apart from the return for labor of superintendence, and representing merely the accumulative power of capital, he enriches himself without rendering a just equivalent, he has gained wealth dishonestly. He has absorbed what rightly belongs to others; to those whose labor created it.

It is, in many cases, extremely difficult to draw the line and say just where the process of dishonest accumulation begins, and how far a large class of capitalists are rendering value by their brain-work for what they receive. But when, in the course of a few years, men are able to count their fortunes in millions, or when the processes by which money is accumulated are obviously such as do not tend to return society any benefit, there can be no possible question that they are receiving from the labor of others, wealth for which they have rendered no substantial return. Take the great landowners and money-kings, and apply the test to their accumulations. What have they given in labor to the world as a return for the produce of labor which they absorb in such ample measure? In some cases they do a considerable amount of head-work it is true, but it is often work that benefits nobody, that does not increase by one iota the sum total of production, or the facilities of distribution. The men who are engaged in struggling for fortunes on the stock exchange work hard after their fashion, in scheming and planning to outwit each other. But their labor is unprofitable to the community. It is non-productive. They are no more use than so many gamblers or tramps, and render no value whatever for what they receive. A landlord who merely lives on ground rents is a thief pure and simple—a cumberer of the earth and a parasite upon industry. A landlord who builds and rents houses does a public service and confers a measure of value in return for the income he draws. The capitalist who is a mere usurer and receives the produce of others' toil, without contributing either by thought or exertion to the increase of the production, lives by legalized theft. But the capitalist who personally gives direction to labor is a producer. Whether he is also in any measure a thief or not, depends entirely on whether the return he gets for his services is adequate or exorbitant. Frequently, not content with the fair value of his own labor of superintendence, he enriches himself by stealing from his employés a portion of their share of the common earnings. It is thus that large fortunes are realized.

Judged by this test of the returns made in labor for the produce of labor, the gains of capitalism are largely the result of the spoliation of the workers, even where they are not, like the fortunes built up by land-ownership, usury or speculation, the result of processes which confer absolutely no benefit on the community. It has often been charged against Labor Reformers that they ignore or undervalue brain labor; that the only "labor" they recognize is that of the wage-earner or the self-employed manual worker. In so far as this has been true

in the past it was the inevitable result of a system which regards capital as a separate interest controlling labor, and
merges the just and reasonable rights belonging to the labor of
supervision in the unjust and unreasonable claim of the capitalist in unlimited profits. It is not by necessary and legitimate brain work that men become rich, but by the power of
monopoly and competition to concentrate wealth in the hands
of those who control the means of production. Were the
system of distribution altered in accordance with the idea
that labor alone should be recognized as entitling any one to
share in the benefits of production, intellectual toil must of
course participate in proportion to its value.

Under the present system, much of the mental work, and as
a consequence much of the physical labor of the world also, is
misdirected, so that it is either valueless or positively injurious.
It is directed not to increasing production or perfecting the
machinery of distribution, but purely to self-aggrandizement,
by methods that are destructive and serve no useful purpose
whatever.

The following news item, which appeared in the newspapers
in the fall of 1885, will serve as an illustration.

" LITTLE ROCK, ARK. Nov. 19.—A war has been in progress for
several days between the Arkansas Telegraph Co., and the St. Louis
Iron Mountain and Southern Railway Co. The telegraph men have been
erecting poles on the line of railway near the city, and railway men have
taken them down as fast as they were put up. Each pole has been put
up and taken down a number of times during the day. Frequently, while
one set of men are digging a hole, the other set are shovelling dirt back
into it. The contest is really between the Baltimore and Ohio and
Western Union, the Arkansas Co. representing the latter."

Though this is a particularly aggravated and pronounced
instance of the waste of means and energy caused by competition, it is by no means an isolated case. It is rather
typical of the entire system and the processes that are continually going on all around us in the name of commercial enterprise. A vast proportion of the labor of the world is as
badly misdirected and as futile in its results as that of the

gangs of telegraph and railroad men kept busy in undoing each other's work. What are the men who "defy competition" and "will not be undersold," the keen, pushing leaders of mercantile enterprise, doing, but seeking continually to cross each other's paths and cut each other's throats, and undo what their rivals have accomplished? Half the energies of the organizers of the world's financial, railroad, manufacturing, and commercial systems are devoted to fighting each other, to filling up the holes that their rivals have dug, and pulling down poles they have erected—to making their work ineffective. Competition implies a continual warfare, which, like all warfare, results in a drain and a tax on productive industry.

Here, for instance, are a dozen wholesale merchants in a line where half their number would be amply sufficient to supply every legitimate demand. They accordingly engage in a desperate struggle, each fighting to keep his connections and take as much business as possible away from his neighbors. Each sends out his drummers to coax, importune, and tempt the retail dealer into making purchases. Most of their work is utterly wasted and unprofitable energy. They are laboring to undo the work of others, just as much as the pick-and-shovel brigades of the rival corporations in Arkansas. And it is so throughout every department in which competition prevails. Why are the prices charged for life insurance by the regular companies just about double what they ought to be? Because these companies, to get business, have to spend a very large portion of their receipts in fighting each other. They put up enormous and expensive buildings for show, and deluge the country with literature printed in costly, elaborate style, extolling themselves and disparaging their rivals. Instead of waiting until people who wish to insure come to them, they send out canvassers on big commissions to drum up business. When one company adopts this expensive system, of course others in self-defence are driven to follow their example, and the result is, that the cost of all this waste and loss is paid by the public, It is all entirely unnecessary—all a useless expenditure of labor and money. But the competitive system demands it, and industry bears the burden.

Wherever there are two or more railroads doing the business that could just as easily be done by one, there is a waste of labor and a loss of capital, though it may not be quite as apparent on the surface as in the case of the battle of the rival corporations in Arkansas. But, practically, it is just as destructive. Supposing the employés of one of the superfluous roads should go in a body, tear up the track, and burn the rolling-stock and freight-sheds of the other line. Everybody would be horrified at the awful waste of material. But a little consideration will show that there would be no more waste or sacrifice in such a high-handed act of aggression than there is in keeping up two roads to do the work of one. The waste lies in the mis-employed labor and capital spent in multiplying undertakings not demanded in the public interest.

In the railway and telegraph world, competition is never of long duration; it is always followed by combination or amalgamation in some form, and then up go rates, and down go wages. The losses to capitalism of the period of competition are made good many times over by systematic extortion. The business of filling up holes dug by others will have to be paid for just as though it were productive industry. What a vast amount of the world's best energies, what countless millions of money, have been sunk in the unprofitable, stupid, wicked work of pulling down what others have built, and filling up where others have dug. The warring armies of laborers in Arkansas, one trying to build and the other to demolish, are representatives of the state of industry and commerce to day, the world over. When will the senseless system cease, and men learn that it is better to co-operate than to compete? to be all builders and none destroyers? Not so long certainly as the selfish, soulless forces of capitalism and individual avarice have the control of industrial organization.

The following passage from "Poor's Manual of Railroads" for 1885 gives some idea of the enormous extent of this waste, from misdirected labor and uselessly employed capital spent

in undertakings not demanded in the public interest, but originated in a spirit of aggression.

"Of the 40,000 miles of line built in the five years ending with 1883,
no small part was built on speculation, and for that very reason paral-
leled already existing lines. The most striking examples of this kind,
examples so often adduced, are the West Shore and "Nickel Plate"
lines. The general demoralization which has prevailed in railroad
circles is due more to the construction of these two, and to the ill-fort-
une which attended them, than to any other cause, or it may be said to
all other causes. * * * Although West Shore and "Nickel Plate"
seemed to be the occasion of the great catastrophe of 1883 and 1884, the
real causes had been long at work in the wonderful success of signal
instances of ' watering,' of which the Pacific lines, the New York Central, and Lake Shore are striking examples. Incited by their success,
our whole people became wild upon the subject of railroad construction,
believing that two or three dollars could easily be made for every dollar
put up, either by the success of their ventures or by the sale of their securities. In this mania or delusion the capitalist and the adventurer
alike shared. The promoters of West Shore, men of capital, put up
their money in good earnest under the idea that they were embarking
in an honorable and meritorious enterprise. The promoters of Nickel
Plate built their line on speculation and for the purpose of selling it,
securities being issued at the rate of two or three dollars for every dollar
of cash paid. No small portion of the 40,000 miles constructed in the five
years ending with 1883 was built upon the same plan and with the same
object. Whatever their fate a large number of them became competitors
for a business for which ample provision had already been made by existing lines. Railroads unfortunately seem to reverse the rule of the survival of the fittest to ' the survival of the unfittest.' They can be used but
for one purpose, and when they go into the hands of receivers they are
to be run so long as the operating expenses can be paid. If the earnings
are not sufficient for this purpose, they are to be eked out by ' Receivers'
certificates.' The country is now at about its lowest depth, so far as
railroads are concerned. The evil done, the remedy has now to be applied."

A very large proportion of the brain labor that is most
highly remunerated is either useless or absolutely injurious to
society, such as that devoted to the construction of the West
Shore and Nickel Plate railroad lines, with the results above
depicted, and the "work" of land speculators, gamblers either
on or off the stock exchange, usurers, corporation lawyers, and

the great majority of politicians. In the same category must also be placed very many of the class who mould public opinion—editors, preachers, lecturers, magazine writers, and college professors. Much of their labor is devoted to inculcating wrong ideas; to making the worse appear the better cause; to justifying and apologizing for social abuses. Ignorantly or knowingly, they prostitute their talents and opportunities to the service of Mammon, and antagonize the rights of labor. The value of their services to society is often in inverse ratio to the remuneration they actually receive. Mental services of incalculable value are frequently poorly rewarded, or not rewarded at all. The great poets, inventors, thinkers—the intellectual heroes and saviors of the race, the men who propound new truths or are quick to grasp the significance of altered conditions and apply old principles in a new way—the pioneers of thought—seldom indeed reap the fruit of their labors. They are fortunate if they win a bare subsistence.

> " Serve not for any man's wages,
>   Pleasure, nor glory nor gold;
> Not by her side are they won
> Who saith unto each of you ' Son,
> Silver and gold have I none;
> I give but the love of all ages,
>   And the life of my people of old.' "

The poverty in which mechanical inventors have lived and died, while leaving to the world inventions which have immensely increased the productive capacity of labor, is notorious. The inventor, a poor man as a rule, toils and struggles for years in bringing his scheme to perfection—sacrificing his ease, his pleasure, and his health, frequently denying himself needed food and rest, bending every energy of mind and of body to the accomplishment of the dream of his life. And when success is at last achieved, it is in the great majority of cases the man of money who reaps the benefit of the invention, while the creative genius pines in poverty and neglect.

If the extent of their services to society were the measure

of the extent to which the product of the labor of others should be at their disposal, a very large class of brain-workers, now honored and wealthy, would have no claim whatever to the emoluments they now enjoy. On the other hand, many who toil on in penury and obscurity, whose creative powers in the departments of invention, literature, and art, or whose faculties for the organization and direction of physical labor have hitherto secured scant recognition, would have a fuller measure of reward. Under the present system, the returns of brain-labor, when exercised by the capitalist, are simply what he can secure under the workings of monopoly and competition ; when exercised by the wage-earner its remuneration is measured by its adaptability to the purposes of capitalism. In neither case does the element of labor-value given to society enter into the account.

We are living under a system of one-sided Socialism. Political economists, capitalistic editors, full-fed optimists, and sleek pulpiteers of the Henry Ward Beecher and Joseph Cook stamp may deprecate with all the energy at their command the theories of Socialism proper. They may exhaust the resources of argument and ridicule in demonstrating the injustice and utter impracticability of the Socialistic system. They may ransack history to show the failure of all attempts to re-organize society on such a basis, or to establish permanently successful communities on the principle of equal rights. They may adduce from theology and science principles which they consider conclusive against the future accomplishment of any such scheme. But in the meantime the practical developments which are taking place all around us are a demonstration of the tendency of modern civilization towards a more perfect system of industrial organization, partaking largely of the Socialistic character. In some of its phases Socialism is already here. Every advance from the primitive system of isolation and self-dependence, every improvement which brings closer together the producing forces, which simplifies the mechanism of exchange and distribution, which facilitates division of labor, and increases the de-

pendence of the individual upon the community, limiting the
scope of his unaided powers, while increasing immensely his
productive capacity, has been an advance towards Socialism
in its co-operative phase. Here again the vocabulary of political economy fails us for the right word to convey the meaning. Co-operation literally implies " working together," but
its modern secondary meaning is the working together of
those who have a common interest in the result of their enterprise proportionate to its returns. This kind of co-operation has not made much headway, but co-operation in the
literal sense—that is to say, industrial organization under the
direction of capitalism—the association of workers together
by hundreds and thousands, under the same control and for
the same ends, and the dependence one upon another of the
enterprises in which they are engaged, gives us practically
Socialism in work in connection with individualism in the
distribution of returns. Under this anomalous semi-Social-
ism the laborer gets the worst of it all around. He has all
the disabilities of individualism and Socialism combined.
His remuneration is fixed by competition, under the law of
supply and demand, without regard to the productive power
of his labor. Division of labor confines his training to one
department, and he loses that general adaptability and capacity for doing many things which the laborer possesses
where work is less specialized. In case of a revolution in his
particular branch of industry, owing to commercial changes
or new inventions, he is frequently unable to adapt himself
to altered conditions, or find occupation outside the narrow
groove to which he has all his life been accustomed. Socialism in production only has reduced him to the level of an
automaton—a portion of the industrial mechanism—and largely
deprived him of the self-supporting faculty, should he by any
chance drop out of his place ; while the compensation for his
loss of self-hood and absolute dependence upon social adjust-
ments which true Socialism would offer in a recognized claim
upon the common production and an assured future, is wanting. The opponents of Socialism, who dwell upon its injuri-

ous effects upon national and individual character, by lessening self-reliance and hardihood, and degrading mankind into
a race of weaklings all looking to be helped and provided
for by the state, completely overlook the fact that the modern
industrial system is doing for the mass of wage-earners, in
this respect, the very worst that State Socialism could possibly do. The tendency of large enterprises to absorb or crush
out smaller ones is so fully recognized at this stage of the
controversy, that there is no need to emphasize it. In every
department the field for individual energy is being continually narrowed, and the possibilities of success for new competitors diminished by the consolidation and welding together
of existing interests.

"Enterprise" has long been regarded by Americans as a
cardinal virtue, sufficient to atone for many defects of character. It is natural that in a new country where much rough,
arduous, and dangerous work had to be done to prepare the
way for civilization, the pioneer and the pathfinder should be
held in high esteem. The circumstances under which America has been settled, the wilderness reclaimed, industries established, the means of travel and communication and all the
agencies of civilized life introduced, not by government instrumentality, but by the unconquerable resolution and energy
of individual citizens, tended to set a high value on the quality of enterprise. When, as was often the case, the wisdom
of any particular course could only be decided by the event,
it is not surprising that Col. Davy Crockett's maxim, "Be
sure you are right, then go ahead," became abbreviated in
the popular acceptation to "go ahead anyhow." Enterprise
that no obstacles could daunt and no failure discourage,—enterprise that flung caution to the winds, and risked everything
on a single chance,—enterprise that took its life in its hand
and braved all dangers, that encountered seeming impossibil-
ities, and set at defiance all precedents and rules, has been
the darling and cherished characteristic of those concerned in
the development of the American continent, from the con-
structors of the Union Pacific railroad down to the advent-

5

urous gold-seekers who faced the perils of the prairies with
the legend " Pike's Peak or Bust" inscribed in straggling and
uneven characters on their wagons. " Enterprise ! "   There
is a fascination for every American in the word.   It tells of
heroic struggles and sacrifices—of the toilsome life of the fron-
tier settler, determined to build up a home for himself in the
wilderness—of the hope deferred of the inventor, racking his
brains to perfect some mechanical improvement upon which he
has spent his all—of the lofty and comprehensive projects of
the great captains of industry, and of the ambitious designs
and day-dreams of the penniless Yankee boy, pacing the
streets of New York or Chicago with the determination to
make his fortune.   In the social struggle, as in war, one brilliant success casts into obscurity a thousand failures.   The
career of the few who succeed, the Stewarts, and Jay Goulds,
and Erastus Wimans, are blazoned forth as examples for the
emulation of young men, and proofs that in America push and
determination are always rewarded ; while those who have
striven and struggled in vain, and live on in poverty, or fill
unknown graves—victims to enterprise—are forgotten.   Just
so twenty years ago the names of Grant, Sherman, and Sher-
idan shone freshly luminous with the glory of battle, while
none but their immediate circle of friends knew or mourned
the privates who fell in the conflict.

> " Some men must fill trenches, ten thousand go down,
>   As unnamed and unknown as the stones in a wall,
>   For the few to pass over and on to renown."

If " peace has her victories not less renowned than war,"
she has also, alas ! her tragedies of defeat, and her long roll of
the vanquished and despoiled.

While, as has been said, the tendency to magnify and
esteem enterprise is a natural result of the conditions under
which American civilization has been created, we have now
reached that stage of social organization in which a much
lower rank must be accorded to it.   Qualities which are of
invaluable practical utility at one period of social develop-

ment may be largely useless or positively detrimental to the general welfare at a more advanced stage. The enterprise which, during the formative period, manifested itself in pioneer work, which laid the foundations of civilized institutions, turned to account the resources of nature, and built up great highways of traffic was a beneficent agency. But when thickly settled communities have grown up, and industry and production are fully organized, the enterprise which was formerly constructive becomes largely competitive and destructive. In many of its forms it is positively injurious, and its sphere of possible utility is greatly decreased. But the current American tradition of "go ahead!" still survives, and men still eulogize enterprise as such with very little discrimination as to its objects. It may be directed towards a wholly unnecessary and even ruinous competition with existing undertakings; it may manifest itself in projects which derange the industrial and commercial machinery, without a single compensating advantage to the public; it may take the form of speculation in grain or stocks, sharp financiering or land monopoly, enriching the operator at the expense of society. No matter how useless or how pernicious in its effects, a bias in favor of enterprise, simply as enterprise, cause it to be regarded with a large measure of favor and admiration, even by those who suffer from it.

The misdirection of enterprise and the consequent waste of material and productive force are owing to the fact that the personal interests of individuals are allowed undisputed control of capital, without reference to the needs of the community. The greed, ambition, passions, or caprices of a very small minority are paramount to the vital necessities and highest interests of the masses, and the disproportion in numbers between the few who exercise control and the many whose means of existence are at their disposal, is constantly increasing. The Chicago *News*, for instance, in July, 1885, commenting upon the labor troubles which then prevailed in that city, called attention to the vast disparity between the numbers of employers and employed.   Owing to the immense accumulations of capital in few hands and the consequent centralization of industry 200,000 out of the 300,000 wage-earners of that city were then employed by about 250 individuals or corporations.   The following passage is full of significance, and is applicable to many other labor centers than Chicago.

"Without some means of settling the difficulties that culminate in strikes, Chicago will sooner or later be called upon to face a general uprising of a large portion of its wage-working population.   Indeed it was feared in the last strike, and in such an event what would the 250 employers of the 200,000 wage-workers in this city do?   The only alternative is to yield or stop work."

In this growing disparity of numbers between capitalists and wage-workers lies the hope of a just and satisfactory solution of the problem.   Capitalism is cutting its own throat very fast.   By killing off small competitors, and continually narrowing the circle of the employers of labor and the accumulators of wealth, it weakens immensely its powers of resistance to the popular demand for justice.   The process will go on and on until some day in the not distant future the representatives of the toiling millions may quietly walk into the offices of the few hundred capitalists and say, "Gentlemen, the people have decided to dispense with you.   We have concluded that you have engrossed the fruits of our labor long enough.   Henceforth we shall conduct the business ourselves, and for our own benefit."

The failure of the system under which capitalism controls labor for its personal advantage, and work and wages are regulated by monopoly above and competition below, to regulate satisfactorily either production or distribution is so manifest that we find so orthodox a political economist as Francis A. Walker compelled to admit it, and to admit also the defects of political economy, and its absolute failure to point out any remedy for existing evils.   In his work on "Money, Trade, and Industry" he says:—

" It would seem that the most important of the questions which political economy is called upon to answer, is the question why the production of a people so often falls below and remains below what would result from the proper application of its labor power and its capital power to the natural agents—land, water-power, mineral resources, etc.—of the country where they dwell ? Why is the actual at times so far short of the maximum production ? Yet there is no question with which political economists have so little concerned themselves. There are scores of systematic treatises on my shelves from which not a hint could be obtained in explanation of the economical situation of the United States at the present moment, and indeed at any time during the past five years— an immense labor power and capital power only partially employed, while natural resources remain unexhausted, and even in a large degree undeveloped, to which labor and capital might be applied to the satisfaction of human wants. Those wants remain unsatisfied ; poverty and suffering result to hundreds of thousands; straitness of means and diminution of comfort to millions more; and yet there is no indisposition of the capitalist to derive an income by allowing the use of his money in production, and no reluctance of the laborer to work. Abounding natural resources, unemployed labor power, unemployed capital power, no lack of disposition to labor, and yet an enforced idleness and resulting poverty and squalor.''

It would be difficult to frame a more forcible indictment of the generally accepted system of political economy than this candid admission by an advocate of its cherished principles. If Mr. Walker's statement be true, that it has no explanation to offer of the present industrial evils, and no remedy to suggest, what claims have its teachings upon the intelligent opinions of those who are brought face-to-face with the practical aspects of this problem, which the writer sets before us so clearly ? How can men who feel bitterly the effects of the conditions he has thus graphically depicted, be expected to rest satisfied with the empty platitudes and time-honored traditions which have wholly failed to meet the living actual issues of the present? How can a system which reiterates with little modification the ideas and principles which were considered applicable to the condition of society before the railroad and the telegraph were in operation, before the era of mechanical invention and manufacturing expansion set in, help us in the solution of an entirely new and complicated set of questions, the very possibility of which was not dreamed of when its theories were formulated? As well might the modern general, in these days of Winchester rifles, Armstrong guns, and iron-clad vessels, base his plan of campaign on the tactics of Frederick the Great or Turenne. It is idle to talk of the wisdom of our ancestors, or the respect due to principles which have so long been accepted by mankind. When all the conditions have altered, the longer that any system has been in vogue the less likely it is to be suitable to the prevailing requirements.

Of late the public mind, or perhaps rather the public conscience, has acquired some vague perception of the truth of the new political economy. If has become the fashion to speak of wealth as a "trust." The millionaire is held morally responsible for the use to which he puts his superfluous riches. If a rich man dies without leaving a considerable percentage of his money to religious, philanthropic, or public purposes, the fact is commented on by the press often in severe terms, as though he had in a sense defrauded the community by withholding what they had a right to expect. Now all this is entirely at variance with the recognized principles of political economy, that whatever wealth a man can accumulate by legal means is indisputably *his* to use as he pleases, to hoard or squander, to give or bequeath as he sees fit, without any one having the right to call him to account. This instinctive sense, that, after all, the community has a claim upon the accumulations of wealth, utterly illogical though it is in its manifestations, is significant of a widespread though undefined revulsion from the formally accepted theories as to property rights. Newspapers which would repel indignantly the charge of "Socialism," and are ordinarily firm sticklers for the rights of capital, will nevertheless write of the responsibilities of wealth, and if a prominent millionaire dies without making the customary benefactions to churches, colleges, asylums, or hospitals, will refer to the matter in a tone which intimates that in their opinion the omission indicates a grave shortcoming in the character of the late lamented. There is room for clear thinking on this phase of modern sentiment. If wealth is indeed a " trust," its possessor cannot have an absolute individual right to it. On the other hand, if he has such a right to it, it cannot be a trust. And if it is a trust, it is surely logical to say that society ought to have the power— seeing that it must clearly have the right—of seeing that the trust is not abused. If a wealthy man be really responsible— as a large class of journalists, ministers, and lecturers of unquestioned economic soundness say that he is—for the use that he makes of his means, should the enforcement of this responsibility be left altogether to public opinion? If he is not responsible, there is an end of the matter. But if he is, why is he left free to deny or ignore this responsibility, and to assert his privilege to " do as he likes with his own ? "

The fact is, that the intuitive sense of justice of the masses has reached a conclusion that is entirely at variance with their theoretical opinions. They feel the wrong and the injustice of unlimited personal aggrandizement, by the operation of the system of monopoly and competition, though they may not be able to reason it out clearly ; and they assert an indefinite, shadowy sort of claim on behalf of society upon large accumulations, which they would be puzzled to justify on the principles that they profess to accept.

The " trust " idea so frequently emphasized of late is important merely as showing the tendency of men's thoughts in relation to the intrinsic injustice of methods, under which individuals are able to heap up wealth in amounts which bear no ascertainable relation to the actual value of the services they render to society. It contains the germ which, expanded and systematized, will revolutionize the relations between labor and capital, and instead of keeping the worker hopelessly dependent upon those who control the means and opportunities of production, will restore to each the right to the full earnings of his labor under the new political economy.

CHAPTER IV.

REVOLUTION OR EVOLUTION

Courage! my brother or my sister!
Keep on! Liberty is to be subserved whatever occurs.
That is nothing that is quelled by one or two failures or any number of
    failures,
Or by the indifferences or ingratitude of the people or by any unfaith-
    fulness,
Or the show of the tushes of power, soldiers, cannon, penal statutes.
What we believe in waits, latent forever through all the continents, and
    all the islands and archipelagoes of the sea.
What we believe in invites no one, promises nothing, sits in calmness
    and light, is positive and composed, knows no discouragement.
Waiting patiently, waiting its time.

WALT WHITMAN.

THE great majority of wage-workers and a good many others are so fully sensible of the injustice of the system of capitalism, that arguments to prove what daily impresses itself upon them by bitter experience may be regarded as superfluous. They know already that they do not get the value of the products of their labor, and that the reason is because those who have monopolized the means of production absorb, as profit, rent, and usury, a vast amount in excess of anything to which they are legitimately entitled as remuneration for brain labor. They see, moreover, that private control of capital results in waste and loss, owing to the undertaking f enterprises which are not required in the public interest—which waste and loss ultimately fall on the producing class. But though there is a widespread conviction of the wrong, there is no adequate general perception of the remedy; and still less is there a determination to forego all other public objects in order to secure it.

Despite the wonderful advances made of late in the direction of labor organization, and a better understanding of the conditions of the problem, numbers of wage-workers are still apathetic or hopeless of any permanent betterment of their lot. Many are thoughtless and indifferent so long as their immediate position is not absolutely insupportable. Others are under the spell of the fatalism of political economy, which teaches that periods of industrial stagnation and distress are natural and inevitable. More are influenced by a perverted Christianity, which disparages sublunary matters as of little moment, and blasphemously regards the consequences of human greed and oppression 'as Heaven-sent afflictions which must be borne in patience, holding out the prospect of a "home beyond the skies" as an incentive to contentment under unjust conditions here. A considerable proportion are disposed to regard the existing system with some measure of favor, because, under the influence of the "self-made man" tradition, they hope, by superior industry, thrift, and enterprise, some day or other to escape from the ranks of labor and become wealthy themselves. And many who are keenly alive to labor's disabilities have not yet progressed beyond the idea of trade-unionism, and regard the question as simply a difference between the laborer and his immediate employer respecting wages or hours.

Among those who realize the necessity for organic change, and are willing to work to secure it, the greatest difference of opinion prevails both as to aims and methods. While the final results sought to be attained are more or less socialistic in their character, the means of operation may be broadly classified as revolutionary and evolutionary.

Hitherto I have as far as possible avoided the use of the term "Socialism," not from fear of arousing vulgar prejudice, but to avoid confusion of thought and misunderstanding. Socialism, as the word is popularly used, may convey so many different meanings, that unless the sense in which it is employed is thoroughly defined, it is liable to lead to misconception. As loosely made use of by the ignorant—though possibly college-bred—writers for the capitalistic press, it implies a suggestion of violence. In its scientific sense it connotes a systematized completeness as to the details, which does not enter into the schemes of many who are more or less Social-

istic in their aims. But to label as " Socialism " any movement or plan which has for its ultimate object the substitution
for wage-servitude and competition, of a system under which
the community shall regulate production and distirbution,
tends to preclude consideration on its own merits, and to
imply more than is intended. In particular, it is calculated,
owing to the systematic perversion of the term by capitalistic writers, to convey to superficial minds the notion of revolutionary violence. Socialism, in the legitimate sense of
the word, relates solely to the system, and has not the slightest
reference to the means employed for bringing it about. It
no more implies insurrection than does " Democracy"—a word
to which, in continental Europe, much the same sinister
significance has been attached. Most of the avowed anarchists are not Socialists in the sense of having any definite
ideas as to the future organization of Society. And many,
perhaps most, Socialists are not revolutionists. They look to
the power of the ballot to accomplish their objects, rightly
arguing that if men will not combine for peaceful political
agitation, it is folly to imagine that they could be induced to
resort to the desperate measure of armed revolt in sufficient
numbers to make success possible.

Of late years the air has been full of the mutterings of approaching disturbance. Associations and publications openly
revolutionary in their object have been established. Again
and again has the long-smouldering discontent of the restless, hungry, dissatisfied element, the "proletariat" of the
great cities, flamed up in incipient revolt, as in the memorable
Pittsburg riots of 1877, the Cincinnati outbreak in 1884, and
the Milwaukee and Chicago riots of the spring of 1886. The
growth, owing to the operation of the system of capitalistic exploitation, of this outcast class—the under dogs of the world's
fight, the wrecks and failures of humanity, the "unfittest " who
do not "survive," the weakest who go to the wall in the struggle, who fear no future in this or any other world, who have
neither hope nor energy nor ambition left—is at once one of
the saddest results of the existing system, and the sure pre-

sage of its overthrow. Like Frankenstein in the story, Capitalism has created a monster which threatens to destroy the classes, if not the system, that gave it life.

The number of men and women who cannot get work on any terms implies a far larger class whose pay has become a mere pittance by reason of competition. The ranks of vice, idleness, and criminality are continually swollen by those who, under juster conditions, would have remained useful members of society. If there is one lesson that is clearly deducible from the history of all countries and ages, it is the absolute certainty of retribution for every form of injustice and oppression. America has already had one terrible experience of the slow but sure Nemesis which overtakes national wrong-doing, in the suffering and loss entailed by the war for the preservation of the union and the suppression of slavery. The record of the proudest empires of the past shows the inexorable working of this law of retribution for wrongs perpetrated and sanctioned by law and public opinion. In Draper's "Intellectual Development of Europe" the causes which wrought the decay of the powerful and splendid Roman Empire are thus summarized.

"Labor was despised; hence the downfall of the Roman Empire. The treatment of the laborers was atrocious. On the murder of one Pendanius, four hundred slaves were put to death, when it was obvious to every one that scarcely any of them had known of the crime. To such a degree had this system been developed that slave labor was cheaper than animal labor, and work formerly done by cattle was done by men. The class which should have constituted the chief strength of the country disappeared, labor becoming so ignoble that the poor citizen would not become an artizan, but became a pauper. The concentration of power and the increase of immorality proceeded with equal step. Crimes were committed such as the world had never before witnessed. An evil day is approaching when it becomes recognized in a community that the only standard of social distinction is wealth. That day in Rome was soon followed by corruption and terrorism. No language can describe its state after the civil wars. The accumulation of power and wealth gave rise to untold depravity among the aristocracy. A citizen had to deposit a bribe before a trial at law could be had. The social body was a festering mass of rottenness. The aristocracy was demoniac. The city

was a hell to the laborer. No villainy that the annals of human wick-
edness can show was left unperpetrated. Remorseless murders, the betrayal of parents, husbands, wives, friends, were reduced to a system
which degenerated into crimes that cannot be written. ''

And so fell the power that for centuries made the world
tremble, and exercised a wider supremacy than any nation of
ancient times. The systematic oppression of the laborer
sapped its manhood, destroyed its strength, rotted the magnificent structure at its foundation, and left it an easy prey to
the barbarian hordes. The description of the causes of
Rome's overthrow presents such a startling parallel to the
causes now at work in every modern land that it reads like a
slightly overdrawn presentation of the evils of American or
European society to-day. Is history repeating itself? Are
the great Empire and the great Republic travelling over the
same broad road that led old Rome to the abyss?

> " Ill fares the land, to hastening ills a prey,
>   Where wealth accumulates and men decay,"

wrote the poet; mourning over the extinction of a once comfortable and happy peasantry at the will of the self-styled
"owner" of the soil. Look where we may, the same sinister
phenomenon presents itself—the accumulation of wealth and
the decay of manhood. Horrible crimes abound—each day's
despatches tell the story. As in the days of Roman deca-
dence, "the concentration of power and the increase of immorality proceed with equal step." Look at the great monopolies—the trans-continental railroad lines—the coal companies—the manufacturing combinations—the telegraph corporations—the land-grabbing rings and the landlords who
own block upon block of property in the heart of our great
cities—the capitalists, who by a stroke of the pen can raise
the price of the necessaries of life. Never since the days to
which the foregoing extract refers did a very few men hold
in their hands such extensive powers over their fellows, or use
them more remorselessly. The claims of manhood are dis-
regarded; only those of the moneyed interests are recognized

by the lawgivers, who are as much owned by the monopolizing class as though they had been purchased in open
market. The whole advantage of the great inventions designed to improve the condition of mankind has gone to the
exploiting classes. If experience can be depended upon as a
guide—if there is any meaning in the warnings of history—
these wrongs must bring retribution in their train. Unless a
thorough reconstruction of the industrial system arrests the
tendency to demoralization by ensuring healthier conditions
for the development of a higher standard of manhood and
womanhood, the same enfeeblement and degradation of the
race which proved the ruin of the ancient civilizations based
upon slavery and caste supremacy will assuredly sap the system reared by capitalism upon a like foundation of industrial
serfdom.

The revolutionary spirit is abroad. Wherever the pressure
is greatest and the depressing effects of the social struggle
most keenly felt, there are spasmodic outbreaks or menacing
demonstrations—the instinctive turning of the crushed worm
rather than the deliberate purpose of those having in view a
definite end. In a large proportion of the now chronic labor
troubles in the large centres a disposition towards physical
violence has been displayed. When the desperation of wage-
workers who see their condition growing more intolerable
takes the form of assaults on those who, like themselves, are
the victims of capitalism, and have no choice between accepting the terms offered them and slow starvation—when unionists, in their blind and unreasoning rage, turn against non-
unionists, or Chinamen, or foreign workmen, and kill or assault them, their acts admit of no justification whatever, of
no palliation even, except the perpetrators have been brutal-
ized and degraded by oppression.

But outside of this form of physical outbreak, forcible resistance to the tyranny of employers, or acts committed in retaliation as a deterrent, cannot be consistently condemned
except by those who are non-resistants on principle. Those
who hold the Quaker doctrine, and believe, theoretically

at least, in turning the left cheek when the right is smit-
ten, in enduring wrong meekly and uncomplainingly, and
in returning good for evil, may logically denounce striking or
locked-out workmen in resorting to violence. But they are
the only ones who can. Among the great mass of mankind
another principle prevails. Non-resistance is voted an impracticable if not a cowardly doctrine—one which would give
this world over to anarchy, tyranny, and brutal oppression.
The maxim that " resistance to tyrants is obedience to God "
is inculcated as embodying a noble rule of action and justifying
the course of Washington, Tell, Hofer, Garibaldi, Toussaint
L'Ouverture, and other revolutionary patriots whose names are
held in high honor. Rebellions against acts of oppression infinitely less mischievous in their crushing and degrading effects
than the cold-blooded and systematic pauperization of American labor have been lauded to the skies as just and righteous.

Because England put a paltry tax of a few cents a pound
upon tea, which did not materially interfere with the comfort
and well-being of the American people, a Boston mob
seized the cargoes of that commodity in the vessels lying in
their harbor and threw them overboard. The act is regarded
by every American as the outcome of a noble and patriotic
determination to resist a tyrannical imposition. Now what
is the difference in principle between the doings of the historic
" Boston tea party " and the destruction of property in the
mines of Ohio or on the railroads of Missouri by men ground
down to the last stages of endurance by the inexorable and
pitiless hand of monopoly ? Why is the one to be honored
and the other condemned ? It is asserted that historical research
has proved William Tell to be a myth. Be that as it may,
his character, whether real or fictitious, has long been held in
high esteem for his successful resistance to the tyrant Gessler.
He refused to bow to the despot's cap elevated to receive the
homage of the people, and the struggle that followed ended by
his sending an arrow through the oppressor's heart and restoring
his country's liberties. That was magnanimous and noble and
heroic in the estimation of the very people who will in the

next breath condemn the people's war on monopoly as the act of wretches who ought to be sent to the gallows. And yet what a light and trifling thing is the exaction of a motion of external homage as compared with the actual deprivation of the means of subsistence and the slow process of moral and physical degradation which the tyrants of monopoly have decreed? If—apart altogether from considerations of expediency—revolutionary courses on the part of oppressed wage-workers are morally wrong, then clearly a great many parallel actions, which the general consensus of opinion has hitherto held to be justifiable and even admirable and heroic, were also wrong. If resistance to oppression is to be held right, it simply becomes a question of degree—a question of how long and how much poor humanity is to be expected to endure before it seeks to retaliate.

While, according to the principles acted upon by the founders of the republic, an uprising of the working-classes to recover their rights by force would be fully justified, it is well that the sound, practical common-sense and right feeling of the great majority are decidedly against violence, except as a last resort. Considerations of humanity and expediency alike point to the employment of every other means before resorting to the dread alternative of insurrection. The horrors of a civil war between sections would be far outdone by the hideous program of the anarchists, were it by any possibility realized. Then war would be brought home to every man's door, and the most sanguine could hardly expect that in the end the lot of labor would be materially bettered. Every condition of success in such a contest is wanting, and stern repression and bloodthirsty vengeance, such as that which characterized the fall of the Paris Commune, would be inflicted by the infuriated victors. The worst possible result would be the achievement of a temporary success by men whose sole aim was the destruction of existing institutions without any definite or well-arranged plan, perhaps without any plan at all, for their replacement. Every thoughtful Labor Reformer realizes that, cruel as are the wrongs perpetrated under the

present social organization, the hardships and miseries
entailed by a sudden stoppage of its machinery would be
infinitely greater.

The abuses of capitalism are so hateful and its rule is so despotic—often so devilish in some of its aspects—that we are in
danger of forgetting the old adage, " give the devil his due."
We fail to remember that, black as the record of capitalism is,
and bitter as are the wrongs that men bear at its hands—yet
nevertheless, in the present stage of the world's development,
it serves a useful purpose. It was not created. It did not
spring into existence armed with all the powers which it has
so badly misused, but was evolved gradually with the growth
of society to fill a function which no other power was then or
is yet capable of filling. Now, in the complicated network of
an advanced civilization, the work of organization, superintendence, and direction must be done by somebody, or chaos
will come again. Just think of the fate of a great city like
New York or Chicago, or even of a small town, if the wheels
of the great machine of commerce and transportation were
suddenly to stop—if, owing to want of organizing capacity
and executive action, the supplies of wheat, cattle, and coal
on which the people are dependent for existence were
no longer forwarded—if the water-works and gas departments were allowed to run themselves—if all the systems
of transit and communication, such as the railroads,
the telegraphs, the express companies, the great manufacturing and wholesale enterprises, were brought to a standstill by
reason of the forcible and sudden removal of the monopolists
and middlemen by whom they are conducted. It would simply mean starvation to thousands and inconceivable hardship
and inconvenience to the survivors before society could re-
adjust itself. Yes, capitalism does, after its fashion, bung-
lingly and badly, and with harshness and injustice enough,
God knows, the needed work of superintendence and direction
—but after all it does it. The monopolist and the middle-
man must be got rid of—utterly abolished at the earliest
opportunity. But to do this without entailing far greater

evils than even their exactions inflict, some means must be found of filling their places and doing their work of organizing, production, and distribution. Are the world's toilers at present fit to undertake this essential task ? The experience of the numerous attempts at productive co-operation unfortunately points in the other direction. Before any hope of such a change in the social organization as will substitute universal co-operation for the wage system can be reasonably entertained, workingmen must have cultivated successfully the business faculty—the power of close calculation, of accurate, shrewd, and conscientious management of public affairs, and learned in larger measure than at present the need of mutual confidence and the value of combination and united action.

In evolution, not in revolution, lies the solution of the problem. No sudden spasmodic change, even could it be accomplished peaceably, could possibly bring those aptitudes for the fulfilment of the duties and responsibilities of a more perfect social state which alone could save the community from a worse fate than the rule of the moneyed interest. Our position may be compared to that of prisoners in the hold of a pirate vessel, robbed, half-starved, and condemned to drudgery. It is possible that by a concerted movement we might kill or master the pirates ; but we are ignorant of navigation, and should we attempt to work the vessel, would be in imminent peril of shipwreck. The pirates, though severe taskmasters, at least keep us afloat.

Power and ignorance do not go well together. The world is not ripe for a social revolution. Were such a general upheaval as would utterly prostrate the power of monopoly and put capital under our feet to come now, it would come too soon, because it would find the masses unprepared. Suppose that, in the present condition of public opinion, the wage-workers throughout this continent rose as one man, overcame the police, the military, and the Pinkerton mercenaries, hung every monopolist upon whom they could lay their hands to the nearest tree or lamp-post, sent their palaces up in smoke,

6

aad confiscated their stolen goods to the public use, what, so far as the condition of labor is concerned, would be the result? Why simply that in a few years later all the evils and abuses which had provoked the outbreak would again be in full blast. We should have a new set of millionaires and monopolists created out of the dominant working-class by the operation of the same conditions and influences which have developed the present taskmasters, and the masses would be no better off than before. The people are not yet sufficiently educated to change the conditions and overthrow the system which breeds monopolists. If the monopolists, as a class, are worse men than their victims, it is the fault of a system under which the baser qualities of human nature conduce to prosperity— while the nobler traits of humanity are often obstacles to success in life. The individuals who have climbed to the pinnacle of fortune over the heads of their fellows, careless of whom they crushed bleeding to earth, may deserve all that a bloody revolution would bring upon them. But their fate would not of itself alter the conditions, and other greedy and unscrupulous men would soon step on over prostrate humanity into their places.

With too many working-men the millionaire is an object of envy. The only reason they have for hating the system is because they do not happen to have drawn prizes in the lottery of life. They desire nothing so much as to become monopolists themselves. "I only wish I were as rich as Jay Gould;" "Ah! if somebody would die now and leave me a million dollars," and similar expressions which we hear every day from men who profess to be in favor of Labor Reform, show how deeply the virus of Mammon-worship has tainted society. So long as the great bulk of the people wish and long to be privileged loafers; so long as envy of the fortunate millionaire, rather than hatred of the infernal system which enables him to become such, inspires the masses, we cannot hope for any material gain either by a forcible or a peaceful revolution.

Now men are not individually to blame for wishing that

they were in Jay Gould's shoes. It is the fault of wrong education—not school education merely, but the teaching of the press and the platform and the whole circle of influences which contribute to the formation of opinion. The acquisition of wealth and position at the expense of others has been held up before us all from boyhood as a perfectly natural and laudable ambition. There is all the more need therefore for true teachings on the subject, to counteract the false education which sets up the millionaire as a man to be admired and envied. We have to create a revolution in public opinion before we can hope to revolutionize the system. We have to change not only men's formally expressed beliefs, but their aspirations and desires—to eradicate the deep-rooted selfishness begotten of competition, and to instil in its place a love for humanity and a strong sense of justice. It is an education of the heart as much as of the head that is needed. Not until this work, now just begun, is accomplished can the old order of things give place to the new.

Bearing in mind the great truth that all human institutions, including government in all its forms and phases, and the entire industrial system, are the product of evolution; that they have not been imposed upon mankind, but have slowly developed in accordance with the necessities of the case, we must look to the same process of gradual change for the improvement of present conditions. The acceptance of the evolution theory as applied to the growth of human society does not, as some have argued, imply a passive acquiescence in abuses in the spirit of fatalism. Evolution is not a blind, inexorable force. The direction of its working is capable of being changed by a change in conditions; and potent among these are the opinions and actions of the social units, still more those of large combinations. "In a society," says Herbert Spencer, "living, growing, changing, every new factor becomes a permanent force, modifying more or less the direction of movement determined by the aggregate of forces." Such a new factor in the transition stage upon which we have entered is educated and organized labor. As in the physical sphere the growth

of an organism is modified by its surroundings, so in the development of social institutions the influence of law, of public
opinion, and of organized effort tends continually towards a
change of structure, and makes a lasting impress upon the
character of the community, far more important and far-
reaching in its effects than the immediate result. A principle
once admitted, a precedent once firmly established, a step once
taken at the parting of the ways, trivial apparently by itself,
is often the germ of momentous and wholly unlooked for
social developments altering the whole trend of progress.

We stand at the parting of the ways. We have reached a
social turning-point. To move forward in the direction in
which we have been progressing, to allow the overgrown and
abnormal development of over-shadowing corporate and individual interests to continue, must before long destroy even
the semblance of democratic institutions and create an absolute plutocracy. There is no middle course—no possibility
of standing still and expecting that the relations between
capitalism and the community will remain as at present.
There can be no " arrested development," no Chinese crystallization of class relationship in the plastic political and social
organization of America.

To assert that because hitherto, since the era of industrial
expansion and socialized production, the working of the law
of evolution has been unfavorable to Democracy, by causing
inequalities in condition which are inconsistent with political
equality, is to ignore the new factors which are just coming
into play—labor organization on a great scale and the growing determination to use the ballot as a remedy for social
abuses. The political power of the masses, so far as this
question is concerned, has been an unused force. Men have
been divided on party lines based on unmeaning distinctions
or obsolete issues, while, under the influence of inherited traditions limiting the functions of government, the vital and all-
important new questions have been left to solve themselves.
The unprecedented interest now being taken in the Labor
question marks another such pivotal point in the course of

American liberty as was reached when the aggression of the slave power aroused the conscience and manhood of the nation against it. The period of vague unrest and chaotic upheavals is passing into the stage of crystallization of thought and directness of aim. Spasmodic local movements for trivial and temporary objects are giving place to general combinations for ends which are becoming more clearly defined. "The chaos of a mighty world is rounding into form;" the ideal of a regenerated society, of an industrial Democracy, as the ultimate goal of endeavor is taking the place of those meager concessions and partial ameliorations of their lot which were lately all that the masses dared to hope for. By evolution under the influence of the "new factor" of the opinion, the political power, and the united action of the laboring masses can this goal alone be reached.

While industrial evolution in one of its phases has been unfavorable to Democracy by degrading the citizen into a wage-serf, in another aspect it has immensely simplified the solution of the problem of social re-adjustment. It has created a system which is well-nigh perfect in its details so far as regards the organization of industry and the mechanism of exchange. For the crude and cumbrous methods of our ancestors it has substituted the nicely-adjusted and smoothly-working organization of forces by which the advantages of division of labor are realized, and the productive capacity of all forms of industry is marvellously increased. To transfer from the organizing and directing force of capitalism to the community the disproportionate share of the advantages of the system which capitalism now retains; to preserve all the social benefits arising from this elaborate mechanism of production and traffic, while abolishing the injustice and spoliation resulting from the control by and in the interests of indi. viduals, is a much less formidable undertaking than to create a social Democracy in a society where individualism in production has prevailed. It is easier to perfect a one-sided socialism than to build from the foundation.

It is recorded that the tyrant Nero once wished that the

Roman people had but one head that he might cut it off at a single blow. The progress of centralization is rapidly reducing the controlling forces of some forms of monopoly to this condition. Every year weakens the power of resistance to an organized attack by the people, because it diminishes the number of those personally interested in maintaining the present situation. In connection with the great railroad and telegraph systems especially, the number of heads continually decreases, and the final process of decapitation will be almost as simple as that longed for by the Roman despot. That "the rich are growing richer and the poor poorer," is a favorite summing-up of the situation of Labor Reform speakers and writers. They should not overlook the fact that the rich are also growing fewer—relatively at least—and the poor more numerous.

There are some who are disposed to regret the centralizing tendency of the modern system, and to look back with regret to the ante-machinery days and lament the loss of the greater opportunities for self-employment which then existed. Such regrets, though vain, are not unnatural. Those living in a transition stage, and feeling the evil effects of the system from which they are passing, as well as of that on which they are entering, are more prone to look back with regret than forward with hope. But a return to the days of individualism is neither possible nor desirable. Whether we like it or not we must make up our minds that the great change in organization induced by nineteenth century improvements and appliances is irrevocable. If revolutions, as has been said, never go backward, still less does evolution. To perfect and round off a system, the development of which in some directions has unduly outstripped its growth in others, is the only possible remedy for transitional evils.

Systems develop rapidly from force of circumstances; while the laws, ideas, traditions, and sentiments of men are slow to take on the change necessary to adapt them to the altered situation. Our industrial system, considered with reference to our political and legal institutions, our modes of thought, and the approved maxims and rules of conduct, is a man in the clothes of a boy. As regards the rights of society and the claims of its individual members, we are dominated by the theories of individualism; while the system under which they grew up has been largely superseded.

Herbert Spencer, in the " Study of Sociology," thus refers to the incongruity frequently presented between the surviving principles appertaining to a past stage of development and the present conditions:

" The illogicalities and the absurdities to be found so abundantly in current opinions and existing arrangements, are those which inevitably arise in the course of perpetual readjustments to circumstances perpetually changing. Ideas and institutions, proper to a past social state, but incongruous with the new social state that has grown out of it, surviving into the new social state they have made possible, and disappearing only as this new social state establishes its own ideas and institutions, necessarily furnish elements of contradiction in men's thoughts and deeds. And yet as, for the carrying on of social life, the old must continue so long as the new is not ready, this perpetual compromise is an indispensable accompaniment of a normal development."

Strange to say, Mr. Spencer himself, in his politico-economical teachings, offers a most striking illustration of the survival of ideas alien to the newer stage of development. The eminent expounder of the evolution hypothesis as applied to social growth is also the uncompromising advocate of individualism, the so-called right of free contract and the doctrine of *laissez faire* in its extremest form. He has since given to the world, under the title of " The Man *vs.* the State," a work which is full of significance in its bearing on the labor question. It is important mainly owing to its admission of truths and tendencies entirely contrary to the views of the author, and as proving how evolution is actually bringing about a change in the relations between the government and the people, altogether at variance with politico-economical theories, but under the irresistible pressure of social exigencies and a demand too strong to be resisted. No one laments this change more than Mr. Spencer. His testimony is that of an opponent of anything in the form of "paternal government," and a thorough adherent of the principle of non-interference. Quoting a very large number of remedial and regulating measures passed by British Liberal governments since 1860, Mr. Spencer urges that Liberalism has lost its distinctive character. Because acts have been passed giving protection to various classes of factory employees, more especially women and children, providing for public school education, nationalizing the telegraph lines, prohibiting the sale of adulterated and unwholesome food, and amending the Merchant Shipping Act so as to prevent sailors being sent to their death in " coffin ships "—because the gross and flagrant evils arising under "free contract" have fairly forced upon British legislators the necessity of taking some action to protect those who cannot protect themselves, Herbert Spencer, under the influence of our surviving traditions of individualism, sounds the alarm that the liberties of the people are in danger from a new type of Toryism. It is amazing that so acute a reasoner in the domain of science should not recognize in this noteworthy new departure in legislation the harmonious working of the law of evolution.

Industrial development has revolutionized England more than any other country in the world, but we look in vain in "The Man *vs.* the State" for any recognition of the vast social transformation wrought by the steam-engine and the electric wire, the spinning-machine and the power-loom. It does not, from cover to cover, contain a single sentence indicating that the author has taken into consideration the enormous social and industrial difference between the England of a century ago, when the old Toryism of divine right and aristocratic privilege ruled supreme, and the England of to-day, with a popular franchise, and what the author calls the "New Toryism," restraining in the name of justice and humanity the greed of the few for the welfare of the many. It is not the part of a philosopher to ignore completely the change of conditions, and to insist upon the adherence to old formulas and traditions of legislation, when the age to which they were suited has passed away, and the surroundings have altogether changed.

The tendency to coercive and regulating legislation which Herbert Spencer deplores is the natural and legitimate result of the working of social evolution, the functions of government being developed as the necessity arises for their exercise. These powers have not been suddenly or arbitrarily assumed—they have been gradually developed owing to the needs of the case. Governments have been by no means eager to increase their responsibilities in the direction and regulation of departments once left to the unrestricted greed of private enterprise, and regulated only by competition. The various measures instanced by Mr. Spencer, far from being willingly adopted by the governing class to increase their power, as he infers, have been fairly forced on them by public opinion. The government of England has not gone nearly so fast nor so far in this direction as it would be warranted in doing by the sentiments of those who, the author would have us believe, are grievously oppressed by the prevalence of paternal legislation.

There is every reason to hope that Mr. Spencer forecasts the future aright in asserting that the tendency towards restrictive legislation of the character referred to is likely to increase in the future, or, to quote his own words, that " kindred measures effecting kindred changes of organization tend with ever increasing force to make that type general, until, passing a certain point, the proclivity to it becomes irresistible." The influence of precedent is exceedingly powerful, and in the reforms already adopted are the germ of a universal collectivism, under which the state, organized upon a popular basis, and acting as the agent of the mass of producers, can organize industry and distribution, and supersede capitalism. The tendency which Herbert Spencer views with dread because it runs counter to his cherished theories, the Labor Reformer should hail with joy as the first step on the way to deliverance from an intolerable thraldom. Further advances in this direction are thus anticipated :

" From inspecting lodging-houses to limit the numbers of occupants and enforce sanitary conditions, we have passed to inspecting all houses below a certain rent in which there are members of more than one family, and are now passing to a kindred inspection of all small houses. The buying and working of telegraphs by the state is made a reason for urging that the state should buy and work the railways. Supplying children with food for their minds by public agency is being followed in some cases by supplying food for their bodies, and after the practice has been gradually made more general we may anticipate that the supply now proposed to be made gratis in the one case, will eventually be proposed to be made gratis in the other ; the argument that good bodies as well as good minds are needful to make good citizens being logically urged as a reason for the extension. And then avowedly proceeding on the precedents furnished by the church, the school, and the reading room, all publicly provided, it is contended that pleasure in the sense it is now generally admitted, needs legislating for and organizing at least as much as work.''

A still more important phase in the distinctly socialistic legislation of England is the Irish Land Act and its amendments, in which the principle of the right of the state to regulate the use of the soil, irrespective of claims of personal ownership, is so fully asserted that it will at a future day be easy to widen the precedent thus laid down into an assertion of complete national ownership. By no violent convulsion, but by directing the force of public sentiment and the political power of the masses to the securing of like changes in American legislation, by the irresistible demand of educated and organized labor that the people's government shall no longer hold aloof from interference with matters hitherto regarded as beyond the scope of governmental functions, meeting first the more pressing exigencies, and rectifying one by one the abuses arising from monopoly and competition, will a better and more equitable social system be evolved.

CHAPTER V.

LABOR AND GOVERNMENT.

God said, I am tired of kings,
I suffer them no more;
Up to my ear the morning brings
The outrage of the poor.

Think ye I made this ball
A field of havoc and war,
Where tyrants great and tyrants small,
Might harry the weak and poor ?
    *   *   *   *   *

Call the people together,
The young men and the sires,
The digger in the harvest field,
Hireling and him that hires.

And here in a pine state-house
They shall choose men to rule
In every needful faculty
In church and state and school.

                                   EMERSON.

WHEN the people of the American colonies threw off the yoke of a foreign monarchical government, and established democratic institutions, they fancied, as many of their descendants of to-day fancy, that they had settled the question of government for all time. So far as machinery is concerned, they secured the full control of the people over the government as far as the sphere of government extended. But influenced by British traditions they limited the functions and the range of government, partly by express constitutional provisions, and partly by the general consensus of opinion which is potent to restrain legislative action even inside of the narrow limits of its constitutional operation. The founders of the American republic had good reason to regard with a jealous eye the powers of governments. They had been so accustomed to identify the idea of government with that of arbitrary and irresponsible power under the monarchical system that it is not surprising that the ideal which found most favor with them was that of a government which should simply maintain order, administer justice, and leave the people as free as possible in carrying on their affairs.

The abuses from which men suffered a century ago were mainly such as arose from a tyrannical misuse of the govern-ing power, from restraints upon freedom of speech or printing, unjust prosecutions, unfair and crushing taxation, and the insolent or overbearing conduct of consequential officials. The yoke of government was heavy throughout Europe. The ambitions of kings and statesmen and the intrigues of courts caused ruinous and ferocious wars. Kings not only reigned in those days but governed, and as a rule they gov-erned badly, having only their own aggrandizement in view. What wonder then that men who felt these evils came to regard government, the general type of which was the mon-archy, as something not merely apart from, but antagonistic to the people—a power requiring to be curbed by every pos-sible means? The idea that danger to popular liberty could come from any other source formed no place in their calcula-tions. In that age of simple social arrangements and self-dependent isolated industries, when men travelled little and dealt almost wholly with their neighbors, and large corporate interests were unknown, the government which interfered least and left industry and commerce to regulate themselves seemed perfection. Little government was needed, and a system that put the ballot in every man's hand and confined the objects of administration to the narrowest scope consist-ent with a national existence was all-sufficient.

But now all this has changed. Side by side with the democratic system of government, under which every man is sovereign, has grown up the commercial, industrial, and finan-cial organization under which every laborer is a wage-serf. It touches the lives and well-being of the people at a thousand points, where the government controls them in one. Not only in America, but the world over does the power of cap-italism bear the real sway and continually encroach upon the functions formerly possessed by the ruler. Well may it be said that "the kings reign but no longer govern." Capitalism is king. The real rulers are not the puppet princes and jumping-jack statesmen who strut their little hour upon the world's stage, but the money kings, railroad presidents, and great international speculators and adventurers who control the money-market and the highways of commerce. Where is the emperor or premier in Europe that has the power of the Rothschilds? What American president or congress ever exercised as much influence over the lives and fortunes of large masses of the people as Jay Gould? Every war, every peace, every commercial treaty is dictated not by the men who do the stage business and dazzle the crowd by their displays of regal splendor and court ceremonials, but by a few shrewd, sharp, long-headed business men who form the power behind the throne. All the diplomatic flummery and formalism, all the pomp and glitter of imperial state, are so much empty sham behind which the hand of the financier and the representative of large corporate interests pulls the wires. The real government of our nineteenth century civilization is not the parliamentary or administrative bodies in the name of which laws are promulgated. It is the industrial and business and social organization which governs by its iron laws that need no popular assent, and cannot, as matters stand, be affected by the vote of those upon whom they press hardly. What law that can be passed at Washington or Albany or Boston has such vital, all-absorbing interest for labor as the unwritten, arbitrary law which says—"You, wage slave, have produced for us, your masters, so much wealth that we are, in fact, suffering from over-production. Therefore it is decreed that the factory shall be closed until further notice." What law duly assented to by the president or state governor, and printed in the statute book, is one-tenth as important to the toiler as the silent informal decree of landlordism, " That whereas the necessities of the public for accommodation have increased, therefore rents are henceforth increased twenty per cent." Where is the law duly formulated in good set terms and redundant legal phraseology that affects the toiling millions as much as do the machinations of the speculators who combine to put up the price of coal, and wheat, and pork? What are the government taxes to the exactions continually levied on industry by the landlord and the usurer, the profit-monger and the capitalist?

Frequently there is destitution and semi-starvation in the land because of the edict of the government—the real "government" of capitalism—which decrees that labor must starve and stint itself to restrict production—that wages must be reduced and factories shut down until the surplus stocks are worked off. Who voted for this measure? What political candidate stumped the country, promising a general restriction of production as a cure for industrial evils? Where, in short, does the idea of self-government and popular freedom apply, if measures of such life and death consequence to the people can be carried out, not merely without the people having any voice in them, but without any one even imagining that these are matters on which they have the right to be consulted. How paltry and insignificant are the party issues over which politicians wrangle and voters spend their time and breath.compared with the questions of work and wages, and freedom to use the natural resources of the earth without being taxed to maintain a host of idlers? Yet we are told that such measures as would secure to labor its rights are "unpractical." The real objection is that they are a great deal too practical for the exploiting classes, who are quite willing that the people should amuse themselves by playing at politics, overturning and establishing sham governments, while capitalism retains the real power in its hands.

The people have in the United States political power; in other countries they are attaining it. But what is the good of it to them, if it is to be confronted and hemmed in on every side by the non-political but organized power of monopolies, rings, and corporations, and the entire social machinery in the hands of capitalism and landlordism? Where is the benefit to the worker of a free ballot, if on all live, practical, bread-and-butter questions he is to be told " Hands off ! This is not a political matter. This must be left in the hands of private enterprise. We cannot interfere with the sacred right of free contract ! "

The growth of popular sovereignty should be so directed as to breathe the breath of life into the decaying systems of government, and substitute for their formal parade and empty ceremonial, a vital, active interest in matters now considered beyond the scope of legislative interference. Let government, as the representative of the whole people, step in and, instead of being controlled by the machinery of capitalism, control it through all its ramifications. In place of the capitalistic rule, which in the true sense now governs the people by prescribing whether they shall work or not, and how much they shall receive, let us have a representative, popular, recognized government, conducted on business principles, doing the same thing not for the profit of a few, but in the interests of all. Instead of the capitalist being "free " to say, " Work on my terms or starve ; buy coal on my terms or freeze ; rent a house on my terms or become a homeless vagrant "—the people should be free to organize every department of labor and distribution through their representatives. Until this kind of freedom can be secured political liberty is to the disinherited a mockery and a delusion. This is the ideal which Labor Reformers should keep steadily in view, not as something to be attained by a ready-made Socialistic scheme, cut-and-dried as to all its details, to be suddenly imposed upon the nation by the power of the majority, but to be reached by the process of development—by the gradual extension of the powers of government, beginning with the departments in which the evils of capitalism are most obvious, and popular opinion is most favorable to a new departure.

The tendency towards Collectivism against which Herbert Spencer and the doctrinaries of the *laissez faire* school protest is the first step in that change of the character and aims of government which will have to be accomplished before it can permanently and effectively redress the evil of one-sided

Socialism. It prepares the government to accept the wider and more important functions to be forced upon it, and breaks down the old mediæval idea of government as a power aloof from and above the people, paving the way for the acceptance of the new radical idea, that government should be nothing more than a committee delegated by the people to attend to their business with as little unnecessary ceremonial or form- ality as may be.

The most perfect form of government in the world will not of itself avail to better the condition of the people. The elec- tion of chief magistrates, legislators, judges, and all the rest of the officials by manhood suffrage or universal suffrage may mean but "the liberty to choose one's jailer." A corrupt Senate is as great a drawback to progress as an obstructive aristocracy. A president or governor in league with money or railroad rings is as deadly a foe to popular freedom and prosperity as any Bourbon or Stuart who ever claimed the "right divine to govern wrong." That Democracy will by its intrinsic merits bring about a change for the better in the conditions under which labor lives, exists, or starves, is one of those fondly cherished delusions which will not stand the test of experience.

Those who have held that the mere possession of power by the people, irrespective of its use, would accomplish their de- liverance have confounded the means with the end, the tools with the work. What should we think of a carpenter who should take great care to provide himself with the very best kit of tools procurable, spend his time sharpening and polish- ing them and getting them into excellent order, and never do a stroke of work with them ? Should we have much pity for such a man were he to find himself destitute and to begin to express his wonder that a carpenter who had so thoroughly equipped himself with the implements of his trade could not earn enough to live on ? Yet he would make no worse mistake than the people who, having equipped themselves with a well-adjusted democratic constitution, now wonder that the machine does not right social abuses. So far Dem-

ocracy has done little more than sharpen its tools. The tools
are necessary for the work, but to get them in order is not
the work itself. It is important that everyone subject to the
laws should possess the franchise. But it is still more important that those who have it should use it well and intelligently to redress inequalities and guard the rights of labor.
All forms of government can be taken advantage of by men
to maintain themselves in power and pervert instrumentalities
designed to be beneficent into the means of plundering and
oppressing the people. But under democracy it requires more
cunning, shrewdness, and deceit to do this than under a mon-
archy, and it needs furthermore the connivance or apathy of a
majority of the people themselves. Democratic institutions
are the beneficent instruments by which it is possible for the
working-classes to redress every abuse of the monopoly and
competitive system. It puts into their own hands the means
of their emancipation. But to revert to the tool simile, the
very best set of carpenters' tools will not build a house or even
a hog-pen unless there is the force, the skill, and the knowledge behind if necessary for the work. So with democratic institutions; there is no benefit to the masses of the
people in having access to the ballot-box unless they use their
votes rightly and intelligently to protect themselves against
the encroachments of capitalism. Machines will not run
themselves. There is no Keeley motor in politics.

Unless the working-people of America make use of their
ballots to kill capitalism, capitalism will kill freedom, even
such theoretical freedom as the mere possession of the franchise implies. Doctrines and ideas utterly antagonistic to the
foundation principles of Democracy have obtained a strong
hold upon the wealthy classes. Propositions for the abolition
of manhood suffrage are tentatively thrown out and hinted at
in influential quarters. The Chicago *Current*, a representative organ of that literary culture which draws its inspiration
from European sources and is distinctively un-American in its
ideals and modes of thought, in the spring of 1885 published
an article assailing manhood suffrage in the most outspoken
fashion. A portion of it read as follows:

7

" At present society is struggling with a manhood suffrage which no
one denies is full of evils. No change is made. The present evils are
deplored not the less, but the fear is general of greater ills to be fastened
upon us (and the worse the disease the more difficult the cure.) Under
the existing regime in large cities a cellar-full of celibates, sleeping in
bunks at the price of five or ten cents a night, doing less than twenty-
five cents worth of work a day, year in and year out, march to the polls
and wield a force equal to that exercised by the heads of twenty-five
families, in each of which families are wife, children, dependent rela-
tives, and domestic aids, each infinitely more useful and promising than
the dime lodger.

There is no doubt that this passage fairly expresses the
opinion of the large and influential class for which the *Current* and journals of its stamp cater. Of all phases of reactionary sentiment that which speaks in the name of ' culture, '
and professes to represent the superior intellect of the community, is the meanest and most malignant. It lacks even
the poor excuse of self-interest, and throws its influence into
the scale against Labor Reform gratuitously. The culture
which looks merely on the outward symptoms of social disor-
ganization, taking no note of their deep-seated causes, is merely
a book-learned ignorance. Capitalism, having produced the
social outcasts whose power in politics is so hypocritically
deplored, by first robbing them of their natural rights and
then defrauding them of the fair value of their labor, now
proposes the crowning outrage of depriving them of the means
by which they might recover their lost heritage. The
Atlantic Monthly some time since published an article in
favor of cumulative voting—as less likely to arouse antagonism
than the actual disfranchisement of the poor. The man of
wealth was to receive additional votes in proportion to his
possessions. No less prominent a political leader than Ros-
coe Conkling has more than once given expression to the
same idea, that property, and not manhood, ought to be the
basis of political power. In a letter dated Utica, N. Y.,
September 1st, 1880, which occasioned some comment at the
time, speaking of the Republican party, he said:—

" Those who compose it, and the communities and States which uphold it, represent an overwhelming preponderance of the material interests of the country, the agricultural, productive, and tax-paying interests, and in every partnership it is wise and safe for those who own the most to keep their share of control. Whenever in a business concern—and the government of every country is in the highest sense a business concern—money is to be expended or obligations incurred, those who are to do the paying had better do the deciding, in the first place, whether the thing is wise at all."

In another letter, dated Utica, September 7th, 1880, addressed to the editor of the Burlington *Hawkeye*, Mr. Conkling said in reference to the administration of the affairs of the Government :—

" In a joint stock association all stockholders and all classes of stockholders should have their full share and full rights; but whenever those who have the bulk, put the whole into the hands of those who own but little, there is much unwisdom in it   *   * When an administration, a Congressional majority or a party represent those who do most of the paying, who carry on most of the business, who feel most of the loss or gain, who have done most and given most, and have in all things most at stake, that administration, that majority, that party is a safer agent to trust than an agent more deeply interested for somebody else."

When, in the height of a presidential campaign, a party leader of Mr. Conkling's standing gives utterance to such sentiments, the one interpretation of which is that men are entitled to political power in proportion to their wealth, we can realize how far such reactionary ideas have spread among the moneyed classes, and how gladly they would, if they but dared, deprive labor of its franchise.

But this tendency is not theoretical merely. The retrogressive and anti-democratic views of capitalism have been carried into practice to a much greater extent than is generally supposed. Under the specious guise of registration laws the attainment of the suffrage is in many states hedged about with restrictions and attended with disabilities which practically deprive a very large proportion of the laboring-class of the right to vote. The insidious provisions of laws which make the payment of a poll-tax a pre-requisite to voting, and require the citizen to lose the time necessary to see that his name appears upon the register—a serious matter often to a poor man, to whom the loss of even a few hours means the deprivation of some home comfort—have disfranchised great masses of the toilers. Shortly after the presidential election of 1880 the New York *Herald* published a table giving the number of males of voting age in each state and the number who actually voted. The figures are very suggestive. In only six states was the proportion of actual voters to the adult male population over 80 per cent. In the pivotal state of New York it was 78 per cent, in Massachusetts only 56 per cent ; and in most of the remaining states the percentage was between these figures. In Rhode Island, indeed, under the un-American real-estate qualification system, the actual voters only amounted to 38 per cent of the adult males. Making every allowance for voluntary abstention and unavoidable absence, these figures indicate but too surely the deprivation of the franchise to which the poorer classes have been subjected by registration laws, shifting upon the individual the duty rightly belonging to the state of securing the right of suffrage to those entitled to it, and by a poll-tax levied under conditions which make it virtually a tax on voting.

Could any statistics show the proportion of instances in which the ballot cast by the laborer was in reality the vote of the employer given under the menace or the dread of loss of work ; could any figures indicate the extent of intimidation practiced by powerful corporations or individual capitalists upon those dependent upon them, the result would be yet more startling. The right conferred on all by the founders of the republic is worse than withheld when it is perverted by coercion or bribery to become an instrument of oppression. Then it may be said that "the spirit of murder works in the very means of life."

The growth of the labor question as a factor in politics, and the deference which each party, however hypocritically, feels called upon to pay to labor in the caucus and the convention, are hopeful signs. From one aspect nothing can be more sickening than to see politicians who have not a single aspira-

tion or idea in common with Labor Reformers and whose interests and sympathies are all on the side of capitalism, posing as
the friends of labor, and inserting in the party platforms,
pledges which they have not the remotest intention of fulfilling, in order to "capture the labor vote." Parties whose
course as a whole has been utterly adverse to the interests of
the masses, owing to whose shameful betrayal of the responsibilities confided to them the evils of the situation have been
intensified, have of late felt it incumbent upon them to recognize the growing disposition of the wage-earning classes to use
their ballots in their own behalf. To conciliate the labor vote
and head off any broad, comprehensive scheme of political
action looking to a radical and organic change in the relations between labor and capitalism, the parties pay Labor Reformers the hypocritical tribute of sympathetic professions
and platforms embodying some of the demands made by organized labor. Under the pressure of party exigencies
millionaires whose lives have been one long course of greed
and grab, lawyers whose ingenuity and technical knowledge
have been perverted to the overthrow of justice and the aggrandizement of corporations, and the whole tribe of venal
and unscrupulous politicians who have ever been the servile
tools of capitalism have been compelled to admit the necessity
of considering in legislation the interests of the laboring
masses. Utterly insincere as these formal professions are,
inadequate as are the palliative measures so far secured by
appealing to the political hopes and fears of partisans, they
nevertheless both indicate and hasten a change in public
opinion which is likely to be much more far-reaching and momentous in its consequences than they anticipate.

Hitherto the politicians have used labor. The time has
come when labor must use the politicians. The politicians
have been able to use labor because working-men have put
party first. When they put labor first and let party interests
look out for themselves they can make the politicians their
obsequious servants. It is the prejudice, the ignorance, the
unreasoning servile devotion to political leaders who have

duped them, and to parties which have always played into the
hands of capitalism, which are alone to blame for the scant
consideration received by labor in politics.

Political movements, like those of natural forces, follow what
is termed by the scientists " the line of least resistance."
Capitalism dominates in public life because it knows no party.
The great corporations and millionaires sit loose to the ties of
partyism.   They look upon politics simply as a means of advancing their own interests, and throw the money-bags into
either scale, according as they think those interests will be
best secured.

The great majority of wage-earners, on the contrary, allow
their partisan feelings to control their political action.   A
little hypocritical deference on the part of the party managers,
the inclusion in the platform of a trivial concession or two in
the shape of resolutions against prison labor or Chinese immigration, a few nominations of professed Labor Reformers for
minor offices are quite sufficient to keep them in line with the
party.   That the whole tenor and aim of its course, with these
exceptions, is opposed to the rights of the people and dictated
by devotion to the money power is not sufficient to shake their
allegiance.

The politicians know that to refuse to give legal sanction to
the encroachments of monopoly would lose them the support
of capitalism.   They have no reason to believe that the de-
fection would be offset in any appreciable measure by increased popular support.   While the money-power is swayed
solely by selfish considerations, the people cling tenaciously to
their parties.   Is it any wonder that the politician seeks to
preserve the equilibrium by giving an inch to labor where he
gives an ell to capitalism ?

The hold which party associations and traditions have obtained over the masses of the American people is the greatest
obstacle to any present advance.   Under this malign spell
many men who, outside of politics, are enlightened in their
views and thoroughly convinced of the necessity of such
social changes as will secure a just system of distribution and

destroy monopoly, may be found, year after year, plunging into the excitement of political contests, fought out between parties both of which are controlled by capitalistic influence, on issues which completely ignore the supreme question of social and industrial re-adjustment. Energy and intelligence which ought rightly to be devoted to the solution of the labor problem are worse than wasted over the petty, misleading, idle issues which partyism keeps in view ; and the attention of the people is distracted by campaigns which, whatever the result, settle no question of real significance, because neither party represents any principle which has any bearing upon the vital needs of the community.

Repeated attempts have been made to organize third parties, to maintain popular rights against the sinister influences of capitalism, which have rendered the Republican and Democratic parties corrupt to the core. The Greenback, Labor, National, and Anti-monopoly organizations have sprung up, rallied adherents to their support, won some local victories, and finally dwindled away and become resolved into their original elements. The absorbing interest and contagious enthusiasm of the great quadrennial fight for the Presidency, involving the personal interests of hundreds of thousands of office-seekers and office-holders, draws away the supporters of the smaller parties. The temptation to share the glory and participate in the spoils of present success is much stronger to the minds of most men than the inducement to stand up for a principle. A grave defect in the American character is its impatience of small beginnings and slow growth. Unless a movement carries everything before it with a rush, and bears down all opposition with the momentum of numbers and enthusiasm, the mass easily become disheartened. They must have immediate tangible results, a growth like that of Jack's beanstalk in the nursery story, a birth like that of Minerva springing forth armed from the brain of Jupiter, or the enthusiasm soon gives place to apathy. When this predominating temperament is considered it is hardly surprising that parties which could offer to their supporters no prospect of immediate triumphs on a large scale, and no stimulus in the way of patronage, excepting so far as these might be secured by demoralizing alliances with one or other of the older parties, have crumbled away under the pressure of the quadrennial struggle, leaving merely skeleton organizations to tell of their existence.

But although in the past these efforts have proved futile against capitalism entrenched behind the rampants of party, there is no reason to despair of the future. If the regular parties have so far been able to hold their following it has only been by repeated concessions and pledges to labor. Slight and insincere as these may be, they nevertheless are an indication too plain to be misinterpreted of the influence of the new factor in public affairs. They are the thin end of the wedge. When the people learn in the process of political education now going forward that the concessions are futile so long as the wage system remains intact, and that the pledges are only made to be broken, a new departure on a broader scale, either within or outside of party lines, may be looked for.

The success of the Irish Nationalists under Parnell's leadership in dictating the policy of the Liberal party of England, overthrowing coercion, and advancing the cause of Home Rule so as to bring it, as the phrase goes, within the scope of " practical politics " is destined to give a powerful stimulus to the action of revolutionary parties on both sides of the Atlantic. If not the originator, Mr. Parnell is at all events the first to carry to a successful issue the idea of the balance of power in politics. He has demonstrated that a small but compact, unanimous, and determined party, holding itself apart from the two greater organizations, never sinking its identity, but willing to co-operate with either or both in turns without merging itself in their following, can virtually make its own terms. So long as the Irish members of the English Parliament were divided on English issues, and adhered to one or other of the historic British parties, Ireland might ask in vain for justice. When Parnell arose, and a handful of Irish members shook themselves free from party ties, set political traditions and public opinion at defiance, and made Ireland's welfare their paramount object, they assured large instalments of reform. They have already overthrown two British administrations, and stand ready to turn out a dozen in succession if need be to secure their object.

The lesson should not be lost upon American Labor Reformers. Had Parnell been afraid of "hurting the party," the land act would never have been passed, coercion would to-day be in full force, and Home Rule would be as far off as it was ten years ago. The American working-man, if he really desires to use the ballot effectively to secure Labor Reform, must get over his squeamishness as to the effect of his action on "the party."

Owing to the differences between the English responsible government system and Democracy, it would not be possible to bring the balance-of-power principle into play so frequently in American state or national politics as in England, where the life of the administration depends upon its retaining a legislative majority. But, on the other hand, parties are so evenly balanced that a much smaller force would suffice to turn the scale at a presidential election. A small matter of 1047 votes in New York State, in the election of 1884, made Grover Cleveland president. The electoral vote of that state is nearly always decisive of the result in Presidential contests. Imagine the organized labor of the Empire state, swung loose from party fealty, as regardless of the issues between Democrat and Republican as the Irish party in Great Britain are of the differences between Liberal and Tory, and looking to the politicians as tools to be used for their ends. Suppose that, under the leadership of a man with something like the genius of Parnell for organization and political strategy, labor were organized as thoroughly for political action as it now is for the purpose of resisting the unjust exactions of employers; that when thus massed into a compact and disciplined force negotiations were opened with existing parties, and a full concession of all the demands of labor—as formulated for instance in such a comprehensive shape as the platform of the Knights of Labor—were demanded as the price of the labor vote. Owing to the unfortunate experience of the past, it would no doubt take some time to convince either party of the sincerity of the movement, and of the determination of a sufficient number of the workers to make it really formidable, to stand by their demands. But if organized labor stood firm; if it showed no disposition to break ranks and fall into the party traces; if the same strictness of discipline and unanimity of purpose animating the Irish Nationalists were manifested, one party or other would speedily show themselves anxious to make terms. It is no doubt probable that the pledges by which they would seek to secure an alliance with labor on a large scale for political action, would be no better observed that many promises given in the past to conciliate the working-class element already affiliated with them. But if, as soon as the disposition to kick over the ladder by which they had climbed to power were fairly manifested, the whole strength of the political labor organization were devoted to punishing their treachery; if, by independent action as a compact force, the Labor Reformers voted their betrayers out of power by a significant and sweeping majority, the lesson would be as effective and as productive of practical results in forwarding the cause, as that administered by the Irish Nationalists to Liberals and Tories in turn. If the men who now unite and make sacrifices and submit to rigid discipline for petty local objects, small increases of pay, amelioration of unfair shop rules, and the like, would but show equal constancy, and equal determination in standing together for comprehensive, far-reaching objects, to be achieved by political methods, they could carry everything before them.

But they wont—not at present. They are afraid it might hurt "the party." So they let the politicians use them instead of using the politicians. Nevertheless the leaven of political thought is working, and the example of what a third party has accomplished for Ireland will exercise a marked influence on American political methods and ideas.

From the parties, as at present controlled, labor has nothing to expect. The American working-man has a great horror of "throwing away his vote," as it is absurdly termed, by casting it for a cause that has no chance of immediate success. He would be willing enough to join a political Labor party, if he thought it could possibly elect a president in 1888; but he has no idea of marching to certain defeat with a forlorn hope, even though the attack may prepare the way for a victory in the distant future. When present success rests between one of two parties the "least-of-two-evils" argument, that specious plea of pessimists and trimmers, appeals with almost irresistible force to minds not under the sway of strong convictions. The temptation to vote for the "best man" of two party hacks without an enlightened idea between them, or to prefer this or that party because of old associations or taking catchwords is well-nigh irresistible. It is so easy to yield to contagious enthusiasm, to train with the old crowd, to follow the band and the torchlight procession; so hard to stand aloof and bear ridicule as a crank and a visionary. But if every Labor Reformer, putting aside all these temptations and excitements, looked at the question solely from the standpoint of how his action was likely to affect the cause he professes to have at heart, he would be very apt to come to the conclusion never to cast a party ballot—unless in pursuance of some such comprehensive strategic scheme as I have outlined.

Under existing conditions, while the claims of labor are ignored as at present, it is an absolute disadvantage to the cause for working-men to vote for party candidates, because it creates the impression that Labor Reformers are satisfied with half-measures. It would be better to let the public see plainly that such makeshift legislation is regarded as inadequate and misleading. Is is better to be unrepresented than misrepresented; better to have it understood that no party politician is entitled to speak for labor than to have some smooth-tongued trimmer pose as one who owes his election to working-men's votes.

In the incipient stages of great reforms the ballot is of use only as a means of giving expression to opinion. It is an invaluable agency to force discussion, ripen the issue, and mark progress. In all other respects just now it is practically useless—that is, so far as securing any radical changes in the wage-system is concerned. We can hope for no immediate victory. The indirect use of the ballot to forward agitation and mould public opinion has been a frequent feature in American politics. The early anti-slavery agitators availed themselves of it. The candidatures of Gen. Butler and Governor St. John in the Greenback-Labor and Prohibition interests in 1884 are instances in point. Neither of these candidates had the ghost of a chance. None of their most enthusiastic supporters ever dreamed that there was even a remote possibility of the election of either of them. They were in the field merely to allow their respective supporters a chance to stand up and be counted—as the practical politician would say, to " throw away their votes " for a principle.

This being the case, in contests where there is no possibility or thought of success, where the object of putting a Labor Reform ticket in nomination would be merely to force the issue and give the adherents of the cause an opportunity to cast an honest ballot, why not vote directly for the principle? Why go to the trouble of selecting candidates, which under the circumstances becomes a meaningless formula? Would it not serve every purpose to drop a platform or a ticket with the simple inscription " Labor Reform," or any other explicit and convenient phrase, into the ballot-box. It is much easier to agree on a principle than on a candidate. A man is sure to have enemies. He has generally a record which presents many points of attack. The selection of candidates arouses jealousies and creates divisions. In voting for a principle simply there is no weakening of strength from these causes. There is nothing to explain away or apologize for. And the moral effect upon parties and politicians of a large vote cast for the abstract principle of Labor Reform, would be far greater than has been produced by any form of political action yet adopted. Supposing that, in any important election, when the votes came to be counted, it were found that there were enough electors who had taken the trouble to go to the polls and cast their votes for the idea, despite the fact that there was no man in the field to represent it, to have changed the result. Would not this action, as to the motive of which no possible doubts could exist, which would testify far more strongly to the sincerity and earnestness of those resorting to it than if there were even a remote possibility of personal advancement as the result, have an influence upon public opinion infinitely greater than could be obtained by the compromises and dickerings by which the "labor vote" is traded off for a few minor nominations or a "labor plank" in the party platform? Its very novelty and boldness—its unprecedented defiance of the traditions of political life—its avowed abnegation of all hope of immediate personal triumphs and advantages, its deliberate "throwing away" of the valueless feature of the ballot—that of promoting the success of one of two corrupt parties—while retaining all which makes it really worth anything to the believer in comprehensive social reform—would force the Labor question to the front as the main issue as no other use of the franchise could possibly do.

Let no one underrate what has already been achieved by Labor Reformers in politics. Considering the difficulties under which they have worked, the apathy and lack of steady determination on the part of the bulk of the laboring class, and the strength of party predilections and politico-economical fallacies, very much has been effected, especially in State legislation. The volume of factory laws, the restrictions on female and child labor, the mitigation of the evils of the convict and imported labor system, the abolition or limitation of the truck system, the abrogation or modification of mediæval conspiracy laws preventing combinations among workers, and the establishment of bureaus of Labor Statistics, have been extremely beneficial in their results. Before labor was as generally organized and as fully cognizant of its rights and disabilities as it now is, the only available method of procuring such ameliorative measures was the one hitherto followed. It was right and necessary to accept from one party or the other such piecemeal reforms as could be obtained in return for political support. But the time is ripe for a change. The concessions made to Labor Reform, important as they are in themselves, are slight as compared with the increased power of capitalism.

The reforms thus far secured have been directed towards modifying the more obvious abuses of the system. They are mere palliatives—excellent so far as they go, useful especially as precedents to establish and extend the principle of the right and duty of society to regulate industry in the interests of the whole people, instead of permitting it to be controlled by a class. But the hour has arrived when educated and united labor must strike more directly at the wage-system itself; when its political force, instead of being divided between parties, each of which seeks to offset enormous privileges to monopoly by niggardly concessions to labor, must be consolidated into a people's party.

Existing political parties are crystallized around dead issues and old-time reminiscences of the slavery and rebellion eras. They trim and fence not merely on the Labor problem, but on all live and important questions. A modern political platform is a marvel of disingenuous ingenuity. It has a verbal bait for every sort of political loose fish. Instead of being the clear expression of the views and aims of men who agree on certain principles, it is the utterance of those who agree on nothing except the desirability of obtaining office—and to that end wish to conciliate as many opposing classes, interests, and sections as possible, without offending any. Consequently it is framed to please prohibitionists, while convincing the liquor-seller that no harm is intended to him ; to placate the tariff reformer, while allaying the fears of the protectionist ; to satisfy alike the bi-metallist and the believer in the gold standard of the currency; and to promise concessions to labor without alarming the capitalist. No matter what pledges may be made in the direction of Labor Reform, the interests of those who, by virtue of their wealth and social position are entrusted with party leadership and put forward for the more important office, are always a guarantee that the claims of the money power will be the supreme consideration.

Instead of being thus treated as a side-issue, Labor Reform must be the main issue.

Commissioner Arthur T. Hadley, of the Connecticut Bureau of Labor Statistics, begins his admirable report for 1885 with the following pregnant assertion :

" The relations between labor and capital cannot be treated as a mere matter of private business, but involve social and political questions. This fact is becoming clearer every day, whether we like it or not. The state of things is this. The men who do the most physical work, as a class, seem to have the least to show for it. Their wages are often barely sufficient to meet the expenses of living. They sometimes cannot get work at all; at best they are working for others with little independence of action, and often with little hope of anything better. In their life, their work, and their relations to their employers, evils and abuses have arisen which it seems impossible for any individual to prevent; while the attempt to remedy them by organized action too often proves worse than useless. In this difficulty there is a demand for public investigation and for legislative interference."

Now, if the Labor problem be a political question at all, it is the supreme and overshadowing issue. If the right and the duty of State interference to remedy evils and abuses be admitted—and at this stage of the discussion there are few who can consistently deny it—it logically follows that this interference cannot be limited in extent or direction so long as these remediable abuses continue. In the Labor Bureaus, in the measures restricting the right of private contract, in whatever of regulative legislation has already been secured, we have the starting point of a new departure—the germs of the social evolution.

To make Labor Reform the supreme issue—the one important end and aim of political struggle with the toiling millions, for which they are ready to sacrifice every other consideration —is the only way by which the power of capitalism buttressed by partyism can be overthrown.

CHAPTER VI.

STEPPING STONES.

As between infancy and maturity there is no short-cut by which there may be avoided the tedious process of growth and development through insensible increments; so there is no way from the lower forms of social life to the higher, but one passing through small successive modifications. If we contemplate the order of nature, we see that everywhere vast results are brought about by accumulations of minute actions.

HERBERT SPENCER.

THE necessity of a gradual change from the system of capitalistic rule and wage servitude to the control by society of the means of production and of all distribution of the gains of industry on the basis of labor-value being admitted, what are the first practical steps to be taken to forward this change? In the political field, simply to do the work that lies nearest to hand in the line previously indicated of enlarging the functions of government and increasing the control exercised by the citizens over the governing body. The most obvious and essential reform to be accomplished in the near future is to reclaim for the government those powers which have been foolishly or corruptly granted to private corporations fulfilling public functions.

Railroads, telegraphs, telephones, banks, insurance companies, and the like were called into being by special enactment. The corporations which conduct these and similar enterprises stand in a very different position to individual capitalists. But for the powers and privileges granted them by the people's representatives, conferring upon them quasi-public trusts, they could have had no existence. They are creations of the law. Those trusts having been violated, and the powers conferred for the public benefit having been prostituted to selfish ends, the people have the right to abrogate them, and to resume those functions, the exercise of which by private individuals has been the most fertile source of every species of political corruption and financial dishonesty.

The modern corporation occupies a wholly anomalous position. It is virtually a portion of the real "government" of the country. It exercises public functions, and is obliged to resort to the government to obtain its franchises and powers ; but it is irresponsible to the public, and there is no adequate means of holding it to account for the exercise of its despotic sway. No system could be better devised to promote corruption, and to ensure the betrayal of the people by their representatives than the relations between the corporations and the government. In the first place, the whole of the immense transportation, money-issuing, and electric-communication systems of the country, on the management of which every branch of industry and trade is dependent, is entrusted to the hands of bodies composed of individuals of large wealth. They are dependent for their corporate existence, and the enormous facilities of levying tribute upon industry which the possession of corporate privileges confers, upon the assent of the people's representatives. As new opportunities present themselves, rings and syndicates for the procurement of charter-powers are organized. Their interests often clash with those of existing corporations or other applicants. Rival sets of railroad or telegraph magnates, each seeking to promote its own aims or cripple its rival, having immense resources at their command, resort to every means of political intrigue and corruption to secure favorable consideration of their claims. They buy legislators and judges like cattle. They enter the political field, and throw their influence into the wavering balance of party. There is no cause which has tended more to debauch American politicians than the struggle of corporations, actual or prospective, for the immensely valuable privileges which are thus trafficked in by public men, in return for party advantage or personal emolument—no class of legislation which has been anything like so fatal to previously fair reputations as that dealing with corporate interests.

Apart from gross cases of positive bribery, such as were isclosed in connection with the Credit Mobilier and Pan-Electric telephone scandals, where stock in corporations was

8

distributed gratuitously in return for political influence, the indirect corruption resulting from the system is an evil of far greater magnitude. The prominent men in politics being mostly wealthy, and having extensive business interests, are frequently holders of large amounts of stock in corporations, acquired before they accepted office without a thought of its being other than a legitimate investment. But how can they be expected to legislate in the public interest, or give unbiased decisions upon questions affecting the companies in which they are stockholders? Even if the particular corporations are not concerned, the heavy personal interest which a very large number of men in representative positions have in the claims of corporations renders it impossible to expect that they will be vigilant guardians of the rights of the people. While these immense interests are permitted to exist apart from government, irresponsible in the exercise of their power, having their ramifications throughout the business and political circles from which public officials are drawn, and continually dependent for public favors upon the very class of men who in their private capacity are concerned in their maintenance, corruption in its most insidious form will be the inevitable result. It is inherent in the system.

There is a great deal of force in the remarks of Gen. Butler, who, in an interview published in the New York *Herald* of February 5th, 1886 regarding the Pan Electric Telephone expressed himself as follows:

" Is a senator of the United States to have no other business relations? A large proportion of the senators are very large representatives of business wealth. They are elected with such business complications, and they must vote in regard to legislation which affects their business interests. When I was in congress a majority of the house was composed of officers and stockholders of national banks, and upon the occasion of a vote being taken affecting the banks, I called the Speaker's attention to the rule of the house that no man should vote upon a matter in which he was personally interested, but it was ruled that as they were only interested in the business of the country, they must legislate concerning the business of the country ; they must vote in regard to it, although their votes might make thousands of dollars' difference to them individually."

When the great majority of public men, owing to their business relations, are thus bribed in advance to support the insatiable claims of monopolies of all soils, how is it possible to expect that the public interest will be fairly considered? The cabinet-minister, senator or congressman who is a stockholder in a national bank, railroad or telegraph company, be his intentions ever so honest, is in a false position. On the one hand, the natural bias of personal interest continually prompts him to favor legislation looking to the aggrandizement and strengthening of monopolies; on the other, as a representative of the people, it is his duty to prevent the encroachments of corporations. A few may be public-spirited enough and sufficiently mindful of their obligations to act independently of pecuniary considerations, but all history shows that no class of men have ever voluntarily used their power against their own interests. It was not slaveholders that abolished slavery, or the owners of Irish estates who passed the Land Act. Gen. Butler's observation gives the key to the situation. Monopolies grow yearly in power, and strengthen their grasp upon the country because the people elect to office men who are identified with them by "business complications," who must either vote against their personal advantage or betray the trust reposed in them.

Americans have been in the habit of congratulating themselves that primogeniture and entail do not exist on this continent, that because the system of hereditary estates descending in unbroken bulk from father to son, generation after generation, has not been as yet established, we are therefore free from the great cause of the disparity of social conditions existing in England. It is a shallow and short-sighted conclusion. Though entail, primogeniture, settlements, tying up estates for a long period of years, and other devices for enabling dead men to control the interests of the living have not been introduced into America, a yet more formidable power for the accumulation of capital to be wielded by the hands of the few as an instrument of oppression, has been devised in the corporation. Men may die but the corporation outlives them. It concentrates amounts of wealth, which if scattered would have little power for evil and places them at the disposal of ambitious money and railroad kings. When corporations were few and largely of a speculative character large fortunes were precarious. They were apt to get dispersed, if not during the lifetime of the accumulator at his death. But the firm establishment of the corporation system has changed all that. Money invested in the stocks and bonds of solvent companies does not disappear in a night, like the unsubstantial investments of the gambler on margins. Any capitalist of ordinary discretion can so place his money that it will be absolutely safe so long as the institutions of the country endure, and go on indefinitely increasing in amount and controlling influence. The Vanderbilt fortune is now intact in the hands of the third generation, and by the will of the lately deceased millionaire, all the railroad stocks are to be retained in bulk. The profits only will be divided, while the capital itself as a power in the railroad and financial world is unbroken.

According to "Poor's Manual of Railroads" for 1885, the share capital of the railroad companies amounts to $3,762, 616, 686, and the funded debt to $3,669,115,772, making a total of $7,431,732,458, of "entailed" capital, so to speak in this one department of monopoly. According to the census of 1880 the estimated valuation of the farms in the United States is $10,197,000,000.

If by any process of law or sudden change in the working of our institutions three-quarters of the farm property of the country were tied up by the English system of entail and primogeniture so that the land could not be sold, seized for debt, bequeathed or otherwise disposed of, but must be kept intact and undivided in the families of the present possessors, the danger to free, popular government would at once be apprehended. Every American would realize that such a system would before long be fatal to the spirit if not to the semblance of political equality. And yet, as the holders of the entailed farms would constitute a numerous, widely-scattered class identified with popular interests, the peril would not be nearly so great as arises from the concentration in the hands of a very few men of the enormous powers represented by railroad capital. It is no argument to the contrary to point to merely personal changes in the management of corporations. It is true that in the despotisms of corporation rule as in those of arbitrary government "Amurath to Amurath succeeds." Vanderbilt II. in the course of nature gives place to Vanderbilt III. Stocks and bonds may pass from one holder to another, one great railroad magnate may be overthrown by a combination among his rivals, and a sudden transfer of the balance of power to a hostile syndicate; but all such merely individual conflicts and changes affecting the depositaries of power in no respect mitigate the injurious exercise of the power itself; in no way decrease the peril to liberty from the existence of the concentrated and increasing control of public functions by a very small number of self-interested, irresponsible persons.

"When we want to drain a marsh we do not take the votes of the frogs," says a French proverb. The great cause why the marshes of monopoly have been so long left to poison with their malaria the public life of the nation is, that we not only take the votes of the frogs, but leave the whole matter to their decision. It is a political truism which no one thinks of disputing, that wealth is the first requisite for election to the United States Senate. Chosen for their wealth, and often by their wealth, it is not surprising that the members of this club of millionaires use their political power principally as a means of strengthening their monopoly power. As Buckle truly says in his "History of Civilization," "There is but one protection against the tyranny of any class, and that is to give that class very little power. Whatever the pretensions of any body of men may be, however smooth their language and however plausible their claims, they are sure to abuse power if much of it is conferred on them. The entire history of the world affords no instance to the contrary."

During the civil service reform movement an expression much in vogue as characterizing the opponents of the measure was, that they were "part of the thing to be reformed." It is just so with the men who, committed beforehand to the interests of monopoly, fill not merely the Senate, but the popular branch of the national legislature, the high executive offices, the judiciary, and the state legislatures. They are a part of the thing to be reformed.

We talk of the "abuses" and "evils" of monopoly. The whole system is one gigantic abuse. It is irresponsible government, it is arbitrary power, it is taxation without representation. Nay, it is worse than these in their naked and undisguised form, because it co-exists with free institutions and reacting upon them, tends continually to debauch the character of public men and pervert the machinery of democratic government into the instrument of spoliation and oppression. Under an honest despotism public officials may be honorable and high-minded men. Under the hybrid or double-headed system of popular government, limited in its scope, side by side with the monopoly government, dependent upon it for unjust privileges, the prevalent type of the successful politician is the shrewd and unscrupulous trafficker in votes and subsidies, the betrayer of the people's rights for his personal enrichment.

The only way to abolish the "abuses" of monopoly is the way in which the "abuses" of personal rule, chattel slavery, and piracy have been abolished—by abolishing 'the system itself.

Instead of granting charters and franchises to private individuals, enabling them to exercise functions which are so far public in their character, that without the express sanction of the state they could not be undertaken, the government should resume their powers and conduct such enterprises as banks, railroads, telegraphs, and telephones as recognized public interest, and legitimate departments of the sphere of administration. If, in order to initiate any enterprise, it is requisite to apply to the government for the granting of special privileges and prerogatives not otherwise attainable by individuals or combinations, it is a sure indication that the undertaking is of a character that ought properly to be carried on by the whole people in their own interests, and not by private individuals for personal gain.

But in order to take even the first steps in this direction, we need such a radical change in public opinion that wealth and social position, instead of being generally regarded as desirable qualifications in a candidate for public office, must be looked upon as a strong *prima facie* cause for distrusting and rejecting him. The slavish adulation of money which permeates every fiber of our social and public life, which dominates the party caucus and convention, and elevates to the controlling position men whose selfish instincts and acquisitive faculties are their only claims to consideration interposes an insuperable obstacle to every proposition for industrial reform at the outset. Just in proportion as wage-workers allow themselves to be carried away by the false estimate of men's worth, and join in paying the tribute of servile souls and beclouded minds to the owners of the money bags, do they help to rivet the chains of industrial serfdom on their own necks. If they will help to elect men to the state legislatures and to Congress because they are rich, it is absurd to expect that the latter will use their influence as politicians to overthrow or weaken their power as monopolists. In supporting the candidate with a " bar'l," the people vote for their own enslavement. Men with " bar'ls " may empty them with lavish hand to obtain political positions, but it is always in the hope of refilling them again and again at the people's expense. Before monopoly can be reformed out of existence, those who profit by it must be voted out of public life.

The advantage of the nationalization of the means of transit and communication are so manifest that only the antagonistic self-interest of the wealthy politicians and the false public opinion created by the influence of seven thousand millions of capital through a hireling press could have prevented its being generally recognized. All competition would cease. The vast amount of waste and loss entailed by the construction of unnecessary lines of railroad and electric communication would be saved. There would be no more probability of the useless expenditure of money and labor in building two or three railway-lines between the same points than there now is of the construction of superfluous wagon roads. Were any municipality to vote away money for the building of an ordinary highway running parallel to one already existing and sufficient for the accommodation of travel, it would be regarded as an utterly unjustifiable and senseless waste of the public funds. The people would stand amazed at the folly of any set of men who, whether through ignorance, indifference, or venality, could sanction such a project. Yet so warped have men's judgments become by the undue exaltation of private enterprise that the syndicate of speculators who go to the legislature or congress and obtain a public franchise endowing them with what are virtually public trusts to run competing railway or telegraph lines involving an enormous needless outlay are regarded with no sort of disfavor and probably lauded as benefactors.

The nationalization of railroads, telegraphs, and similar enterprises would place the working employés in a far better position that at present. Instead of being subject to the fluctuations of the labor market, liable to have their wages reduced in order that the monopolies may pay dividends and to be treated as human machines, the working-force of railway or telegraph lines owned and managed by the government would be able to bring their political power to bear, to secure a just scale of wages and equitable treatment.

No government dare deal with its employés as W. H. Vanderbilt did with his wage-slaves during the freight-handlers' strike at New York and other Eastern cities, or as Jay Gould did with the telegraphers, or more recently with the employés on his South-Western roads. No political party would venture to justify the " iron law of wages " in relation to government employés. The politico-economical doctrine that labor is a commodity has been practically repudiated by the government. The wages of civil service employés are not fixed by competition—do not fluctuate with the state of the labor-

market, but, so far at least as the lower grades of the service
are concerned, are arranged on the principle of paying something like the value of the labor performed. That some of
the higher officials are paid extravagantly high rates, owing to
the prevalent over-estimate of the value of executive ability
as compared with ordinary work, is no valid argument against
the change, since the same conditions now prevail in the commercial world. The high salaries or emoluments of post-mas-
ters and collectors of customs in the principal cities are paral-
leled by the scale of remuneration of railroad, bank, and insurance officials and the superintendents of large manufacturing
and commercial businesses. The cause and the justification
of high salaries is the competitive system under which it is
essential to the success of business undertakings to secure at
any cost alert, energetic, and keen-witted men of organizing
capacity, diplomatic tact, and the qualities of judgment and
resolution which characterize the capable general of an army.
These qualifications of business leadership, in their highest
form and most perfect combination, are so much in demand,
because of the necessity which the enterprises concerned are
under of fighting each other. The energies and talents which
command so high a recompense are mainly devoted, not in
any direction which benefits the public, but to outwitting and
circumventing rivals. In short, the tendency of the competitive system and the survival of the fittest is to evolve a class
and kind of capacity, the social value of which is very slight,
while its value to the individual or combination in whose
service it is employed is very great. This kind of capacity
may be styled "business generalship." Now this fitness for
leadership in commercial and industrial war commands a high
price, just as the rare combination of qualities which constitute the successful military commander does in time of war
or in the presence of conditions which render war probable.
But as in an era of assured peace the estimation set upon the
services of the military leader would decline, so, as the system
of government ownership became substituted for that of
monopoly, and the industrial war of competition died out, the

services of the Napoleons of railways and finance would depreciate.

High salaries for the class of positions in the public service requiring a measure of organizing talent and responsibility of superintendence are directly traceable to the demand which exists in all departments of business for men of unusual tact, resource, and executive ability to be utilized mainly in wasteful and injurious struggles for supremacy between conflicting interests. The purely adventitious value thus imparted to commercial generalship is responsible for the unjust difference in the salaries of officials and the unduly high estimate placed on the class of talent supposed to be possessed by those chosen for leading administrative positions. When the competitive features disappear, mere capacity for organization and acquaintance with business methods, which will be all that is requisite, can readily be procured at a much less exorbitant rate. There will be no need to pay responsible administrative officials twenty, fifty, or a hundred times as much as the lower grade of public employés.

When once the nation has assumed the ownership of the means of transit and communication and the duties of a public character now performed by other corporations, the sphere of government will be rapidly widened and extended. Many other enterprises are so closely bound up and identified with these that the necessity of embracing them in the system of state ownership will follow as a matter of course. Coal and other mines, for instance, are largely owned and operated in connection with railroads, and the monopoly system results in combinations by which the supply of fuel is restricted and the price kept up for the benefit of the railway corporations. If once the railways were expropriated, a demand for the government ownership of all mines owned and operated by railroad companies would naturally follow. The immense resources of mineral wealth which have been alienated by faithless and corrupt guardians of the public welfare, owing to the apathy of the people, temporarily dazed and bewildered by the changes in the industrial system, and unable to forecast the results of a delusive "progress," must be reclaimed by the government, and worked in the public interest. Such monopolies as the Standard Oil Company and the natural gas corporations will be abolished, and the supplies of these free gifts of nature regulated by the government, instead of being made a means of extortion.

Following up the idea of the gradual extension of the functions of the State, the next step would naturally be to nationalize those departments of industry closely connected and interwoven with the systems brought under government control. Grain elevators, wharves, warehouses, express companies, steamboat lines, and other undertakings dependent upon railroad traffic would be absorbed. Then would follow the extensive branches of manufacture which supply plant for the railroad and telegraph lines, such as steel and iron works, car and locomotive factories, telegraph, instrument manufactories, and the like. The printing, binding, and engraving offices which furnish the supplies of stationery consumed in connection with the departments of traffic and communication would also come under government ownership. In short, the circle would continually and rapidly widen. The organization of modern commerce and industry is so complete, and the different departments are so dependent on each other, that every fresh extension of the sphere of government control would suggest and justify a further inclusion of some similar or closely allied industry. The economy of forces, owing to the absence of competition, and the better condition of the laborers in government employ as compared with those serving individual capitalists would popularize the change among the working-class, and petitions and movements in favor of fresh expropriations would give an impetus to the general tendency in favor of state-controlled co-operation which nothing could withstand. In a hundred directions the opportunities for converting private into public enterprises would be seen and sought for. Simultaneously with the movement for nationalizing the larger monopolies and their associated and dependent industries, the same pro-

cess would be going on locally by the assertion of the rights
of the individual states and municipalities to own and direct
the smaller enterprises of a public character. Already there
is a strongly developed feeling among Labor Reformers
against the government and municipal contract system. It
puts a premium upon the employment of cheap labor and gives
the unfair and grinding employer an advantage in competing
for public work. All that the body awarding a contract looks
to is securing cheapness in construction, and in place of the
interests of labor being secured by stipulations providing for
the payment of fair wages the contractor is left free to obtain his labor on the best terms he can. If he can procure
cheap, non-union, convict or foreign labor in sufficient quan-
tities, he is enabled to underbid his rivals who may be willing
to pay the current rate of wages. Thus the system becomes
an engine of oppression and the means of keeping the scale
of wages at a low level. It is grossly unfair that in undertaking work for which the whole community is taxed, the
laborer paying in greater proportion to his means than those
of any other class, the rights of labor should be so conspic-
uously ignored as they have been.

Commissioner Arthur T. Hadley, in his report of the Connecticut Bureau of Statistics for 1885, strongly condemns the
contract system in factories in the following terms :—

" A manufacturer employs, let us say, a thousand hands in a large
number of different rooms. He cannot, of course, come in direct personal
contact with the whole number. Paying by the piece he is able to give
a stimulus to each individual laborer to do his best. But this does not
suffice to insure their work being organized and directed in the best
manner. To remedy this he says to the foreman of a room, ' I will give
you a certain gross sum for a certain amount of work to be performed
in your room. Make what terms you can with the workmen, I will pay
their wages; and your profit will be the difference between the amount
paid in wages and the gross sum offered.'

" Under this system the owner has to furnish the capital and pay the
workmen. The contractor makes the arrangements with the workmen,
and in supervising their work has every interest to see that everything
is done as economically as possible. The great advantage of the system
is the stimulus which it gives the foreman to become a contractor. It

enables a man without capital to grow rich; in some instances, to absorb the lion's share of the profits. As far as it goes it is a system of co-operation.

"But it is co-operation going only down to a certain point and then stopping abruptly. There is every danger that its effect upon the vast majority of workmen, who are not contractors, will be bad. The contractor is in some respect in a different position from the employer. Dealing with but a few men, and not having the permanent reputation of the firm to sustain, he is likely to economize by crowding down wages to the lowest possible limit. This is not a necessary consequence of the system. The best firms are wise enough to avoid it. But it is at any rate a frequent consequence, and may fairly be considered the usual one."

These objections to the contract system in private manufacturing enterprises, so forcibly presented by Commissioner Hadley, apply with tenfold force to the public contract system. The cutting down of wages to the lowest possible point may not be a necessary consequence of contracts between manufacturer and foreman as at present entered into. But supposing the manufacturer were to call for tenders from a number of competitors for the position of foreman, on the understanding that the man who would undertake to turn out the most work for the least money would obtain the appointment, then the grinding down of labor to the lowest living or starving point would be not merely the frequent but the inevitable result. The foreman-contractor may squeeze the laborer for his personal gain after he has obtained his position. But the public contractor, under the competitive system, is compelled at the outset to place the wages of his employés at a low figure in order to obtain the contract. And while the individual employer may for his own reputation secure a measure of equity in the arrangements between his foreman and his working-men, the national, state, and municipal governments, not being held responsible by public opinion for the oppression resulting from the contract system, and aiming solely at cheapness, not merely take no measures to prevent injury to the rights of the laborer, but render it essential that the contractor should engage the cheapest labor obtainable before he can enter upon his undertaking.

The opposition to a system which thus arrays the people, in their collective capacity as an employer, against the just demands of wage-workers, will naturally strengthen the movement for the public control of corporation enterprises. The abolition of the public contract system, and the undertaking of the work now performed by contractors by the national, state, and municipal bodies on their own account, would be an important step towards the broader reform. Its influence would be greatly felt in molding public opinion, and concentrating the power of the working-class in favor of the change. When post-offices, custom-houses, court-houses, jails, city halls, school-houses are built, harbors, bridges, light-houses, and breakwaters constructed, streets graded, paved, and drained, under the direct control of public officials employing and paying all workers, without the intervention of the middlemen who now enrich themselves by cheapening labor, the advantages gained by the workers would be so obvious that the further extension of the sphere of public as opposed to the private enterprise would be insisted on. Simultaneously with the movement for the nationalization of the railways, telegraphs, and banks of issue, the local governing bodies, states, counties, cities, and villages would be urged to extend their powers over local corporate enterprises, such as street railways, elevated railways, bridges, ferries, gas companies and the like. As in the case of the larger public concerns of a national character to be expropriated by the general government, the principle of the thin end of the wedge would apply. When once a beginning is made, other branches of industry or systems of distribution, closely affiliated with or dependent upon those taken, will one by one be absorbed.

While the people are asserting their right to control, in the interests of the community, those public undertakings now perverted as the instruments of oppression; while they seek to use their political power through the government to destroy monopoly and limit the power of capitalism, there is another and equally inportant phase of the movement to be accomplished by other means. It will be remembered that in the second chapter the writer endeavored to show that the evils of present industrial conditions were caused by monopoly above and competition below—monopoly of resources, of means of employment in the hands of the few, and competition among those dependent upon them for liberty to labor. Now, while monopoly is being assailed by substituting government ownership for individual control, striking first at the points where the power of resistence is weakest and the influences ranging themselves on our side are most powerful, the war against competition amongst workers must also be pushed.

By perfecting labor organizations, establishing a more thorough community of sentiment among workers of all classes, and bringing to bear the pressure of an enlightened public opinion, with the coercive power of the boycott behind it as a last resort, labor can successfully combat the arrogant pretensions of capitalism to "do as it likes with its own" and "conduct its business in its own way." Organized labor, making its strength felt by united action, utilizing every advantage, availing itself of the most effective methods of industrial warfare in place of the crude and often unsuccessful plan of strikes, can secure, to a great extent, the control of capital and supersede the capitalist. The success of co-operation in certain branches of industry, when wisely undertaken by men having the requisite skill, experience, and capacity, is no longer problematical. The wonderful expansion of the system in England has done much towards cheapening the necessaries of life and securing to the toiler larger returns for his expenditure. In Great Britain and Ireland, at the end of 1883, there were altogether 1461 co-operative societies. Returns from 1291 of these showed a total membership of 729,957 persons. Their sales for the year were £29,336,028, the net profit realized being £2,434,996. Compared with the figures for 1873 a very remarkable increase is shown. The societies have gained 88 per cent. in membership, 87 per cent. in sales, and 119 per cent in profit. During the twenty-two years from 1862 to 1883, inclusive, the total sales were £305,515,659, on which a net profit of £24,247,077 was

realized. Though these societies are mainly distributive, the
returns include a number of productive enterprises conducted
in connection with the stores. The English Co-operative
Wholesale Society, the sales of which in 1884 amounted to
£ 4,675,371, has undertaken to manufacture its own supplies
in several departments. Though productive co-operation
is merely in its infancy, the results already accomplished
wherever it has been established are sufficient to show its
immense possibilities as a means of bettering the condition of
labor.

The report on co-operative production published in the
annual of the English Co-operative Wholesale Society gives
details for 1885 respecting the enterprises founded under their
auspices, from which may be gained some idea of the benefits
to the worker from association in production. The Crumpsall
Biscuit works, opened in 1873, employ about 70 persons ; value.
of supplies £21,352 ; percentage of profit on capital, 19 3-8
Shoe-works, Leicester, established in 1873 ; number of employés about 600 ;   value of supplies, £110,996 ; percentage
of profit, 10 1-8.   Shoe factory, Heckmondwike, established
1880 ; value of supplies, £19,960 ; percentage of profit, 5 7-8.
Soap-works, Durham, established 1874 ; value of supplies,
£16, 570 ; percentage of profit 9 7-8.

It must be borne in mind that the profit here given is in
addition to interest at the rate of about 4 per cent included
in the expenses, which are deducted before the profit is
reckoned. That the system under which these results have
been obtained is not pure co-operation, but a hybrid scheme,
retaining some of the features of capitalism, giving large
"profits" to non-workers who simply utilize it as a means of
investment, and paying employés "wages," like any other
employer, without giving them an interest in the result unless
they are shareholders, does not in the least destroy the
evidence afforded by these figures as to the power of workers
by combination to retain the large percentage of the wealth
they create. When in the course of a few years co-operative
enterprises, starting heavily handicapped by their inexperience

in the ways of commerce, having to create for themselves a business connection and to compete against private capitalists with every advantage on their side, can produce such results during the early period of struggling for a foothold, what may not be hoped for when the difficulties of the pioneer stage of the movement are overcome, and increased experience and intelligence have smoothed the friction attendant upon first experiments ?

It is true that productive co-operation requires a much higher standard of intelligence, discipline, and organizing capacity than does distributive co-operation. Those engaging in it undertake a far greater risk. To start a co-operative store involves merely the investment of a few dollars each on the part of the great body of its members. If there are no profits, or even if the concern fails, they sustain no serious loss. But with productive co-operation the case is widely different. Those who undertake to be their own employers risk not only what little capital they may contribute, but their means of livelihood. They must have not only enough capital to purchase material and pay current expenses, but sufficient to subsist on until they can market their products. They require a degree of self-confidence and mutual reliance, and qualities of perseverance, hopefulness, and readiness to incur temporary reverses without discouragement which are only found among picked men. The difficulties in the way of both productive and distributive co-operation are greater here than in England. Americans are more migratory in their habits. There is seldom that feeling of permanent settlement and fixity of location among the working-people of this continent which is necessary for the success of co-operative enterprises. The man who has already been compelled to make several changes of residence to secure work and who regards himself as a temporary resident, not knowing when he may again have to remove to a distant point, is not likely to interest himself in undertakings which are essentially local. Where this liability to change of residence prevails, working-men have not the same opportunity of making themselves

thoroughly acquainted with each other's characters, and acquiring the confidence in the integrity and fidelity of their
associates which exists where men have been brought up
together and expect to live and die members of the same
community.

There are a large number, of course, to whom these observa-
tions will not apply, men who, have steady employment and
comfortable homes of their own, who are thoroughly identified with the localities where they live. But for some reason
or other, whether it be the contempt for petty economies and
trifling percentages which is a legacy of the " good times "
of inflation, or the kindred American aversion to small beginnings and gradual progress, and the unattractiveness from
that standpoint of a system which dispenses with the
glitter and display of competitive trade, co-operation on this
continent has not hitherto attained anything like the propor-
tions which it can boast in England.

In the present condition of labor there are few departments
of industry in which much can be expected in the way of
productive co-operative work at present. The conditions are
against it as a general measure. Here and there a band of
picked men, having the necessary capital and experience, and
under exceptionally favorable circumstances in regard to
finding a market for their products, may succeed, as some
have already done, in working out their independence of
capitalistic control. But in the great staple lines of manufacture, in those departments where huge corporations, counting
their capital by the millions, already hold the position and
command the channels of distributions, the attempt would be
hopeless. The capitalists who control the cotton manufacturing interest or the iron and steel trade, would speedily crush
out a co-operative rival, even if they had to sell at a loss for a
time to do it.

But in every direction in which co-operation offers a fair
chance of success, wherever a branch of manufacture exists
which can be carried on with comparatively little capital and
begun on a small scale, then the attempt at self-emancipation

from wage-thraldom ought to be made. If, instead of wasting money upon strikes, which drain the resources of labor unions, the amounts were carefully laid by until an opportunity to start a few men in some co-operative enterprise presented itself, the benefits achieved would be infinitely greater. The manner in which, during any extensive disturbance of the relations between capitalism and labor organizations of different classes of workers, totally unknown to each other perhaps even by name, render mutual assistance, is a splendid tribute to the great principle of the solidarity of labor. The sums of money proffered from far and near, the few cents from each individual swelling into the hundreds and thousands and tens of thousands of dollars, present a noble testimony to the thoroughness with which the wage-workers have learned the lesson that " an injury to one is the concern of all." But how much more satisfactory would the result have been had the amounts thus lavishly poured into the treasuries of strike committees been devoted to organizing co-operative associations. When, in addition to the money payments to support strikes, the loss of wages is also taken into account, the enormous waste of means and of energies, which might have been devoted to the permanent amelioration of the condition of labor is still more apparent. The census returns give statistics respecting 762 strikes which occurred in United States in 1880. In 414 of these contests the number of persons engaged was 128,262. As regards the majority of strikes no returns as to direct or indirect losses were received ; but full reports as to the 226 strikes involving 64,779 persons show that the time lost was equal to 1,989,872 days, work, and the unearned wages for this time, $3,711,097. The report of the New York Bureau of Labor Statistics for 1886, shows that the wages lost in strikes during 1886, as far as reported, amounted to $2,538,544, in addition to strike allowances and disbursements by unions to the amount of $329,080. The cost to labor organization of the strike on the Gould railway system in the South-western states during the spring of the present year is estimated at one hundred thousand dollars, the lost wages at one million. During the protracted strike of the Hocking Valley miners in 1884-5 upwards of ninety thousand dollars was contributed by the labor organizations of the continent in aid of the strikers. Had a like amount been put into any form of co-operative industry where a favorable opening seemed to present itself, the failure to achieve any beneficial result could not possibly have been more signal; and had the enterprise succeeded an advance would have been made towards a permanent solution of the labor problem.

But, unfortunately, in the past it has generally required the excitement of an open conflict with capitalism, and the knowledge of the urgent needs of men engaged in industrial warfare, to rouse the sympathies of wage-workers sufficiently to induce large contributions for such purposes. Just as in national affairs hundreds of millions of dollars can be raised for war purposes when men's passions and resentments are aroused, where it would previously have been impossible to procure a tenth or a hundredth part of the sum for objects that might have conduced to a pacific solution of the difficulty, so in the case of labor agitations a lack of foresight and imagination renders men, who are easily moved to action by present emergencies and the excitement of conflict, slow to undertake remedial measures gradual in their operation. Those who will freely give in aid of a strike without hope or thought of any return, without stopping to consider the prospects of success, turn a deaf ear to appeals for co-operative schemes, and perhaps justify their refusal to aid them by expressing doubts as to the feasibility of the project or their chances of getting back their investment. In the one case workingmen contribute ungrudgingly and unquestioningly, in the other they hesitate and criticise and tighten the purse-strings for the fear of possible less.

What can be accomplished by co-operation, as the term is usually applied, however, covers but a small portion of the field of labor reform. The number of enterprises in which co-operation under present conditions would be likely to succeed is limited. In many departments the competition of accumulated capital, which has so remorselessly crushed out the small manufacturer and the small trader, would render co-operation impossible. The difficulties of the system, such as the want of cohesion, discipline, and mutual confidence, naturally increase in proportion to the extent of the enterprise and the multitude and complexity of its details. In those departments of modern industry in which operations are conducted on a large scale, requiring vast amounts of capital and the employment of thousands of men under the same management, each separate establishment again being a member of a combination controlling the trade co-operation, would be an impossibility. Were it possible even to secure the means to make a venture in the same line on a smaller scale, and produce as cheaply as the larger capitalistic manufactories, the co-operators would occupy no better position, and probably, from lack of business experience, might occupy a worse position, than numbers of small enterprises which have been unable to stand the competition of their wealthier rivals.

In the case of these enterprises the solution must be sought in substituting the control of the community for that of capitalism. In place of the absolute ownership of the means of production being vested in individuals, the people must assert the supremacy of the public good over private interests, the right of society to step in and regulate the distribution of the earnings of productive industry.

The rule of King Capital has already begun to pass by evolution from an absolute to a limited monarchy.

To the insolent demand of the capitalist, when called to account for some act of arbitrary oppression, to be allowed to " conduct his business in his own way" and " do as he likes with his own," the answer of recent discussion is an emphatic " No! " It is virtually admitted that the abstract rights hitherto claimed for capitalism are practically untenable, and that labor must be allowed some voice in fixing the conditions of work and wages. The consensus of public opinion, never before brought so fully to bear upon the labor question as

during the last year or so, is fairly epitomized by the pre-
viously-quoted utterance of Prof. Arthur T. Hadley : " The
relations between labor and capital cannot be treated as a
mere matter of private business, but involve social and political questions." A few years ago such an expression would
have been regarded as revolutionary. Now it is echoed by a
thousand presses and pulpits. The propounders of palliatives
are studying how to hedge round and limit the heretofore
absolute power of capitalism with checks and restrictions.
The drift of public sentiment is all in favor of permitting the
creators of wealth some voice in its distribution—some
guarantee against the power which they have called into existence being used unjustly against them.

Industrial partnerships, boards of arbitration, securities to
employés against arbitrary discharge—all such proposals are
in the line of social evolution, and assert a right on the part of
society to interfere with the management of what have hitherto been looked upon as strictly private enterprises. But the advocates of these and similar amelioratives have little idea of
the conclusion to which their logic leads. There is no finality
about such proposals. They are steps towards collectivism.
When once the principle they embody is admitted, it is simply a question of increasing by degrees the extent of the control exercised by the community, and decreasing in proportion
the power of the individual capitalist, until the latter at length
becomes little more than nominal, preparatory to its final
extinguishment.

" It is the first step which costs." As the granting of tenant
right in Ireland is but the prelude to the overthrow of landlordism, so the admission of the wage-earners' interest in productive enterprises, in addition to a weekly wage fixed by
competition without reference to the intrinsic social value of
his labor, will form the leverage for the destruction of capitalism. When, either by legislation under the stress of a quickened public conscience or by more thorough organization and
discipline among the workers themselves, the share of labor
in the products of industry is fixed proportionately to the re-

turns, and when permanency of employment is secured, a long stride toward collectivism will have been taken.

Fixing the share of labor, by whatever means of legislative authority or of industrial combination it is accomplished, is virtually fixing the share of the capitalist-employer. That accomplished, the next step will be to eliminate the factor of usury from the calculation, and by successive re-arrangements to bring matters to the point where " the share of capitalism " is reduced to a reasonable remuneration for the actual labor of superintendence and direction.

When this stage is reached, and the industries now controlled by capitalism are practically socialized, each in the hands of its group of workers, a few additional regulations for government supervision will be all that is necessary to bring them into line with the expropriated enterprises under government control. Two movements, both of which are making great headway—the one, the assertion of increased jurisdiction by the government over matters formerly considered beyond their scope; the other, the disposition on the part of wage-workers to closer organization and more emphatic assertion of their claims irrespective of legislative action—would thus close in as it were upon capitalism from above and below simultaneously, and meet and merge in each other. It is often assumed that there is an antagonism between these movements. The advocates of the *laissez faire* school are accustomed to deprecate looking to government action, and to urge upon working-people the advisability of doing everything themselves—forgetful that under Democratic institutions the government should be simply the instrument for accomplishing the people's will, and that in acting through government agency the people are doing the work themselves just as much as if they established any other agency for the purpose. To abandon all governmental methods of reform is to deliberately throw away the immense advantage put into the hands of the people by the possession of the ballot. That this weapon has been misused in the past is no reason for discarding it now, for the same increased intelligence and capacity for organization and discipline which are essential to the success of any other method of operation will secure it in the political sphere.

Though apparently opposed to each other, government interference and popular organization are not really so. They are opposed only as the two blades of a pair of scissors are—approaching each other from opposite directions, it is true, but working together and to the same end. The opposition to government interference is a survival of the caste idea. When the rulers represented a privileged class and governed in their interest, the masses of the people being unrepresented, it was natural to regard them as separated by a social chasm from the body of the nation, having diverse and antagonistic interests, and therefore to be intrusted with as little power as possible, and jealously prevented from encroaching on the domain of individual rights. But with the development of political Democracy the situation is reversed. It is unrestricted private rights, swollen by the concession of unjust privileges into monopolies, which threaten liberty.

The advocates of *laissez faire* have not been slow to note a seeming inconsistency on the part of those who favor government interference yet denounce the government under existing conditions as the facile and corrupt instrument of monopoly. It is a seeming inconsistency only. Before administrative interference, would be possible it would be necessary to popularize the government—to get rid of the last vestiges of the Old World idea of the State as something elevated above the people—to uproot the exotic tradition that a certain amount of ostentation and display is requisite to preserve the prestige of rulers, and to make Democratic simplicity an established fact in place of a byword and a sneer in the mouths of reactionaries and Anglomaniacs. As has been previously explained, it is the influence of monopolies reacting upon government and the absence of any strong countervailing public sentiment that has made it corrupt. The inconsistency lies with those who quote the existing corruption as a reason for perpetrating the condition which fostered it.

The first step in establishing the control by the people of the means of production and transit should logically be the nationalization of the land. The greatest and most pernicious of all monopolies is that involved in private land-ownership; the reform which more than any other would tend to redress social inequalities by lessening the stress of competition among workers would be the appropriation of all land values to public uses. So far as can be judged by present aspects it is not probable that this will be generally accomplished until the change from capitalism to collectivism has proceeded very far in other directions, although approaches toward it may be made simultaneously with other advances.

The agitation for land nationalization has made wonderful strides of late, but public opinion has not ripened on this question to the same extent that it has in regard to the other phases of Labor Reform. There are obvious reasons why this should be the case. Social, like natural, forces follow " the line of least resistance." The numbers of those who either are or think themselves to be interested in the maintenance of individual property in land are much greater than the numbers concerned in upholding railroad, telegraph, and money monopoly and industrial capitalism. It is good generalship to attack the enemy's position at its weakest point; necessary to capture the outposts before assailing the citadel. But while the full accomplishment of land reform by the substitution of public for individual ownership may be deferred until collectivism has made progress on other lines, it is altogether feasible that ground may be broken for the change by the gradual transfer of the burden of taxation to the land. As " incidental protection " was the stepping-stone to a high tariff, so "incidental " land taxation may be the beginning of the broader system of public — not necessarily national — land-ownership.

Hitherto in the discussion of the land nationalization question, stress has been laid upon its ultimate results in abolishing speculative land values and placing the occupation of the soil within the reach of all. The matter has been presented from a bro   int. as was of course necessary

Last line illegible in original edition.

in laying down a great principle unfamiliar to the people. To inculcate the elementary truth that the soil rightfully belongs to the whole people, and to show how, by the exercise of the taxing power, they can reclaim the rights which have been usurped under the system of private land-ownership, was the first work essential to be undertaken in order to secure a foundation for intelligent political action. But the benefits and blessings to accrue from the abolition of personal land-ownership have perhaps seemed too abstract and too distant to secure for the measure that cordial and earnest support from the masses which is requisite for its practical adoption. There are a great many who readily yield a formal assent to the land nationalization doctrine, as embodying an important truth which will some day or other prevail. But it does not come home to them as a question demanding present and persistent attention—an issue to be fought out here and now, and from the successful carrying out of which they can expect personal and immediate advantages, as in the case of the shortening of hours labor or of financial reform.

To interest the people it will be needful to give more prominence to the objects that can be accomplished with the money raised by land taxation, to show that long before any general or comprehensive all-round scheme of vesting the ownership of the soil in the government, or even imposing *all* taxes on the land could be achieved, local improvements unattainable on the present basis of taxation can be secured by the free use of the taxing power as a means of appropriating the unearned increment to public uses. A scheme for a free street car service to be maintained by a special tax upon the holders of land upon both sides of the line was recently broached by the American Tax reform League of New York. The street car and rapid transit system has enhanced enormously the value of land in the large cities by rendering it possible for those who gain their living in the business centres to live several miles away. It brings land in the suburbs, which would otherwise have little more than agricultural value, into the market for residence purposes at high prices, and increases the value of property all along the business streets, which thus become great arteries of traffic. It is aptly argued that the landowners who are enriched by the system should be called upon to defray the cost of providing free street-car accommodation for the public, just as the landlord of a large business block pays for the maintenance and working of the elevator.

I merely cite this proposition as an instance of the manner in which the idea of the appropriation of land values to public uses can be popularized by setting before the public the tangible concrete benefits attainable even by its partial application. In place of the abstract and far-away ideal of a complete system of land nationalization, to which men can be induced by argument to give a languid assent, just as they do to the doctrine of the millennium, with about as little active interest in bringing the one about as the other, Labor Reformers must put before them such presently attainable objects as free street cars and ferries, parks, libraries, museums, recreation grounds, schools, and institutes for special branches of education and artistic culture, to be established and maintained by special taxes on land values. When once the principle is established and a beginning made in one locality, the laboring masses will very quickly seize upon the idea, and the demand for public and benevolent institutions to be paid for by taxing ground rents will grow by what it feeds on. A hundred ways will be discovered in which the enormous yearly value of the soil in the larger cities can be devoted to its legitimate use in increasing the facilities for travel, providing opportunities for knowledge and amusement, developing the public taste, and making life easier, brighter, and more pleasant for the masses of the population, by whose presence alone these values have been created.

Land reform must begin in the larger cities, for two reasons. It is there that the consequences of land monopoly are most severely felt and the people most in need of the advantages which the judicious expenditure of ground rents in works of public utility would secure. It is there too that the monopolists, if richest, are also fewest in proportion to the total population, and the disinherited strongest in voting power. When the experiment has been found to work successfully in New York or Chicago, and it is seen that no real danger to the public interest is involved, and that the small property owner is touched but lightly, getting a full return for his increased contribution in his share of the general advantages, while the burden falls on the very rich, smaller municipalities, where the extremes of want and wealth are not so marked, will follow. Thus the system, unattainable as a complete and symmetrical plan of universal application, will be gradually developed in accordance with the principle of evolution.

I did not set out to pen a " Utopia " or " New Atlantis," to picture an ideal state of society based upon principles of abstract justice, with every detail of social adjustment precisely set forth. There has perhaps been somewhat too much " utopianizing " in the discussion of the industrial future. We want to consider not what would be absolutely the best and most perfect system to draft for an entirely new social state, but to take all existing conditions into account, and to indicate what broad general lines of action can be most successfully followed, what already existing streams of tendency can be taken advantage of to further our ends, and how apparently opposite and conflicting movements can be made to harmonize and converge, and every power which nature or social organization has placed in the hands of the people be utilized to its full extent in moulding the institution of a true industrial Democracy. Those who condemn Socialism as impracticable, and praise existing institutions as the outgrowth of the wisdom and experience of the past, forget that these very institutions were not suddenly forced upon society, but were gradually evolved out of previously prevailing systems. The teachings of history are appealed to against Socialism. Men who, as students of those teachings, have seen constitutional government evolved out of despotism as

> " Freedom broadens slowly down
> From precedent to precedent ;"

who have witnessed the decline of feudalism by the growth
of the middle classes; who recognize in the overthrow of
personal slavery the result of a development of the sense of
justice and humanity to a degree unknown to the nations of
antiquity, show themselves strangely blinded by prejudice
when they assume the finalty of the capitalistic system. The
admitted inadequacy of any scheme or any number of
schemes formulated for the reconstruction of society proves
nothing. It would be impossible in the very nature of things
that the work should be accomplished in this way, just as
impossible as it would have been for William the Conqueror
or Henry VIII. to have imposed upon the English people by
the exercise of his despotic power the system of constitutional
government which they now possess. The very wildest and
most Utopian socialistic system that ever emanated from the
brain of a French doctrinaire seems no more visionary and
beyond the reach of possible attainment to the hard-headed
and hard-hearted political economist, than the actually exist
ing social and political system would have appeared to the
most liberal and enlightened of our forefathers a few hundred
years ago. Ideas and principles of individual conduct, of
social relations, of the rights and duties and responsibilities
of the citizen, which are now the common property of the
mass, and the veriest truisms, would have been absolutely in-
capable of comprehension by the men of classic or mediæval
times.

That social order and government should exist without
hereditary castes and classes, that the ordinances of public
worship should be maintained without state endowments by
the voluntary contributions of the people, and that the
necessary rough and menial labor should be performed without men being allowed to hold their fellows in personal bondage would to the mailed baron or cloistered monk of the
Plantagenet era have seemed paradoxical and subversive of
all human experience, and contrary not merely to established
usages and conventional opinions, but to the order of nature
itself. Yet these great changes have been wrought by the

process of evolution going forward without pause or rest, in which each phase of mental activity, each triumph of mechanical skill, each stage in the uphill struggle between the forces of progress and reaction is but the germ of new and undreamed-of further developments—the foothold and vantage-ground for fresh advances. Though it is impossible even to outline the final form which social institutions based upon the principle of a just return to each for his labor will assume, it is within the power of each and every man to aid in rough-hewing the material for the edifice, assured that in leaving the ultimate result to the shaping of the future he will be building better than he knows.

CHAPTER VII.

STUMBLING-BLOCKS.

Master, what of the night ?
   Child, night is not at all
   Anywhere, fallen or to fall,
Save in our star-stricken eyes.
Forth of our eyes it takes flight,
   Look we but once nor before
Nor behind us, but straight on the skies,
   Night is not then any more.
                    SWINBURNE.

IN such a contest as that upon which the Labor Reformers have entered, nothing is to be gained by ignoring or belittling the obstacles in the way of success, whether they are internal or external in their character. In all movements in connection with the onward progress of humanity the drawbacks and the difficulties have always been great and apparently insuperable in proportion to the magnitude of the change sought to be accomplished. Arrayed openly against us are the selfish interests not only of the few who actually benefit by the existing state of things, but of the much larger number who either think they benefit by it now or hope to do so at some future time; the influence of political and economic traditions; the instincts of the timorous and the naturally conservative; the stolid apathy of the large class who can only be roused by extreme pressure; and the bitter hostility of the supercilious and cynical "culture" which apes European models and cultivates undemocratic habits of thought, from the ranks of which capitalism recruits its host of literary hirelings and professional henchmen. In our own ranks there are the weaknesses resulting from want of education and discipline, from lack of an understanding of the real object and significance of the movement, and consequently a lamentable shortcoming in directness of aim and steadfastness of purpose, and from waste of strength, which should be reserved for more important conflicts, in petty and irritating skirmishes, which, even if successful, are not calculated to effect or lead up to any permanent change in labor's relation to capitalism. Many are still under the spell of bourgeois political economy, and regard capitalism as a beneficent instrumentality for finding labor employment, needing indeed to be occasionally checked when too grasping, but by no means to be wholly subverted. Others, while willing to employ every other agency, are indisposed to resort to independent political action, and at elections are partisans first and Labor Reformers afterwards.

It is a common assertion of Labor Reformers that on this continent at least the masses have the solution of the problem in their own hands; that as soon as the working-classes are practically unanimous in demanding their rights they will be able to secure them. This is to a certain extent true, but it is not so reassuring a statement as at first sight it seems. If the masses had at all times understood and acted upon their true interests there never would have been any labor problem in America. Had they had the foresight to resist the insidious beginnings of the monopoly system, and to give to democracy its full interpretation as securing social as well as political rights, capitalism would now be non-existent as an industrial and political force. Unfortunately the masses are only just beginning to think and act in their own interests, and the task that in the formative stage of American institutions would have been easy is now arduous; the once plastic materials are set and hardened, and the opposing influences have become strengthened and inwrought into the very fibre of our social and national life.

But it is well to keep the fact prominently in view that to-day there exist no industrial or social evils which the people, were they enlightened, united, and determined, could not remove. In former times, and in Europe to-day, emperors and statesmen, with large armies at their call and hosts of officials and spies, have by brute force kept down struggling nations, and taxed them to pay for their own subjection. Land monopolists in densely peopled countries have taken advantage of the ignorance of the mass to rob them of everything but a meagre subsistence. The money-power has used its control of the tools of trade to add to its glittering heaps from the penury of the toilers. But never before in the world's history have we beheld the forces of oppression and craft and greed grinding into the dust a people who are kept down by no armed force, who have no superstitious veneration for monarchical "divine rights," who boast of their universal intelligence and education, and who have actually the power of legislation and government in their own hands. That is the exceptional and anomalous feature of the situation in America.

The power of capitalism has been increased enormously by modern invention and progress. One by one it has captured and wrested to its own selfish purposes the very agencies to which our forefathers looked for deliverance. The railroad and the telegraph have become instruments of extortion. The "free press" has become perverted and subsidized as an agency for misleading and deceiving the people. Industrial expansion means simply increased profits to the capitalist; smaller pay relatively to the amount of production, longer hours and greater uncertainty of employment, to the worker. "The Great West," with its hundreds of millions of untilled acres, regarded as the heritage of the landless and oppressed, has fallen into the hands of monopolists, thus closing the outlet for the swarming population of the great centers, and intensifying the competition which cheapens flesh and blood in the market. The great ocean and land transportation routes, with their wonderfully cheap rates of fare, instead of being the highways of deliverance for the down-trodden, have become in the hands of monopoly the means by which it can mobilize its forces and overwhelm resistance to its exactions by forwarding fresh throngs of competitors to any point of conflict. And the nominally "free ballot," in the case of very many workers, merely serves as a reminder of their degradation when the forces of bribery, menace, and coercion are employed to make its exercise a mockery or nullify its effects.

But more potent and insidious than these influences is the power of old ideas, traditions, sentiments, and habits of thought, survivals of a past age, relics of a time when the questions now pressing for solution had not been thought of The hand of the dead past thrusting itself from the mould and moth-eaten cerements of antiquity into the struggle of to day! Specially applicable to the opposition encountered at every stage of the conflict for industrial emancipation is the powerful utterance of Nathaniel Hawthorne upon this subject.

"Shall we never, never get rid of the past ? It lies upon the present like a giant's dead body ! In fact the case is just as if a young giant were compelled to waste all his strength in carrying about the corpse of the old giant, his grandfather, who died a long while ago and only needed to be decently buried. Just think a moment and it will startle you to see what slaves we are to by-gone times—to Death if we give the matter the right word. For example, a dead man, if he happen to have made a will, disposes of wealth no longer his own, or, if he die intestate, it is distributed in accordance with the notions of men much longer dead than he. A dead man sits on all our judgment seats, and living judges do but search out and repeat his decisions. We read in dead men's books. We laugh at dead men's jokes and cry at dead men's pathos. We are sick of dead men's diseases, physical and moral, and die of the same remedies with which dead doctors killed their patients. We worship the living Deity according to dead men's forms and creeds. Whatever we seek to do of our own free motion a dead man's icy hand obstructs
10

us. Turn our eyes to whatever point we may a dead man's white im-
mitigable face encounters them and freezes our very heart. And we
must be dead ourselves before we can begin to have our proper influence
in our own world, which will then be no longer our world but the world
of another generation with which we shall have no shadow of right to
interfere."

All the weight of tradition and precedent arising out of altogether different conditions than those which now confront
us is thrown against Labor Reform.   The battle will be more
than half won when we emancipate ourselves from this thraldom to the ghosts and shadows of the past. Why should new
questions be judged by old precedents ?   Why should we on
this continent and in this bustling industrial age be ruled by
the judicial interpretations, the legislative maxims, or the
social and economic formulas originated by the idlers and
parasites of society at a time when the world was supposed to
have been created for the benefit of the rulers and the rich—
and the people to have no rights whatever but that of sweat,
ing and fighting for their benefit ? How strange that inherited
traditions and ideas should have such a hold that men who
are themselves workers, themselves sufferers from caste oppression, should be largely guided in their conduct by the public
sentiment and code of principles inculcating respect for birth,
money, position, vested rights, etc., created by the dead, and
no doubt damned, old despots and sycophants in the middle
ages ?

Among the modern instances of the survival of these anti_
quated modes of thought as reflected in our laws, customs, and
every-day actions and expressions, may be noticed the tendency
previously alluded to, to regard governments of any kind as
something separate from and above the people, differing essentially from other social and public agencies by which the will
of many is carried into effect by the action of the few delegated to act for them and in their name—the maintenance of
a costly and useless diplomatic service—the constitution of the
Senate by which it is rendered irresponsible, except indirectly,
to the electors—the enormous and glaring contrast between

the rewards offered to the late General Grant and other military commanders, and the recognition awarded to the equal bravery and devotion of private soldiers—the placing of military, political, and official services generally on a higher plane in public estimation than the equally or more valuable arduous and dangerous work of the industrial classes—the power vested in the judiciary to qualify or set aside the legislation of the people's representatives, usually exercised in servile deference to the interests of capitalism—the relic of the "divine right" idea embodied in the arbitrary power of the judges to punish for contempt of court and their assumed immunity from criticism—and generally the disposition on the part of the professional, educated, and influential class, who largely mould public opinion, to regard labor either patronizingly or disparagingly as a separate class or interest deserving perhaps of some recognition, but necessarily subservient and inferior to other and more important interests. It may be said in reply to the latter statement that as the writer, in common with other Labor Reformers, uses the term "working-class" freely, others are not to blame for making the distinction. The phrase is distasteful, but it embodies a fact, and recognizes an existing distinction which ought not to exist. There is a "working-class" only because there is another class or classes who, although they may do some measure of useful and necessary labor, derive the principal portion of their subsistence and their social importance and influence from their control of capital and their alliance with capitalism. The interests of labor are those of the great body of the people.

Legislation against monopolies is not class-legislation ; laws creating and subsidizing them are ; legislation in restraint of the extortions of the usurer and the speculator is not class-legislation, but the opposite. Legislation reclaiming the land from the absolute control of private individuals ; restoring the function of issuing the people's currency to the State which should never have parted with it ; nationalizing the railways, telegraph lines, and mines, is the very reverse of class-legislation. It is legislating the privileged class who grow rich on the unrequited toil of others out of existence. It is law-making in the interests of the bulk of the people as against those of a handful who now arrogate to themselves the right to dictate on what terms the rest shall find the opportunity and means to work which bounteous nature gives freely to all.

The extent of the usurpations of Capitalism, and the inroads of a perverted sentiment upon Democratic principles, is in no respect more noticeable than in the attitude of the public towards labor. We speak for instance of a "self-made man," meaning one who has risen to the position of a capitalist. Nobody would ever think of applying the term to one who remained a wage-worker, although in intelligence and intellectual cultivation he were the peer of any in the land. The pulpit and the rostrum pay a hypocritical tribute to "the dignity of labor," but the sentiment is belied by every action of those who utter it, which tests their real feeling. No actual wage-earner, however competent or worthy, could hope to be elected president or senator, or to be chosen for any of the more responsible positions in the gift of the administration. The letter of the Declaration of Independence pronounces all men by birthright free and equal ; but the unwritten law of political custom and precedent makes a social position, of which the constitution knows nothing, an invariable prerequisite to the attainment of high political office. So familiarized have the people become with the idea that labor is necessarily a subordinate order, that the nomination of a working-man for Congress, instead of being regarded as an ordinary and natural circumstance in a Democratic country, would be looked upon as a notable concession to class interests, and would doubtless be deprecated as the extreme of demagogism in many quarters. Yet the filling of important positions by the election of lawyers, merchants, manufacturers, and bankers—the representatives of capitalism whose interests are antagonistic to popular rights—is regarded as a matter of course. Even working-men themselves, to judge from the political action of most of them in the past, consider it quite natural and fitting that the wealthy classes and their allies should monopolize the

higher public positions to the exclusion of actual workers.
There is a general tacit acquiescence in the political tradition
which entrusts the administrative and legislative power entirely to the hands of the comparatively small class who have
special interests apart from those of the people, and ostracizes
completely those who live by their labor, because they are
working-men. With such a principle actuating both political
parties, with an electorate so wedded to partisan issues and
blinded by party feeling that they passively submit to this
discrimination against labor, what else than legislation for the
benefit of capitalism can be expected ? How can labor fairly
hope for justice or consideration when the ballot put into
its hands is used in elevating to public positions the men
whose interests and sympathies are bound up with the system that crushes it to earth ?

In a real Democracy, the people would choose for the leading positions in their gift men thoroughly identified with the
views and aspirations of the masses, tried and true champions of popular rights. Instead of riches or social position
being a passport to office, they would furnish the best of
reasons for declining to intrust with power those concerned
in the maintenance of special class interests, apart from and
opposed to the general good. Yet, owing to a singular
perversion of the popular judgment, the causes which should
tend to make the claims of a candidate regarded with distrust and aversion are apt to contribute in no small degree
to his popularity and success. After having thus thrown
away the protection given by the ballot—having made money
and the influence which comes of close association with and
devotion to capitalistic interests an essential requisite for
high representative functions, what right has labor to complain when its reasonable claims are scouted and its remon-
strances ignored by the rulers it has unwisely chosen because they were not identified with labor?

When a wage-worker is elected to one of the State legislatures he is regarded as a representative of labor interests.
The party which nominates and elects him takes special

credit to itself for having made this much of a concession to the claims of the working-class. It is looked upon as a special act of condescension, entitling them to the gratitude and establishing a claim to the support of organized labor. Capitalists by the hundred, and professional men, who are the close allies, sometimes the obsequious hirelings, of capitalism, are chosen without a thought that there is anything of a concession to class interests, anything extraordinary in the selection. In short, it seems to be taken for granted that, as a rule, a certain social and pecuniary standing only to be found outside the laboring-class is a pre-requisite for legislative honors; while the choice of a wage-earner is an exceptional and grudgingly made concession to the newly-awakened spirit of Labor Reform.

" But," it will doubtless be urged, " many of these capitalists and professional men began life as laborers. Look at the long list of self-made men who have attained the highest politicals station. Abraham Lincoln, Andrew Johnson, Henry Wilson, Ulysses S. Grant, James A. Garfield were all at one period of their lives working-men. Their humble origin was no bar to their political advancement. In fact it was rather in their favor. A presidential or congressional candidate always finds it to his advantage to have risen from the ranks."

The " self-made-man " tradition is dear to the American heart; but it embodies a radically false and un-Democratic notion. It ought not to be necessary for any one to " rise in the world," in the sense of ceasing to be a wage-worker or a manual laborer, before he can hope to be recognized as worthy to fill an important representative position. The very phraseology so often employed, " rising from the ranks," conveys the idea that manual labor, if not exactly dishonorable, is, at all events, less dignified, less compatible with true manhood, than intellectual toil or dignified leisure.

When a man has ceased to be a working-man in the conventional sense, and either accumulated wealth or attained professional or social standing; then, but not till then, can he look for political advancement. While he remains a wage-worker or a self-employed manual laborer, even his own fellow-craftsmen would rather give their votes to the self-made employer or the professional henchman of capitalism. Far from being an argument to show the estimation in which labor is held, the worship of the self-made man is an emphatic corroboration of all that has been alleged as to the disabilities of labor, politically and otherwise. It proves conclusively that it is necessary to escape from the necessity of labor in order to win honor or consideration. It degrades labor, as a condition to be endured only as long as it is inevitable—bringing out into strong relief its irksomeness and repulsiveness as compared with the wider scope and increased esteem enjoyed by the fortunate few who succeed in emancipating themselves.

The whole tendency of modern education and public opinion on this subject is utterly demoralizing. The ideal of the teacher, the platform, orator, and the press is the self-made man who, from being a farmer, laborer, or mechanic, has " risen " above the necessity of work, by accumulating wealth. Ambitious youths are urged to " be somebody." The professions or mercantile life are held out as the goal of endeavor, and productive labor is belittled, by implication at all events, as an unworthy career for any man of enterprise, or, at best, as a mere starting-point or stepping-stone to something better. The examples adduced for imitation are all those of men who have become wealthy or prominent by abandoning manual toil for other and inferentially more honorable pursuits. While a hypocritical verbal homage is paid to the dignity of labor, the practical lesson inculcated is the exceeding desirability of evading its demands, and as quickly as possible climbing out of the ranks of producers to a position of greater honor. The effect of such teaching is to foster a selfish individualism, and a contempt for honest toil, as a monotonous round of drudgery affording no scope for ambition other than the prospect of shirking it.

It is not uncommon to hear people speak of the opportunities which men of greater shrewdness and resource than the average possess of rising to the position of capitalists as an evidence of the satisfactory condition of labor. The lot of the wage-worker, it is said, cannot be so very unendurable, because a large proportion have in the past risen from a dependent position to that of self-made men. Suppose it were alleged that the convicts in Sing-Sing prison were very cruelly treated.

"Nothing of the kind, I assure you," says one. "The prisoners in Sing-Sing have nothing to complain of. It is very easy to escape. Any man of ordinary strength and cunning can break out."

"But men are continually being starved and beaten."

"Perhaps. But they are escaping all the time. A very large proportion scale the walls and run away."

What would be thought of the logic of such a plea? Yet practically it is exactly that of the argument put forward when the case of those who have risen from the condition of laborers to that of capitalists is adduced in reply to the complaints of the disabilities of the working-man's lot. We are told that escape is easy, that shrewdness and business capacity and industry will enable almost any one to rise above the need of living by his own labor. The hope of escape from the prison-house of toil is held up as the justification for the abuses and wrongs suffered by those who remain in captivity. The ablest and the most intelligent workers are bribed into acquiescence with existing evils by this prospect, while the fate of the vast majority who, in the nature of things, must remain dependent on their labor, is rendered more unendurable and hopeless by the selfish efforts of the aspiring to raise themselves, in place of uniting with their fellow-workers to elevate their class.

The moral effect of the struggle of individual workers for personal advancement by the mode in which it is generally sought is largely evil. It is men's worst qualities oftener than their best which enable them to rise under present conditions. A man of parsimonious, niggardly disposition is more likely to succeed in the attempt than one who is gen-

erous and open-handed. Outspoken candor and a free, independent bearing frequently result in loss of employment, or
keep men in inferior positions, while the obsequious spy and
tale-bearer is advanced and rewarded. Absorbing devotion
to money-getting, to the exclusion of other objects, usually
accomplishes the end in view; while men of higher minds,
whose interests, instead of being centred on purely selfish
purposes, include domestic and social enjoyments and intellectual pursuits, fail for lack of the concentration of effort in
the one direction. The self-made man, as a rule, is a grasping
and sordid creature, the predominant traits of whose character
are avarice and a domineering harshness of disposition. As
in the time of slavery the slave-overseer made the sternest
of task-masters, so the laborer turned employer is usually less
considerate and more greedy and overbearing than he who
has always belonged to the capitalist class. So far as the
great majority of workers are concerned it would be infinitely
better for them if the line were drawn as absolutely and im-
passably between classes as in the castes of India, than that
they should be mocked and deluded with the possibility of
rising into the capitalist class, which in any event can only be
realized by a small percentage at the expense of the best
qualities and finest feeling of humanity, and to the detriment
and disadvantage of the remaining workers.

The self-made man belongs to the earlier stages of American industrial development. It is a mere truism to say that
the conditions have so changed within the last generation that
the opportunity which once appeared to offer itself to every
industrious and saving mechanic, clerk, or laborer of attaining
a comfortable competency is now restricted within very much
narrower limits. The proportion of those without other
means than their physical or mental capacities for labor who
can entertain a reasonable expectation of achieving an independent position continually decreases. The following testimony as to the diminution in number of those who control
capital and production, notwithstanding the enormous increase
in the volume of wealth, is supplied by the census of 1880 :—

" In illustration of the wide diffusion of petty productive establishments it is interesting to observe that while, the settled area of 1840 was
but a little over one-half that of 1880, and the value of the manufactured products perhaps not more than one-seventh or one-eighth, there
were almost as many grist-mills at the former as at the latter date, and
an even greater number of saw-mills. The figures for the two censuses
were as follows :

	1840.	1880.
Grist-mills	23,661	24,338
Saw-mills	31,650	25,708

This fact shows strikingly the tendency to the concentration of productive industry during the last forty years, due chiefly to the increased
facilities for transportation."

Obviously this increased concentration of capital in fewer
hands, combined with the operation of land monopoly in closing the avenues to self-employment, renders the great masses
of the laboring people more and more absolutely dependent
upon employers, and widens the chasm between classes.

But although the chances for individual advancement are
thus lessening year by year, the public sentiment and social
aspirations which were begotten of conditions that have largely passed away yet survive. Men quote the examples of
those who have become wealthy under the former state of
things as an encouragement to personal effort, and forget that
the circumstances which enabled them to achieve success are now entirely altered ; that one by one the ways of
escape from the ranks of wage-labor are closing up, while the
multitude of competitors below is ever on the increase, and
the pressure of monopoly above grows more intense. It will
take many years more to eradicate the " self-made-man " tradition, and to inculcate the stern and salutary truth that for the
overwhelming majority of the producers there is no hope of
substantially ameliorating their condition as individuals, except by united effort for the elevation of their class.

A bugbear which has for long prevented even those who
suffer worst from the effects of the competitive system recognizing that the only permanent and effective remedy is the
substitution of collectivism, is the stereotyped assertion that
it is " contrary to human nature." It is assumed by so-called

philosophers and politico-economical writers that the existing social order is based upon certain inherent and ineradicable instincts which must in the long run triumph over any system founded in defiance of them. This supposed instinctive selfishness, meanness, and general depravity of human nature has done duty so long as a reason why mankind should travel along complacently in the conventional ruts, that it is time to examine the premises on which it is based.

The truth is that human nature, instead of being fixed and unchangeable, is a most variable thing. What was contrary to Greek or Roman human nature is found to be quite in accordance with that of modern civilization. Ideas which were repulsive to the general sense of society in the middle ages are now the universally accepted principles of government and social organization. Human nature is undergoing continual modifications as the environment of any particular section of humanity is changed by new conditions. Instead of being a standard by which to estimate the practicability of institutions, it is perpetually altering its requirements. The pessimist's argument is a most fallacious one.

There is no respect in which the present era differs from previous ages more than in the growth of a spirit of philanthropy. Compare the utter callousness of the ancients to human suffering and degradation, the terrible cruelties which were then a matter of daily occurrence, with the quickened conscience of modern society to the wrongs involved in the *direct* infliction of pain. The pagan civilization of Greek and Roman made no provision for the destitute, the sick, and the afflicted. Hospitals, alms-houses, orphan asylums, institutions for the blind, the decrepit, and the insane—all these were' undreamed of in the classical ages. In Sparta the deformed and sickly infants were exposed to perish miserably rather than permit them to become a burden on society. In ancient Rome, at the height of its glory and opulence, the principal amusements of the citizens were the sports of the arena, in which thousands of slaves, prisoners, or Christians were slain in gladiatorial combats or torn to pieces by wild beasts in a single day to glut the "natural" craving of the populace for the excitement of wholesale bloodshed. Roman ladies of the highest rank gloated over these hideous and revolting exhibitions with far less sympathy or care for the feeling of the victims "butchered to make a Roman holiday" than is often excited in the audience of a modern theatre by well counterfeited suffering. Swinburne says of one of the Roman empresses :

> She loved the games men played with death
>   Where death must win,
> As though the slain man's blood and breath
>   Revived Faustine.
>
> Nets caught the pike, pikes tore the net,
>   Lithe limbs and lean,
> From drained-out pores dripped thick red sweat
>   To soothe Faustine.
>
> All round the foul, fat furrows reeked
>   Where blood sank in ;
> The circus splashed and seethed and shrieked
>   All round Faustine.

Such was "human nature" two thousand years ago. Such were the fiendish barbarities practiced by the most civilized of the ancient nations, not at the caprice of a single despot, be it borne in mind, but in gratification of a general popular passion. Now the great mass of humanity everywhere would stand aghast at the proposal to sacrifice even a single human life for no other end than the amusement of the people.

A retrospective glance at the state of society during comparatively recent historical periods affords ample testimony that the disposition of mankind grows milder and more compassionate, and less tolerant of cruelty and injustice, as civilization progresses. The historian Macaulay observes that there is scarcely a page of the history or lighter literature of the seventeenth century which does not contain some proof that our ancestors were less humane than their posterity. After detailing the harshness of domestic discipline, the horrible cruelty with which many crimes were punished by the law, the brutal sports frequently practiced, and the pestilential condition of the prisons, he says:—

But on all this misery society looked with profound indifference. Nowhere could be found that sensitive and restless compassion which has in our time extended a powerful protection to the factory child, to the Hindoo widow, to the negro-slave ; which pries into the stores and water-casks of every emigrant ship ; which winces at every lash laid on the back of the drunken soldier; which will not suffer the thief in the hulks to be ill fed or over-worked; and which has repeatedly endeavored to save the life even of the murderer. * * The more we study the annals of the past, the more we shall rejoice that we live in a merciful age ; in an age in which cruelty is abhorred, and in which pain, even when deserved, is inflicted reluctantly and from a sense of duty.

This, if somewhat on the optimistic side, is a measurably correct presentation of the extent of the change which has been wrought for the better by the growth of the sentiment of humanity in the last two hundred years. How absurd, in view of this fact, is it for the opponents of collectivism to argue that there is any quality inherent in human nature which renders impossible a social development under which the misery and hardship inflicted by the competitive system will disappear. The answer to the cry that "you can't change human nature " is that it is always changing. There is no single advance, either, in politics or in social organization, that has not at the outset been denounced on the same ground of its being contrary to human nature. The early overthrow of the American Republic was predicted for the reason that democracy was unnatural. The people, it was said, would not respect a government of their own creation; they must be overawed by the pomp and splendor of royalty, or anarchy would result. But a century's experience has shown the fallacy of this reasoning. Against the abolition of slavery the same stock argument was used. Rev. Dr. Nehemiah Adams, in his "South side View of Slavery," written in 1854, says: "The two distinct races could not live together except by the entire subordination of one to the other. Protection is now extended to the blacks ; their interests are the interests of the owners. But ceasing to be a protected class, they would fall a prey to avarice, suffer oppression and grievous wrongs, encounter the rivalry of white immigrants which is an element in the question of emancipation here and nowhere else. * * As an ardent friend of the colored race, I am compelled to believe that, while they remain with us, subordination in some form to a stronger race is absolutely necessary for their protection and best welfare." Tens of thousands of pro-slavery pulpits and presses reiterated and emphasized in every form the idea that the subjection of the black man to the white was in harmony with natural conditions. Again have the predictions of the pessimists been falsified by the result.

Fortunately for the future of the race, human nature is progressive, and susceptible of improvement. Were it othewise we should never have emerged from savagery. To live in fixed habitations, to pursue steady industries, to refrain from acts of aggression on neighboring tribes is contrary to the nature of the savage. But slowly and gradually, through the influence of civilization and Christianity, these traits are eradicated. In the same manner the special vices of our age, the fierce commercial competition which loses sight of humanity in the struggle for wealth, the greed which absorbs millions of the earnings of others and never cries "enough," the moral obliquity which talks of the right to "do what it will with its own" regardless of the general good—all these phases of the human nature of the present are destined to pass away and give place to more humane and reasonable dispositions. A century hence our descendants will look with pitying wonder upon our system and methods, and deplore the ignorance and blindness of a generation which, regarding itself as enlightened, permitted a few monopolists of the resources of nature and the tools of trade to dictate to the great mass of toiling humanity the terms on which they would be permitted to exist. They will be astonished that men having political and physical power on their side should have tamely submitted to industrial slavery. But as likely as not this same enlightened posterity of ours will in their turn be shaking their wise heads over some further proposed innovation to rectify abuses now undreamed of, and repeating with a sapient air the old familiar formula—" It won't do. You see it's contrary to human nature."

Since the doctrine of evolution has come into fashion the position of those who hold that the substitution of co-operation for competition would be opposed to the natural order of things has been reinforced by the scientific principle of the " survival of the fittest." Writers in the interest of capitalism have eagerly seized upon it to justify the existing inequality of conditions as a result of the natural superiority of the fortunate few. The starvation and wretchedness of those who are pushed to the wall and trodden under in the struggle for existence are held to be the legitimate consequences of their inferiority. This process is regarded as necessary to ensure the perfection of the race by weeding out those unadapted to their surroundings. Scientific smatterers are apt to confound " survival of the fittest," with the survival of the best. The phrase as commonly used is deceptive. In the scientific sense it implies neither moral, mental, nor physical superiority—simply adaptation to existing conditions. In the modern industrial and commercial world the very qualities which go to constitute true manhood are often calculated to retard success in life. Other things being equal, the man who is sordid and penurious in his habits, unscrupulous in his transactions, but shrewd enough to keep within the law, and devoted heart and soul to money-making to the exclusion of higher considerations, will have a better chance in the struggle for existence than he who is generous and humane, who would scorn to take an unfair advantage of a competitor, and who studies to improve his mind and to cultivate the social and intellectual side of his nature rather than to amass wealth.

That in accordance with present conditions, the cunning, the heartless, and the mercenary are most likely to succeed, is not an argument in favor of our accepting the " survival-of-the-fittest " doctrine as a permanent bar to social reform. It is rather the strongest incentive for us to labor to change the environment which evolves such a type of "fitness." When the advocates of capitalism advance this plea for the spoliation of the masses, they are treading upon dangerous ground, and putting forth a weapon which may readily be turned against them by the anarchist. Morally, there is no difference between obtaining property wrongfully by cunning and taking it by force. In a state of chaos and disorder, the survival of the fittest would make those possessing physical strength and numbers masters of the situation. Change the environment from one of unequal laws, framed in the class interests of the wealthy, to one of no law but the right of the strongest, and the position would be reversed—the "fittest" of to-day would be the inferiors and the weaklings who must succumb to the superior bodily strength of the desperate and hungry multitudes. In the following verses, penned some years ago, the present writer endeavored to illustrate this point.

THE POLITICAL ECONOMIST AND THE TRAMP.

Walking along a country road,
　While yet the morning air was damp,
As unreflecting on I strode,
　I marked approach the frequent tramp.

The haggard, ragged, careworn man,
　Accosted me in plaintive tone:
" I must have food—" he straight began;
　" Vile miscreant," I cried, " begone!

" 'Tis contrary to every rule
　That I my fellows should assist;
I'm of the scientific school,
　Political economist.

" Do'st thou not know, deluded one,
　That Adam Smith has clearly proved,
That 'tis self-interest alone
　By which the wheels of life are moved ?

" That competition is the law
　By which we either live or die ?
I've no demand thy labor for,
　Why, then, should I thy wants supply ?

" And Herbert Spencer's active brain,
  Shows how the social struggle ends:
The weak die out—the strong remain;
  'Tis this that Nature's plan intends.

" Now, really, 'tis absurd of you
  To think I'd interfere at all;
Just grasp the scientific view—
  The weakest must go to the wall."

My words impressed his dormant thought.
  " How wise," he said, " is nature's plan !
Henceforth I'll practice what you've taught,
  And be a scientific man.

" We are alone—no others near,
  Or even within hailing distance ;
I've a good club, and now right here
  We'll have a ' struggle for existence.'

" The weak must die, the strong survive—
  Let's see who'll prove the harder hittist,
So, if you wish to keep alive,
  Prepare to prove yourself the fittest.

" If you decline the test to make,
  Doubting your chances of survival,
Your watch and pocketbook I'll take,
  As competition strips a rival."

What could I do but yield the point,
  Though conscious of no logic blunder ?
And as I quaked in every joint,
  The tramp departed with his plunder.

It behooves the economic champions of capitalism to consider well whether the systematic degradation of labor is not likely in the long run to result in a struggle for existence, fought out with other weapons than those which now result in the survival of the shrewd and unsrupulous, while the mass are victimized. Either men will, by the power of peaceful and intelligent combination, so regulate matters that it will be no longer possible for a few to enrich themselves by taking advantage of the "natural superiority" of their acquisitive faculties under the competitive system, or the

11

people will re-assert the old-fashioned right of the strongest as against that of the most cunning.

Against Labor Reform is arrayed the enormous influence of a venal and subsidized press. The modern " first-class " journal, and a large proportion of those published on a less pretentious scale, voice the opinions not of the people, but of the wealthy and influential class. The press, never backward in glorifying its mission, is apt to draw somewhat self-complacent and boastful comparisons between the complete equipment and ample facilities of the journal of to-day and the limited sphere of the press as our fathers knew it; but the modern improvements have been dearly purchased at the sacrifice of independence and outspokenness. The widening of the scope of journalism has been accompanied by an enormous increase of its expenses. James Gordon Bennett, the elder, started the New York *Herald* on a capital of $500, and Horace Greeley floated the *Tribune* to sudden success upon a similarly slender amount. Nowadays it is necessary to risk a fortune in the endeavor to establish a daily journal in a large city; and success, if it comes at all, is the result of a long-continued and lavish outlay. The modern daily or " high-class " weekly newspaper is as strictly and necessarily a capitalistic institution as a bank, a railroad, or other large corporate enterprise requiring a heavy cash expenditure before the hope of a return can be entertained. The newspaper proprietor therefore, at the very outset, is committed by interest and sympathy to the side of the money-power. Frequently he is heavily concerned in other financial enterprises, especially if the journal is established on the joint-stock principle.

Again, advertising patronage is the very life-blood of the newspaper of to-day. As every one knows, the competition between publishers as to cheapness has practically resulted in furnishing to the public the printed page for the price which the white paper costs the newspaper. The expense of obtaining the news and editorials, printing and distribution must be made up from the revenue received from advertisements.

The result is that to the natural bias of wealthy newspaper proprietors in favor of capitalism, is superadded the influence of the advertising class, that is to say, the well-to-do and moneyed people, the manufacturing and business corporations, the rings, syndicates, and speculators. The newspaper must conciliate the favor of those who hold the purse-strings or, as hundreds and thousands of honest and independent journalistic ventures have done, go down for want of financial support. Being thus absolutely dependent for life, not to speak of prosperity, upon the good-will of a capitalistic constituency of advertisers, it is tied hand and foot, so far as the utterance of new ideas likely to be unacceptable to any considerable proportion of them is concerned. The vast majority of influential daily newspapers are abject and servile in their devotion to the money-power. They instinctively or deliberately range themselves on the side of capitalism in every struggle between the people and their oppressors. Not only do they systematically suppress anything like the individuality of early journalism in treating of social reforms, and taboo, as dangerous, discussions which seem to run counter to bourgeois prejudice or interests, but they deliberately set themselves to distort and suppress facts, and to pervert public opinion in reference to the Labor Reform movement. They habitually malign the reputations and asperse the motives of the best and most honest of the advocates of labor's rights. It is true that at times political considerations intervene, and that their malignity toward the cause is veneered over with a hypocritical and badly simulated affectation of sympathy, and a patronizing tone that is more insulting and exasperating than open hostility. But when any occasion arises which tests their professions of friendship, all such flimsy and superficial disguises are thrown off, and the real animus of intense and bitter class hatred manifests itself.

" You can hear in every one of its utterances the clink of the dollar and the lash of the party whip. The great dominant press of the land has no sympathy for the masses," said Wendell Philips. Every large and important newspaper is edited from its counting-room. The press as a whole truckles and cringes before wealth as it formerly did at the feet of the slave-power. It is simply a huge capitalistic machine. Intellectual honesty in the editorial chair is an impossibility. Neither talent nor brilliancy, neither scholarship nor literary reputation will enable its possessor to retain a responsible position in journalism unless he is prepared to sacrifice his convictions and to prostitute his intellect in the service of Mammon. A few years ago even so powerful and distinguished a writer as Hon. Carl Schurz was compelled to resign the editorship of the New York *Evening Post* because he dared to take the part of the Western Union Telegraph operators at the time of their strike against the tyranny of Jay Gould. The case attracted much attention owing to Mr. Schurz's political prominence, but it is by no means an exceptional one. It is not indeed often that the editor-in-chief of a leading newspaper allows his conscientious scruples to stand in the way of his doing the dirty work of capitalism; for in most instances he must become known as a zealous, or at all events a pliable and unscrupulous tool before he has an opportunity to attain such a position. But in numberless cases men in subordinate places have been compelled to choose between stooping to the degradation of a mental prostitution, which is as much more debasing than physical harlotry as the faculties of the mind are nobler than those of the body, and sacrificing their prospects of advancement in their profession. The honest, earnest, and conscientious men are weeded out; the cynical, slavish, and selfish, those who value their convictions as Castlereagh did his country, because they can sell them, remain.

The despicable subserviency of the press to the influence of wealth, its utter want of principle and consistency in dealing with questions bearing on the condition of labor was strikingly manifested in two instances during the labor troubles of the spring of 1886. The sudden growth and popularity of the system of boycotting employed by the laboring people as a means of retaliation for acts of oppression or conduct deemed prejudicial to their interests aroused a strong feeling of antagonism on the part of the employers and the bourgeoisie generally. This speedily found expression through the editorial columns of the daily press. The system was denounced as " un-American." The Anglomaniac wealthy classes of the Eastern cities, who devote themselves assiduously to aping English fashions in dress, equipage, and demeanor, and carefully eliminating every trace of Americanism from their speech, aspect, ideas, and sentiments, suddenly developed a profound admiration for " American" traditions, and denounced the boycott as a pernicious foreign importation. Dudes wearing London-made clothes, and speaking with a carefully cultivated English drawl and lisp, and high-toned "society " dames clad in the latest foreign fashions, attended by liveried flunkeys, drove round to Mrs. Gray's boycotted bakery in New York to testify by large orders their appreciation of her adherence to to the " American " principle of managing her business in her own way. Not content with editorial denunciations of boycotting, two New York journals, the *Evening Post* and the *Times*, established anti-boycotting funds for the prosecution of the trades-unionists engaging in the practice. The criminal code of the state was overhauled in order to discover an enactment under which this " un-American " system could be suppressed by the law. In short, the unanimous influence of the leading journals was thrown against the boycott with a virulence which was evinced by the supplementing of the ordinary methods of journalism with functions rightly attaching to the public prosecutor.

" Look here, upon this picture, and on this."

In the annual report of the New York Bureau of Labor Statistics for 1885, page 305, the following testimony is borne respecting a grievance to which labor is subjected :

" An abuse which has existed for some time and of which the working people of the state bitterly complain is called black-listing. In brief this means that an employer has discharged a man because he was a prominent member of the uuion which ordered a strike and had taken an active part in it, and then notifying other employers in the same line of his action.   If they are of a similar mind the unfortunate man is unable to obtain work at his trade, and is either forced to leave his native town and seek work elsewhere or else get into some other business.   This abuse is a fruitful source of intemperance.   Many trade-unions and labor organizations provide for victimized members by starting them in some small business.   Frequently a man is suspected and discharged without a moment's notice.   When the unlucky victim asks for an explanation of this summary treatment he is curtly informed that the firm does not propose to give a reason.   A case of this kind happened at Buffalo while the Bureau was conducting an investigation in that city.   A manufacturing company in Brooklyn entered into an agreement with several of the largest manufacturers by which a man cannot get employment without the written consent of his former employers.   It was charged that should a man secure work in any of these shops the company can pursue him and secure his dismissal.

" From the evidence it would appear that in most labor troubles, the most reasonable, conservative, and sensible men are selected to serve on committees.   These men, while honestly intending to do justice to their employer and acting in a peaceful manner,   are really putting themselves at the mercy of the employers if they are bad ones.   This has been demonstrated by the fact that they are the first ones put on the black-list and thus compelled to leave their homes in search of work.   The man who counselled moderation and frowned down talk about the destruction of property and extreme action is discharged, while the men who advocated these actions are retained.   A poor return for the advocate of law and order."

This system is of long standing.   While it is essentially the same in principle as the boycott, it is infinitely more injurious and more productive of hardship in its results.   A boycotted manufacturer or storekeeper can always come to terms and be reinstated in the favor of his customers by complying with their demands, generally of a reasonable character ; the black-listed employee is permanently deprived of his opportunity of earning a livelihood at his trade.   But when has the press denounced black-listing ?   When has any newspaper outside of the Labor Reform press waged a war of suppression upon it as " un-American," raised a fund for the relief of black-listed working-men, or clamored for the prosecution as criminals of vindictive employers who resort to this cowardly means of retaliation upon working-men who dare to call their souls their own ?

During the recent Missouri Pacific strike a number of mercenary desperadoes, hired and armed by Jay Gould ostensibly for the purpose of guarding his property, without provocation fired upon an unarmed crowd of citizens at St. Louis, killing about eight persons.   This massacre was viewed by the newspaper hirelings of capitalism as an ordinary, if a deplorable incident of the general disturbance.   There was no outcry of horror, no demand for the exemplary punishment of either the immediate perpetrators or the instigator of the crime.   When, a few weeks later, on the 4th of May, 1886, seven policemen in Chicago were killed by the explosion of a dynamite bomb thrown by some one at an Anarchist meeting, the entire press gave vent to a furious, insensate howl for blood and vengeance.   Nothing that has occurred for many years has illustrated the un-Democratic and slavish spirit of American journalism more than this vindictive outburst of indiscriminate wrath.   The case was prejudged against men on trial for their lives.   Every editor became a public prosecutor, and the tremendous influence of the daily press as a whole was directed to secure the conviction upon utterly insufficient evidence of those who were perhaps guilty of no worse offense than the use of language which, though reckless and bloodthirsty, was certainly not more so than the expressions habitually employed by these exponents of " law and order " in denouncing Socialists and Labor Reformers.   The shout of savage exultation with which the verdict secured by such influence was hailed, resembled the yell of a band of Comanches triumphing over a prisoner at the stake rather than the utterance of civilized beings contemplating the infliction of the extreme penalty of the law.   Had the evidence, instead of being weak and untrustworthy, clearly brought home to every man a direct participation in the throwing of the fatal bomb ; were the whole community convinced beyond a shadow of a doubt that justice and public safety demanded the execution of the criminals ; even then the hideous brutality which found in the death sentence of the seven convicted Anarchists a subject for ghoulish rejoicing and heartless jests would have been equally indefensible.

While launching indiscriminate execrations against Anarchists and Socialists the average newspaper editor is absolutely
blind to the fact that Anarchism is a mere surface symptom
of a deep seated social disorder.

> I du believe in freedom's cause
>   As fur away ez Paris is,
> I love to see her stick her claws
>   In the n infarnal Pharisees.
> It's wal enough agin a king
>   To dror resolves an' triggers,
> But liberty's a kind o' thing
>   That don't agree with niggers,

wrote James Russell Lowell in satirizing the editor of thirty
years ago. His successor of to-day, in commenting on Russian Nihilism, German Socialism, or Irish agrarian outrage, can
realize that these manifestations of revolutionary feeling are
not causeless, but have their provocation in the intolerable
grievances to which the people are subject. But in dealing
with similar outbreaks in America the conditions which render the outcast and degraded populations of our large cities a
favorable soil for the propagation of Anarchist ideas are
ignored, and the old crude and brutal methods of suppression
of free speech and the liberty of the press—vindictive legal
penalties, the policeman's club, and the soldier's bayonet—are
the only remedies which these cowardly betrayers of popular
freedom have to propose.

Akin to this malign influence of organized mendacity is that
of the literary and so-called "cultured" class generally. The
whole tone of university education is bitterly hostile to organized labor. It draws its inspiration mainly from foreign
sources, and preserves the traditions of the European industrial and social system. The shallowness of what passes as
modern intellectual culture is shown by its lamentable failure
to meet the problems of the time, or even to make an attempt
in that direction.

This is an age of book-making, of strenuous intellectual
activity. Yet never since the dark ages was there a greater

lack of creative power or originality, of the boldness and mental grasp necessary in dealing with a new situation. We have fallen upon a period of mere criticism and imitation, of a dead-level of conformity to established formulas and rigid adherence to narrowing modes of thought. With the modern literary school, the Fawcetts, Howellses, Jameses and other pretentious pigmies who essay to fill the places of the robust and powerful writers of the last generation, the form of expression is everything, the idea nothing. The absence of a lofty purpose and the lack of the inspiration of a noble cause emasculate and enfeeble the productions is sued by the thousand by men who are mere book-makers, who write not because they think deeply or feel strongly, but simply as a profession. The ardent faith in humanity and the intense individualism and self-poise of the old school of New England literature, now well-nigh extinct, has been replaced by the supercilious and cynical polish of conventional European culture. In place of a literature touching the strongest and most deeply-seated emotions, dealing with great problems of life, and appealing to the hearts of the mass of mankind, we have the " society " novel and the " society " poem, written for a class and embodying the caste idea. Elegant trifling, pretty conceits, dissertations on drawing-room manners, elaborate criticism of trivial details of social etiquette and nice shades of distinction in character, form the staple of this nerveless, marrowless, soulless literature.

" He would have left a Greek accent slanting the wrong way and righted up a falling man," wrote Thoreau of Capt. John Brown. The literary class are greatly concerned about the absolute correctness in form of their utterances and the finish of their style, but there is no help in them for prostrate humanity. The literary degeneracy of the age is due partly to the enervating influence of imported ideals of life and culture, and the reactionary distrust of Democracy fostered in those hotbeds of snobbery and caste feeling—the universities; and partly to the almost universal craving for the material gains of authorship. Shallow and near-sighted observers often point complacently to the great rewards of professional authorship in these days, when a single book frequently wins fame and a competency for the writer, in contrast to the time when the garret and the debtor's prison, the crust of dependence and "the key of the street" were too commonly the returns which a thankless world made for works which have since become classic. They do not see that, in proportion as authorship has become a trade in which fortune awaits the successful aspirant, it has developed the huckster spirit among its votaries. As in the case of journalism, the literary guild have become to a very great extent, either instinctively or from sheer self-interest, the upholders of existing social injustice and the opponents of organic change. The whole range of influences and cramping conventionalities which surround the modern professional writer are hostile to freedom of expression and to the effective treatment of the new issues which have arisen. Men who write in the hope of large pecuniary rewards, and aim at social position; who have set their hearts on immediate popularity and success, are under heavy bonds to say nothing opposed to the interests or the prejudices of the moneyed and comfortable class. They dare not array themselves on the side of the struggling poor, or grapple with the question which is now overshadowing all others in its importance, except to deal in platitudes and falsisms, restatements of outworn economic dogmas, and recommendations of palliatives utterly inadequate to meet the case, such as form the stock-in-trade of the "labor" articles in the magazines. Not from those who have "given hostages to fortune" in a different sense from that in which the term is generally employed, who are looking anxiously for the favor of the wealthy, the press they control and the society they dominate, can Labor Reformers expect anything but opposition and misrepresentation. As the Garrisons and the Phillipses, in their long struggle to awaken the conscience of the American people to the iniquities of slavery, had to face the hostility of the pretentious and pharisaical "culture" of their day, so those who are enlisted in the conflict against the oppressions of capitalism must be prepared to encounter the hatred of the servile and self-seeking

The culture of the college and of literary coteries is narrowing and dwarfing in its effects. It tends to prune and to polish away whatever of native vigor exists. It represses anything like spontaneity and naturalness. It limits instead of broadening the range of sympathies, and cultivates a spirit of pessimistic optimism, if the paradox is permissible. By this I mean a complacent satisfaction with existing conditions, as viewed from the standpoint of personal and class interests, combined with indifference or despair as to the possibility of ever substantially bettering the lot of the many. Its creed is that the mass, even though nominally free, can never become intelligent, or fit to govern themselves—that they must be led by "statesmen," and amused by giving them the semblance of political power while the reality is exercised only by the few. While perhaps rendering a hypocritical homage to Democracy in its narrowest sense of "the right to choose one's jailers," the class who claim a monopoly of culture and enlightenment are strenuously opposed to the idea of a true Democracy of equality of social rights and opportunities. The exaggerated estimates set upon talent, diplomacy, tact, shrewdness, and the like qualities, which are so extravagantly rewarded under the competitive system, as compared with ordinary industry, is upheld by their teachings. The pernicious and undemocratic view, that government is necessarily a science of infinite complexity, involving abstruse problems, and demanding qualities higher and more valuable than the ordinary business capacity and good sense of the average educated citizen, finds extensive currency in their utterances upon public affairs. In short, the tenor and aim of the bulk of modern American literature is to accentuate class distinctions; to exalt wealth, social influence, genius, and statesmanship; to build up a bourgeois aristocracy; and to depress the simple citizen, upon whose plodding industry the stability of the whole fabric rests, to the level of European subjecthood.

The influence of wealth has corrupted our literary and educational institutions to the core. The practice which so largely prevails of millionaires bequeathing or giving during their lifetimes large endowments to colleges and academies naturally enlists these powerful factors of public opinion on the side of capitalism. The occupant of university chairs and like lucrative positions, whose salary is paid from the donations of merchant princes and railroad magnates, cannot, any more than the hired journalist or popularity-hunting book-maker, honestly employ his talents in searching for the truth. He is paid to find the best defence he can for an existing system, not to boldly and freely examine all sides of the question and fearlessly announce his conclusions.

Owing to the same insidious influence the Church has also been largely perverted into an ally and an instrument of the money-power, and the apologist for the very worst of its oppressions. There are noble exceptions, but for the most part the ministry are the servile tools of the rich men's social clubs and Sunday opera companies, which make a mockery of religion by calling themselves churches. The modern fashionable church is a capitalistic institution, membership in which is sought for its commercial and social advantages. The pastor, absolutely dependent on the favor of the rich and influential, becomes the obsequious sycophant of wealth, and the ready defender of the system which he, in common with his patrons, has a personal interest in maintaining. The professed expounders of a gospel abounding with the sternest and plainest denunciations of usury, extortion, land-grabbing, and oppression of the poor, wrest the scripture to justify every species of craft and villainy by which the poor are wronged. The religious "liberality" of the millionaires, so highly praised, and so often advanced as a plea in justification of the system—the "beneficence" that endows churches, missions, theological colleges, Bible and tract societies, and the like, with the wealth upon which even the most tenacious grasp must relax at the touch of a skeleton finger, is, in fact, a subtle, insidious, but none the less effective means of wholesale bribery, by which professional religionism is suborned to the service of Mammon.

In the Church of the Strangers in New York, endowed by the late Cornelius Vanderbilt, there was, and probably is now, a bronze plate on the wall near the pulpit, bearing the following inscription :

Erected

To the Glory of God,

and in memory of

CORNELIUS VANDERBILT,

By the

Church of the

Strangers.

"The name of God," says an indignant newspaper correspondent, " is placed on this tablet in small letters at the end of an insignificant line, while that of Cornelius Vanderbilt stands out on a broad brazen belt in the full obtrusiveness of flaring capitals."

It is not often that good taste and religious feeling are so flagrantly outraged on the surface, but the spirit that dictated this piece of ostentatious irreverence pervades the fashionable religion of the day. In how many of our wealthy churches are the glory of God and the rights of humanity alike subordinated to the exaltation of the millionaire !

The stumbling-blocks in the way of Labor's emancipation are mental rather than physical. Bulwer Lytton, in his work on "England and the English," sums up the matter admirably in speaking of those influences which there retard popular progress. "You have observed," he says, "that the worst part of these influences is in a moral influence. This you can counteract by a *new* moral standard of opinion. Once accustom yourselves to think that

'Rank is but the guinea-stamp,
The man's the gowd for a' that'—

once learn to detach respectability from acres and rent-rolls —once learn indifference for fashion and fine people, for the 'whereabouts' of lords and ladies, for the orations of men boasting of the virtue of making money—once learn to prize at their full worth a high integrity and a lofty intellect— once find yourself running to gaze, not on foreign princes and lord mayor's coaches, but on those who elevate, benefit, and instruct you, and you will behold a new influence, pushing its leaves and blossoms from amidst the dead corruption of the old. To counteract a bad moral influence, never let us omit to repeat that you must create a good moral influence. Reformed opinion precedes reformed legislation. Now is the day for writers and advisers; they prepare the path for true law-givers; they are the pioneers of good; no reform is final, save the reform of mind."

CHAPTER VIII.

THE SOLIDARITY OF LABOR.

Labor is of no country.
KARL MARX.

Laborin' man an' laborin' woman
 Have one glory an' one shame;
Everythin' that's done inhuman
 Injures all on 'em the same.
LOWELL.

THAT all labor has a common interest is one of the truisms of the Labor Reform movement. Loudly proclaimed, en- thusiastically preached, blazoned forth in the mottoes of labor unions, and ostensibly of universal acceptance, it is too seldom acted upon, or its full significance realized. The world of labor is pervaded by the spirit of class and division. The short-sightedness which looks only to trifling immediate ad- vantages, small increase of pay, petty advances of one class of workers at the expense of others, the prejudices of race and creed, and the divisions of party politics, have tended to keep asunder men whose larger interests are mutual, and whose future depends on united, harmonious, and well-directed action. These divisions have been cnnningly fostered and exaggerated by the influences at work in the cause of capitalism. False issues are continually being raised, and jealousies assiduously promoted in order to prevent the laboring-class from presenting a united front to the common enemy.

And no wonder. The solidarity of labor means the annihilation of capitalism. When all who toil are practically unanimous in demanding the social reorganization of industry, and the recognition of labor-value as the only right to subsistence, the day of those who now claim the lion's share of production, as possessors merely, will be over.

The American labor question is complicated and rendered difficult of solution by the results of Old-world systems of misgovernment and industrial oppression. Immigrants by the hundred thousand yearly seek our shores. The extension of the ocean transportation-service and the shortening and cheapening of the voyage has mobilized the labor-forces of the civilized world, and given a literal significance to the saying of Marx, that "Labor is of no country." Whether we accept that doctrine in the sense in which it was uttered or not, we have no alternative as regards the fact that the barriers of race and language and distance, which formerly restricted competition, are breaking down on all sides. We are entering upon an era of industrial internationalism. Narrow our sympathies, cherish our old-time prejudices as we may, the solidarity of labor as a force at the disposal of capitalism is an established condition which cannot be gainsaid. When Italians and Irishmen work side-by-side on the railroads, and Hungarians, Poles, and the miscellaneous cheap labor of South-eastern Europe compete with the American and English-speaking working-men in the coal mines and coke-ovens of Pennsylvania and Ohio—when the French Canadians swarm in the textile factories of the East and the pine forests of the North-West, and the Southern plantations are drawn on for their dusky contingents when unskilled labor is on strike—when the Pacific states, barely reclaimed from Indian savagery, have to be defended against the flood of Mongolian semi-barbarism, the inadequacy of any action based upon national distinctions or the lines of color and creed ought to be apparent to all.

Capitalism is cosmopolitan. It has no patriotism and no prejudices. It will levy its tribute from black or white, European or American, Protestant or Catholic with indiscriminating impartiality. The vampires of the London money-market, having drained the life-blood from Turk and Egyptian, seek fresh victims on the Western Continent. English and Irish landlords, conscious of their waning power, and alarmed by the diminution of their rent-rolls, cross the Atlantic and acquire millions of acres of virgin soil in order to command the product of the labor of Americans, and perpetuate here the system of landed estates which is tottering to its fall in their native country. There is no more mean-spirited and despicable class of reactionaries than the American millionaires, whose sympathies are notoriously hostile to the popular cause in Europe. The most detested of Scottish landlords is the American, Ross Winans, who by his rapacity and petty despotism has done more to arouse public opinion against the system than the exactions of native landlords. The idle and luxurious class of Americans abroad were conspicuous among the upholders of that gilded sham, the Second Empire in France, as to-day they are prominent in courtly and aristocratic circles in England. The instinctive sympathy of the wealthy and ruling classes of different countries with each other has at times produced the most far-reaching results in shaping the course of events. George Otto Trevelyan, in his "Early History of Charles James Fox," points out how the fellow-feeling of the British upper classes for the French aristocracy at the time of the Revolution affected the policy of England.

"That sympathy was stronger and more practical in its effects than the compassion which our nation felt for the Protestants of Holland in the day of the Spanish fury, or for the Huguenots in the days of the dragonnades; for the patriots of the Tyrol, of Hungary, of Naples; for the slaves of South Carolina; for the victims of Turkish cruelty in Greece and of Russian cruelty in Poland. The silken bonds of common pleasures and tastes, which seem trifling enough at the moment, proved stronger under the test than the ties of religious faith or political creed; and while the Democrats of Paris were appealing almost in vain to the brotherhood which, according to the Jacobin program, was to unite against their tyrants all the peoples of Europe, there was nothing fictitious or shallow in the sentiment of class fraternity which instantly and spontaneously enlisted the gentry of Great Britain in determined and implacable hostility to the French Republic.''

Mr. Trevelyan probably lays too much stress on the purely sentimental phase of the matter, and too little on the community of interest and the dread on the part of the British upper class that the example of a successful French Republic might become contagious and inspire a similar attack on their own unjust privileges. But be this as it may, whether the bonds between the wealthy and influential castes of all countries are those of instinctive sympathy or keen-sighted self-interest or both, there is no question that the solidarity of capitalism thus created is one of the most formidable influences with which the movement for the rights of labor has to contend. The commercial and financial interests of the principal nations are so interwoven, and the associations between the leisured and moneyed classes so much closer than formerly, owing to the facility of travel and communication, that an international public opinion, which is distinctively a class opinion, has grown up, and exercises a tremendous pressure upon local movements. Voiced in the great capitalistic newspapers, and through that monopoly-machine, the Atlantic cable, its influence is powerfully felt in antagonism to every agitation for popular rights. Thus the Irish national movement—which is first and foremost a movement for industrial reform—has been systematically misrepresented, its leaders have been maligned, its reverses magnified, and the abuses and drawbacks incidental to any widespread popular agitation grossly exaggerated. This was more especially the case during its earlier stages ; since it has obtained a headway which presages success these tactics are no longer available, though the old animus is still noticeable.

International capitalistic opinion is largely responsible for the infatuated financial policy pursued by the American government during the war of the Rebellion and subsequently, by which the bondholders were enriched by receiving payment in gold for advances made in depreciated currency. The capitalists of America, in any contest with the masses, can always count on receiving the moral support of the ruling classes abroad, and in return are always ready to throw their influence into the scale with that of the opponents of social reform elsewhere. In short, whenever and wherever throughout the civilized world there is a movement on the part of the oppressed to secure a measure of justice, the forces of opinion are concentrated and brought to bear against it. The whole power and pressure of international capitalism, acting though a thousand channels of influence, is directed to crush it.

The forces of labor, on the contrary, have in the past been divided by countless lines of cleavage in all directions, by differences of party, nation, and creed, of sex and color, of occupation and locality; by jealousies between skilled and unskilled brain and manual workers; and by finely-drawn grades and distinctions between those of the same trade. National and race differences, and the prejudices attaching to them, are much more strongly marked among the working-class than among the wealthy. It is a frequent remark that travel, education, and social intercourse have done much to assimilate the richer elements of American and European society. The angles of national prejudice have been rubbed off. The old-fashioned antipathies between Briton and Frenchman, American and European have subsided under the influence of a common caste feeling and a similar standard of conventional polish. The " gentlemen " of one country differ much less from those of another in dress, demeanor, and modes of thought than do the working-classes, among whom, excepting in so far as they may have been influenced by Socialistic teaching, the "foreigner" is generally regarded as an enemy.

John Leech's often-quoted illustration of life in the English mining district—" ' Who is 'e, Bill? ' ' A stranger.' ' 'Eave arf a brick at 'im ! ' " is hardly an overdrawn exemplification of the feeling that even now obtains among the less-educated element of the working-class, though it may not find expression in so crude and summary a fashion. When, under the stress of the terrible Irish famine in 1847 and the subsequent period of impoverishment, the exiled Irish peasantry swarmed into the British industrial centers by the hundred thousand, they endured cruel persecution at the hands of English and Scotch working-men. Instead of recognizing the ties of common interest, a narrow-minded national and sectarian animosity against the new-comers was aroused. The antipathies of race and religion kept them from seeing that the unwelcome competition of the Irish was caused by the relentless oppression of landlordism ; that the system which they, in common with other classes of Englishmen, had sustained in Ireland was responsible for the exodus. In place of seeking to destroy the cause, they directed all their antagonism against the victims who, like themselves, were sufferers from the greed and tyranny of land-monopolists. In the United States the same jealousy of the native-born against foreigners, and more especially against the Irish, found vent in the aptly-named Know-Nothing movement.

That the condition of both English and American labor was for the time rendered less endurable by the Irish influx, and the increased stress of competition, is undeniable. It was well that it should be so. The lesson was needed then as it is needed to day, to teach us that the wrongs perpetrated upon the toiling poor in one land inevitably react upon the condition of labor elsewhere—that we cannot, by any measure short of the destruction of the causes of poverty wherever they exist, secure a selfish immunity from their operation. When it is endeavored to shut out by a protective tariff the products of "the pauper labor of Europe," the American working-man is confronted by the pauper laborer himself, transported by the million to American soil, to compete with him for his place at the loom, by the forge, and in the mine ; to crowd the reeking tenement-house, and swell the population of overgrown cities. What an insult to the intelligence of the mass is this cry against the "pauper labor of Europe!" Had America been true to her democratic traditions there would be no paupers in Europe. No system of class prerogative could have withstood the example and influence of a genuine democracy with equal rights for all. And no amount of foreign immigration could injure the American working-man, if monopoly did not bar access to the soil and control every avenue of employment.

The endeavor to organize labor has developed not a little friction between the skilled and the unskilled classes. The spirit of selfishness, which seeks only the advancement of some isolated branch of industry, strongly pervades many unions. "I do not believe in putting a $3 a day man in the same organization with a $1 a day man, and to our isolation from other organizations we owe our success," said Peter M. Arthur, chief of the Brotherhood of Locomotive Engineers.

This is the old characteristic appeal to selfishness, and pur-blind, narrow-minded selfishness at that—the familiar "every man for himself, and the devil take the hindmost" of individ-ualism, addressed to a would-be aristocracy of labor. It is not easy, nor is it in fact possible, to draw any well-defined line between skilled and unskilled labor. The two classes shade imperceptibly into each other. Among the mass known as unskilled, there are always a large number who have a half-training in some line of mechanical industry, who, at a pinch, can do the rougher and less finished parts of the work of a skilled mechanic. They cannot command mechanic's pay, because they are not up to the standard of the trade unions; but let a strike of carpenters or machinists or brick-layers occur, and the employers of labor can often obtain from these half-trained laborers enough men to enable them to carry on their work. In proportion as so-called unskilled labor is organized and brought into close affiliation with skilled labor, the latter can prevent their places being taken by men having a rudimentary or partial knowledge of their trade. But if a policy of trade isolation were the rule, each trade looking out for itself only, and the unskilled and half-skilled being at the mercy of competition, the skilled mechanics would very soon find out that their power to sustain themselves was greatly weakened. Leave the man with a smattering knowledge of carpentry or printing or black-smithing, the jack-of-all-trades, with a natural bent for turning his hand to anything, and making himself generally useful, free to compete with the skilled artisan, and take his place in the case of labor troubles, as he would be if the spirit of trade exclusiveness prevailed and the skilled laborer refused to make common cause with the unskilled, and the isolated union of any special branch would soon find out class selfishness to be as mistaken a policy as personal selfishness. In helping to protect the unskilled in their rights, as street-car employés, teamsters, railroad laborers, and similar vocations, the mechanic and artisan are protecting themselves from the competition of those belonging to the ranks of the unskilled, who could, in an emergency, do their work.

The skilled mechanic often needs the co-operation of organized labor as a whole in his contests with capitalism. The success of the most potent weapon against an unfair employer—the boycott—absolutely depends on the action of a numerous and widely-spread body outside of the particular industry concerned. No isolated trade-union, however powerful, can bring this instrument effectively to bear upon an oppressor.

Again, the rate of wages paid to one class of workers infallibly affects the rest in more ways than one. Not only does it tend to level the average up or down, by affording a criterion and standard of comparison by which employers in other departments are guided, but it acts either as an incentive or a deterrent in the choice of a calling. A considerable and permanent reduction in the pay of unskilled labor would very soon so intensify the pressure of competition on the part of the young, to obtain a training in the better remunerated branches, that not even the closest trade-union could maintain the rate.

This holds true also with regard to the labor of women.

There is no class who feel more keenly the disabilities of competition, or who have been reduced to more abject servitude
from the want of united action than female workers. Their
low rate of pay necessarily and inevitably reacts upon male
labor. At first sight it might be supposed that the miserably
inadequate wages received by women in factories and stores
could not in any possible way affect the position of the carpenter, the blacksmith, or those of other trades in which
women cannot engage. A little reflection will show this to
be a mistaken idea. The extensive employment of poorly
paid female labor in the avocations open to men and women
alike, results in reducing the pay of the men. The male
factory operative, salesman, clerk, or telegrapher, cannot obtain decent living wages so long as women are able and
willing to work at the same employments at a much lower
figure. What is the consequence? Naturally, men who find
themselves in this position seek other employments; youths
choosing a trade avoid these underpaid industries to a
greater extent than they would otherwise do, and give the
preference to others in which the market is not flooded by
poorly paid and unorganized female workers. As women, because of their willingness to work cheaply, crowd out men
from the lighter callings, the competition in those departments of labor still purely masculine is necessarily increased,
organization rendered more difficult and less effective, and
the number of non-unionists multiplied. There is no laborer,
therefore, however remote his particular trade may seem to
be from " woman's sphere," and however secure from in-
vasion by low-priced female labor, but has an interest in
seeing women's wages increased, and women enrolled in the
ranks of organized labor. It is not so many years since the
feeling largely prevailed among trade-unionists that the way
to deal with the difficulty was to exclude the female worker
from their callings. It is creditable to the growing intelligence of wage-earners that a more chivalrous, reasonable, and
humane spirit now prevails, and that instead of seeking unfairly to restrict the scope of female labor, the demand is now
for " equal pay for equal work."

The fatal error in the complacent self-sufficiency of trades-unionism is its failure to recognize the utter inadequacy of its methods to permanently protect the laborer against the consequences of monopoly, centralization, and the improvement of labor-saving machinery. Notwithstanding that the skill and training of one handicraft after another has been rendered almost or quite valueless by the perfection to which mechanical appliances have been brought, displacing large numbers of artisans, and reducing others to the position of mere drudges and machine-tenders, there are those who can not or will not see that the only adequate remedy is the union of all workers for the overthrow of the wage system; and by obtaining control of the land, machinery, and other means of production, securing to labor the gains now absorbed in increasing measure by capitalism. Monopoly and competition make man the slave of the machine; unless the worker, under the increasing pressure caused by further inventions and denser population, is to sink into yet more hopeless degradation, social re-adjustment must reverse the conditions and make " the machine the slave of the man."

The large class of brain-workers, who exercise an immense influence, have not, as a rule, realized that the emancipation of labor ought to have as much interest for them as for the manual toiler. They have held aloof from the Labor Reform movement as being something that did not concern them— partly from a feeling of false pride and superior social position, and partly from a fear that to identify themselves with it would endanger their prospects. Setting aside for the moment the considerations of humanity and sympathy with a just cause, and looking at the matter from a standpoint of pure self-interest, there is no class which stands more in need of the temporary benefits of organization and has more to gain by the permanent and thorough reformation of the industrial system than the intellectual proletariat.

The position of the vast majority of journalists, stenographers, school-teachers, book-keepers, copyists, clerks, agents, and the like, is even worse than that of the average mechanic. Their earnings are frequently less, their hours longer, and their subserviency to their employers more abject. No organization protects them from the effects of unlimited competition. There is everywhere a host of men and women, young and old, of all degrees of talent and capacity, seeking employment in these callings. They jostle each other in shoals whenever a vacant situation is advertised, no matter how small the salary. They advertise their own degradation, and tempt the unfair employer to grind them into the dust by the frequent announcement, " employment an object rather than salary." Brains without means are a drug in the labor market quite as much as hands, and there is no sort of check such as that interposed by trade-unionism to the operation of the law of supply and demand.

All large publishing centers abound with literary hacks, well educated and clever, who, being without other resources than their brains and pens, are as completely at the mercy of the capitalist as any member of an unorganized trade when brought into competition with cheap labor. They will write anything to order for a pittance. They peddle articles and poems round the newspaper and magazine offices for anything they can get. Publishers drive hard bargains with them, beat them down to starvation prices, and frequently realize thousands or tens of thousands of dollars on works which have earned for the writers nothing more than a meager subsistence during the time they were actually engaged in their production. Yet how few brain workers, despite the intellect on which they pride themselves, can see that their grievances and disabilities are the same as those of the manual laborer ! They will grumble among themselves about the unappreciative public, and the miserably underpaid position of intellectual labor, but the idea of combining to fix a fair price for their work never enters their heads. Still less have they realized the need of uniting with other classes of workers to alter the social conditions which place labor, whether of brain or of muscle, at the mercy of wealth. In questions between the toiler and the capitalist, most of them ostentatiously take the side of capitalism.

The extent to which the substitution of machinery for hand-work has revolutionized the industrial system and intensified competition may be gathered from the report of the United States Labor Bureau for 1886, in which it is stated that the mechanical industries of the country are carried on by steam and water power representing in round numbers 3,500,000 horse power, each horse power equaling the muscular labor of six men; that is to say, if men were employed to furnish the power to carry on these industries, it would require twenty-one million men, representing a population of 105,000,000 to do the work now actually performed by 4,000,000 representing a population of 20,000,000. The same authority estimated the total number of workers out of employment during 1885 at 998,839. But the basis on which this latter calculation is made, is an obviously misleading one, as the result is arrived at by taking only the total of the establishments, such as factories, mines, etc., which were absolutely or partially idle during the year. It leaves out of sight the large number of working-men not having regular employment or places open for them in a particular establishment as soon as work is resumed. As a calculation of the number of employés laid off owing to hard times, it may be correct; but manifestly a statement of the number of working-people thrown out of employment by the shutting down of factories and mines is very different from and less comprehensive than an estimate of the total unemployed labor force. But understated as it clearly is, the fact that one million workers at least were in enforced idleness, while four million more were doing the work which, prior to the era of mechanical expansion, would have required the labor of twenty-one million, is sufficient to show that organization on the lines of trades-unionism is powerless to deal with the altered conditions caused by the perfection of labor-saving machinery. So far, machinery has benefited capitalism only at the expense of labor. Considered as a consumer indeed, the laborer benefits by cheapness of production, but it is a good deal like the advantage which the Irishman of the story received from lengthening his blanket by sewing to the top the strip which he had cut from the bottom, so as to make it long enough at both ends. Where is the advantage of cheapness of production to the army of the unemployed and half-employed, or to those whose labor has been so cheapened by competition that their purchasing power is correspondingly lessened?

The cause of the trouble we are told is "over-production." The workers of the world, according to this theory, have been too industrious. By their superfluous energy there have been accumulated vast surplus stocks of food, clothing, fuel, and manufactured articles of every description for use and ornament, for necessity and luxury. Periodically there is a glut of every salable commodity, and in order to restore the equilibrium between demand and supply, production and consumption, mills, factories, and mines are shut down or run on short time, or the force of workers is reduced. Industry in many departments is brought almost to a standstill. Great distress in consequence prevails among multitudes thus suddenly deprived of the means of livelihood, and many others who are fortunately able to keep the wolf from the door find their income materially reduced, or their small savings, accumulated during more prosperous years, gradually melting away. That destitution among workers should not only co-exist with a superfluity of the articles produced by their industry, but should actually be caused by it, is a sufficient proof of the deep-seated injustice of the present relations between labor and capitalism. Under a fair system of distribution there could be no such thing as over-production. Still less could poverty be caused by it. The greater the production the more prosperity would be enjoyed by the industrious classes.

Under the wages system, the worker is dependent on the capitalist-employer, and he in turn on the purchasing power of communities largely composed of other wage-workers. The crude and drastic remedy of diminished production implies a considerable diminution of the amounts paid them as wages, and a consequent diminution of their purchasing power. Thus the evil perpetuates itself. For instance, the boot and shoe manufacturer, having a surplus stock that he cannot dispose of, shuts down; the woolen manufacturer, and the hat manufacturer do the same. But the employés of the one are the customers of the other. The hatters and woolen mill operatives have less money than ever with which to buy boots and shoes, and the shoemakers must make their old clothing, blankets, and hats last them for some time longer. And so it goes all round, and the very steps taken by individual employers to protect themselves from the consequences of stagnation tend to prolong and intensify it. It is always it her a feast or a famine, too much work or not enough. As boon as " hard times " are fairly over, a boom in productive industry takes place. Merchants' stocks are exhausted and orders come pouring in to the manufacturers. Mills, factories, and mines are worked to their utmost capacity; prices go steadily up, and so, after an interval, do wages. Under the stimulus of an increased demand new enterprises are undertaken. In place of scarcity of employment there is abundant work for all. Employers, in their eagerness to " make hay while the sun shines," run their workshops and factories night and day. The long hours of toil are further lengthened by inducements being held out to employés to work over-time. Under the temptation of extra pay, or the fear of offending their employers by a refusal, men work twelve or fifteen hours a day, allowing themselves barely time for needed rest and refreshment, and no time whatever for mental improvement or social recreation. The wheels of industry and commerce revolve at high pressure, and short-sighted politicians and publicists are loud in their congratulations on the prosperity of the country, ignoring entirely the fact that all this crowding on of sail and expenditure of surplus productive energy is simply preparing the way for the inevitable return of hard times. The inflation period is generally of short duration. Present demands are soon supplied, and goods again begin to accumulate in the factories and warehouses. The competition between producers is no longer as to which shall turn out goods most rapidly and in greatest volume, but which shall sell the cheapest. Production slackens, wages fall, employés are discharged. Enforced economy diminishes the purchasing power and causes further stringency and greater distress among workers, and so the vicious circle is completed. Those who, reluctantly in some cases and willingly in others, crowded two days' work into one, now think themselves fortunate to obtain one day's work in two.

These recurring periods of inflation and stringency teach the absolute inadequacy of private enterprise, and supply and demand, for the regulation of production and distribution. Each manufacturer or association of manufacturers act strictly in their own interests in suspending or slackening production during a period of stagnation, and in crowding on sail when times mend ; yet the result is adverse to the interests of society as a whole. Only by a systematized organization of industry regulating production on the basis of the needs of the community, and distributing the work to be done in supplying those needs more evenly in point of time can the alternation of prosperity and depression be prevented.

The eight-hour movement is a most important step towards such a general re-adjustment of production and distribution, as well as a temporary palliative for some of the worst evils of the competitive system. The establishment of an eight-hour working day would, in most industries, secure an opportunity to work for all. Ten hours being, as a rule, the present day's labor, the substitution of eight would mean, either the addition to the present working force of one-fourth, if the existing rate of production were to be maintained, or the lessening of production by one-fifth were no increase made in the number of workers. No doubt it would operate to a partial extent in both directions. An increase of the present labor force by one-fourth would hardly be possible, but it would largely exhaust the reserve force of unemployed labor, whose competition tends to the reduction of wages; and the limitation of production resulting where the deficiency was not made up from this source, would be the best guarantee

against glutted markets and undue competition. The temporary individual loss ; of pay which would be sustained in many
branches is the bugbear in the minds of many, which prevents
their seeing the immense ultimate gain of shorter hours. Taking the working-class as a whole, there would not be even a
temporary loss and even supposing wages were never raised
above the present hour-rate, there would be no permanent
loss. When the unemployed and partially employed are considered and an average struck, it will be found that eight
hours all round is as much work as the toiler can get. It is
really not a question of the working-class, as a whole, working
less or more, but of the even distribution of what work there
is. We already have not, indeed, shorter hours, but an increase of the number who cannot count on steady employment, and a lessening of the average receipts, owing to the
loss of opportunities to labor. The eight-hour movement, if
successful, would equalize this decrease. The system of long
hours, when it suits the convenience of employers, and short
hours or no hours at all for many as a direct consequence, is
the worst possible that could be devised in labor's interests.
If men refused to work for more than eight hours, they
would not so often be told a little later on, that there was no
work for them.

Now even if what some of the opponents of this great
reform say were true, "that the laborer could not obtain as
much for eight hours, work as he now gets for ten," this would
be a desirable thing. It would certainly be to the advantage
of the laborer to have steady and certain work for eight hours
daily, even at the same rate of pay per hour as at present,
rather than ten hours for a year or two with a shut down for
several weeks or months sprung on him unexpectedly. But
it is not true that the pay would not be increased. If there
is anything at all in the doctrine of supply and demand, it follows that by limiting the supply of labor, as the eight-hour
system would do, and so bringing it down to the level of the demand, the power of the laborer to obtain higher wages would be
thereby increased. Experience shows that the trades in which

the hours are shortest are the best paid.   The natural effect of limiting the time worked by each laborer is to increase the market value of his services just as surely as the arbitrary limit put on the production of coal or iron or cotton goods keeps up the prices.

Only by a united general movement, including the great bulk of the laboring-classes, can the shortening of the hours of toil be effected.   Once secured, the now superfluous laborers, instead of being a standing menace to employed workmen, would become allies and not competitors.   Organized laborers, as a whole, would secure a degree of control over the distribution of the products of industry such as it could obtain in no other way under the wages system.   And, after all, the question between present conditions and the socialism of the future is simply one of degree.   Labor, in fixing its own remuneration, virtually fixes the share of capitalism in the joint product.   By advancing step by step from partial to full control, and by such measures as shorter hours and arbitration on the basis of a recognition of labor's right to a specified share in the proceeds, the point will at length be reached where the " share" of capitalism can be minimized to the amount fairly due for labor of superintendence.   The socialization of capital will then be an accomplished fact.

It is often assumed that the powerful agricultural interest is solidly arrayed against Labor Reform, that the " territorial democracy " will to a man oppose the nationalization of the land, which underlies all other and less important though perhaps more immediately attainable phases of social readjustment.   Those who criticise the Labor Reform movement on this ground are right in calling attention to a point which has been too frequently overlooked, namely, that the most important industry is that of agriculture, and that any popular movement, to be successful, must enlist the sympathy and co-operation of the tillers of the soil.   But they are wrong in supposing that the true interests of the urban laborers and those of the farmers are so far apart that they cannot in the future act together.   Far from being a crushing argument against the possibility of a succesful political agitation, the large representation and powerful influence of the farming community in politics is one of the strongest grounds for hope.

The great majority of farmers are in every sense of the word working-men, and as such have every reason to sympathize with the wage-earner of the cities rather than with the capitalist class. They are subject to many of the same grievances which press so hardly upon city labor. All the forms of monopoly combine to tax the farmer's industry just as they do that of the citizen, and some of them bear down far harder on him than on any other class. Railroad monopoly in particular is the means of robbing the agricultural producer of a very large portion of his earnings. It was among the farmers that the first strong feeling of hostility to the power of the great railroad lines to levy taxes at will upon industry was developed. The question of the control or ownership of railroads by the people is one which affects the farmers in a more vital degree than it does the city working-man. The money monopoly is another matter in which farmers and other workingmen have mutual interests opposed to those of the capitalists, usurers, and speculators. When by basing money upon gold the supply is kept artificially scarce and dear, who suffers more than the farmer? The scarcity of money and the exorbitantly high rate of interest have brought absolute ruin to many a once prosperous farmer, and reduced many others to hopeless bondage to the mortgage-holder. When times are dull owing to the scarcity of money, the farmer is unable to sell his wheat or his cattle at a fair price. He must live and pay running expenses, and is obliged to resort to the usurer. Who should be more anxious to bring about the establishment of a national currency, adequate in volume to the demands of trade, which the dealers in money could not contract and expand at will, than the farmer?

There is no doubt a measure of force in the argument that rural landowners will not be favorably disposed towards the proposal to lay the whole burden of taxation upon the soil.

Let us give all due weight to it. But, on any possible calculation, the number of the agricultural class who would be benefited by the continuance of private land-ownership is **far**
more than off-set by the number who would be advantaged
by its abolition. Those who advance this argument have in
mind the conditions which prevailed a quarter of a century
ago rather than those which now obtain. According to the
last United States census the total number of persons engaged
in farming was 7,670,493, of whom only 2,984,306 were even
nominal owners of their farms. Of the latter a very large
proportion are heavily mortgaged. The "territorial democracy" is a misleading phrase—a tradition, and nothing more.
The available arable land still ungranted is on the verge of
becoming exhausted. The number of tenant-farmers, and the
landless class in the country is increasing, and immense areas
have fallen into the possession of railroad corporations, land
companies, and individual speculators, who hold it at a high
price.   On this point Thomas P. Gill says in an article on
" Landlordism in America," which appeared in the *North
American Review* for January 1886 :

> When there are no more far-distant patches of government land to
> be had by the hardy settler, he will have none but this high-priced land
> to choose from.   How is he to possess himself of it ?   He simply cannot
> possess himself of it.   Never again will such a man have the opportunity
> of winning by his toil and his courage a free home for himself in the
> United States.   The land will become the privilege of capital, and the
> hardy settler will have no alternative but to rent a farm and work it as
> a tenant, with no hope of coming nearer to being its owner after a life-
> time of labor than he was the first day he broke its verdure with the
> plow.   Thus, from the day—now officially declared to be at hand--that
> the public domain is quite exhausted, the manufacture of a tenant-
> farming class will go on in the United States at an enormous rate. * * *
> It is a fact that there cannot be a moment's doubt about—the tendency
> to landlordism in the United States is inevitable and immense.''

It is not only the actual farmers of to-day we have to consider, it is the whole agricultural class ; those born and brought
up in the country, or coming in from abroad, who desire or
expect to farm on their own account. In the near future, far

from being a bugbear and an obstacle to the alliance between the agriculturist and the city wage-worker, the land nationalization doctrine will prove the very strongest incentive to the large majority of the rural residents co-operating with organized labor for the overthrow of landlordism. It is manifestly and clearly in the interests of the small farmer who wants more land, of the tenant farmer, of the farmer's son, and of the farm laborer that they should have the opportunity to obtain access to the land locked up for speculative purposes, by the imposition of a heavy tax on land values, so as to make it unprofitable for any one to hold land which he does not cultivate. Before long, urban labor, now fighting the battle alone, will find an invaluable and invincible ally in the great bulk of the farming class, whose interests as producers outweigh their interests as landowners.

CHAPTER IX.

THE STONE WHICH THE BUILDERS REJECTED.

God never scooped the Mississippi valley to be the grave of freedom, nor poured Niagara for its requiem.—*Wendell Phillips*

LABOR, in working out its own emancipation, will regenerate the world. In solving the labor problem, the other vexed questions which have so long pressed for solution will be settled. All the various forms of social and moral evil which afflict humanity are traceable to caste-rule and the spoliation of the laboring class. War, intemperance, prostitution, and crime are due either to the greed begotten of capitalism, the selfishness, arrogance, and luxury of the moneyed and influential class, or the abject necessity, ignorance, and debasement of the disinherited. With social and political equality established, and every man and woman secured in the enjoyment of the full earnings of their labor, the motives which prompt and the conditions which foster these evils would largely cease. 13

Labor Reform underlies all other reforms. To imagine that
drunkenness and vice and law-breaking can be cured while a
large part of the population are plunged into hopeless degradation by the working of the capitalistic system is the veriest
social quackery. Temperance reformers tell us that drunkenness is the great cause of poverty. The two are closely
connected, but it is far oftener poverty that is the cause of
drunkenness. Mental and physical exhaustion, consequent
upon long hours of labor in a vitiated atmosphere, naturally
drive men to seek relief in stimulants. Unhealthy domestic
conditions, the filth and squalor of crowded tenement houses
and reeking alleys, the evil examples and contaminating
associations forced upon the decent poor who find refuge in
such quarters, combined with the hopelessness of their lot,
and the feeling that struggle and strive as they may, it is
impossible to better themselves, make social wrecks and outcasts of numbers who under more favorable conditions might
have lived and died useful and respected citizens. The temperance reformers, well-intentioned, but superficial and possessed with one idea, wholly overlook these deep-seated
causes of intemperance. Full-fed, handsomely paid, and well-
conditioned orators of the Gough and Murphy type may draw
crowds by their eloquence, and exhaust the powers of oratori-
cal persuasion to reform the drunkard, but the few who can
be reached by such methods are but a drop in the bucket
compared with the number who are yearly sinking into the
abyss. It is the conditions of labor and living in the great
cities that make drunkards and prostitutes. The terrible
picture of the evils of the lot of New York working-women
presented in the report of the New York Bureau of Labor
Statistics for 1885, is more eloquent in its practical matter-of-
fact treatment of the subject than the most highly-wrought
denunciations of the social crime which dooms them to slavery or shame. Moralists and preachers combat the "social
evil" just as they do intemperance, by missions and exhorta-
tions; and respectable society thinks that it does its whole
duty by subscribing liberally to evangelize the slums and

establish Magdalen asylums and homes for the fallen. And oftentimes those who give most liberally and lament most sanctimoniously the increase of vice, are the grinding and conscienceless employers whose exactions have made the lives of the seamstresses and shop-girls in their employ miserable, and driven them to barter their honor for bread.

It is true that the criminals and outcasts do not all come from the needy and dependent class. Professional criminals often graduate from comfortable homes, and the perpetrators of great financial crimes and breaches of trust, which have latterly been alarmingly frequent, are necessarily men of influential positions and good education. But, nevertheless, the prevalence of crimes against property among the class who have special advantages and opportunities is no less the direct outcome of the capitalistic system than the vices of the degraded poor.

They are traceable to the wrong ideals of life and worldly success which are held up before the young from their very cradles. The whole tendency of modern education—not merely in the restricted sense of book-learning, but in the broader significance which includes every influence which shapes men's thoughts and contributes to their intellectual and moral development—is to make rascals. The teachings of the fireside and the school, the newspaper and the platform, by inference if not by precept, encourage the spirit of acquisitiveness. The boy from his earliest years is exhorted to "be somebody"—to aspire to "rise in the world." The examples of men who have become wealthy after the customary fashion, by business shrewdness or the acquisition of some profitable monopoly, are continually quoted. Even in the church and the Sunday-school religious precepts are intermingled with worldly-wise counsel. A spurious Christianity inculcates the gospel of greed and grab. Wealth is everywhere honored without reference to the sources of its acquisition so long as its owners can keep clear of the law, while honest poverty is despised. Social position, political honors, public estimation are all dependent on the possession of money or of talents which the owner is willing to devote to the service of capitalism.

Now, under existing conditions, this striving and straining after wealth is perfectly natural. It is wasting breath to reiterate the customary moral and religious truisms, which every one accepts but nobody acts upon, with regard to the vanity of earthly possessions, and the folly of those who make haste to be rich, so long as riches are not merely the passport to every means of distinction and honor, but the only security against the abyss of wretchedness and degradation into which those without other resources than their labor often fall. It would be as effective to preach moderation and altruism to a crowd upon a vessel in danger of sinking, rushing for the boats and fighting for the possession of life-preservers. The intensity of the strife has been vastly increased by popular education, which, by making the masses more intelligent, has made them more capable of looking ahead and anticipating the evils of poverty. The wholly uneducated man seldom concerns himself much about the future ; but even a moderate degree of education, with the increased capacities for observation and reflection which it brings, induces the habit of anticipation. This fear of abject poverty is far from being wholly selfish. It is interwoven with, and derives its strength from, the warmest affections and most powerful emotions of our nature. Many a man who would face unmoved the prospect of an old age of penury and dependence, is daily tortured by anxiety at the thought of the terrible fate which might befall his family should he be suddenly removed by death, or overtaken by sickness or misfortune, rendering him unable to provide for them. In this world of paradoxes and contradictions men's best and worst motives are often inextricably mixed. Could we trace the secret incentives of the actions of many who are apparently hard and selfish, and destitute of kindly sympathies in their relations with their fellows, it would often be found that the over-mastering motive of their lives was to secure wife and children an assured position which should place them above the fear of poverty. It is the possibility of beggary and wretchedness overtaking those near and dear to them which is the great stimulus to money-getting in the case of very many who would not be influenced by love of ease, pleasure, or social distinction, or any of the varied enjoyments and opportunities which riches bring in their train.

What a world of terrible significance there is in the common phrase that a married man has "given hostages to fortune!" Poor Burns realized it to the full when he penned his half-humorous, wholly pathetic apology for accepting the beggarly pittance of an exciseman's position:

> " These movin' things ca'd wives an' weans
> Wad move the very hearts of stanes."

To know that failure in the battle of life brings privation and suffering untold to those of your own flesh and blood, to picture their fate should bereavement cut them off from their sole dependence, to follow them in imagination to the abodes of poverty in the crowded tenement, or up the stifling alley exposed to the most revolting daily associations; to fancy them pleading for the bitter bread of charity, or seeking with unaccustomed fingers to perform the ill-paid drudgery which alone offers the means of existence to the untrained worker; to see them subjected to the slights of fair-weather friends, and the insults and sneers which poverty that has "seen better days" has always to encounter, struggling to maintain their respectability while beset with temptations and surrounded by evil examples—this is the haunting dread which steels the heart and stifles the conscience of many a husband and father in his dealings with the world. Is it any wonder that, with such a peril ever present to the minds of those who exercise ordinary reflection or are capable of a thought beyond the immediate requirements of the passing day, men who have others dependent on their exertions will strain every nerve to acquire a competency, and that the temptation to do so by illicit methods, such as the " borrowing " of trust funds, or even engaging in crooked speculations, appears to them in the light of a providential opportunity.

The current bourgeois morality is the fruitful parent of financial crime. When those who have made enormous fortunes by stock-watering or cornering grain, by the tricks of the exchange or the purchase from venal legislators of immensely valuable public franchises, by land-grabbing or usury, are not treated as criminals, but honored as enterprising citizens, the natural effect is to confuse the moral sense, and to blur the distinction between right and wrong in business matters, otherwise than as it may be preserved by the often uncertain and always erratic and arbitrary line of legality. The volume of unpunishable financial crime is much larger than that of the recognized offenses against law conceived and executed in the same spirit. The changes in the social system, and the tone of public opinion which would either do away with the possibility or remove the main incentives for the one would be equally effective as against the other.

It has been said that "you cannot make men moral by act of Parliament." The phrase has become hackneyed in the mouths of cynics and pessimists, but it embodies at least a half truth which no evolutionist will deny. In a politically, self-governed community, all law, to be effective, must be the outcome and embodiment of a public opinion strong enough to enforce it. It must be the expression of the will, not of a mere temporary accidental majority, but of the deep-seated and matured conviction of the mass. In the present state of public opinion no law, however definite and drastic, however carefully drawn and hedged about with elaborate provisions for its enforcement, could establish a system of social equality and full industrial rights. The people are not prepared for it. What is first needed is a change of their habits of thought, a gradual breaking with bourgeois traditions, and the adoption of the grander, nobler ideal of a social condition in which " all men's good shall be each man's rule," in which poverty and wealth shall be alike unknown, and co-operation shall imply equity of distribution instead of merely associated effort. The vexed questions as to the precise relations of the workers to the state, of the greater or less degree of supervision or control to be exercised by the central authority, and the details of the mechanism of exchange and distribution, may very well be left to solve themselves according to the law of evolution. The present and pressing work is to so direct the current of men's thoughts as to render possible the beginnings of the vast and complicated social changes which are needed for the regeneration of society.

That the change is possible who that has witnessed the overthrow of the slave power and is a spectator of the social revolution now in progress in Britain and Ireland can doubt? in the eyes of some the written constitution of the United States presents an insuperable obstacle. But there are two or three facts in the constitutional history of the country which are significant of tremendous possibilities. No paper constitution, however carefully guarded against innovation, can permanently shape the institutions of a people or prevent their being moulded according to the national genius and requirements.

The framers of the constitution, in their anxiety to avoid giving the people too large a share of power, provided for the election of the president, not by the voters directly, but by electors chosen by the people of each state specially for that purpose. These electors at first exercised an independent freedom of choice, but at a very early stage in the progress of political evolution the people demanded the right of electing the president, and practically nullified the provision entrusting that duty to the electors by pledging them in advance to vote for a particular candidate. Outside of and supplementary to the written constitution grew up the national party convention system, under which bodies entirely unknown to the organic law, assumed the function of selecting the men between whose claims the people on election day decide. An elaborate and highly organized political mechanism has thus been developed which engrosses the real power, while the recognized constitutional officials only exercise a shadowy ministerial duty.

Again, the written constitution makes no provision against

the re-election of a president for any number of successive terms. Here again the unwritten law of precedent and usage supplements the positive enactment. The feeling against a third term in the case of Gen. Grant, as a menace to political freedom and an insidious and perilous innovation upon established custom, could hardly have been stronger had the proposition involved a direct violation of the documentary law.

Note another phase of this curious accretion of usage having all the binding effect of law which has spontaneously grown up around and become incorporated with the constitutional system of the United States. Though, since the transfer of the real electing power from the electoral college to the people, several thousand electors have been entrusted with the duty of casting the formal vote for president with no other guarantee than a pledge of honor that the views of their constituents would be carried out, in no single instance has that pledge been violated. Even in periods of abounding political corruption, when the honor of politicians had become a by-word, when other obligations to constituents or to the country were set at naught, men of the very same class as were trafficking in their political influence for their own pecuniary benefit in other capacities have always religiously observed the trust reposed in them in the matter of recording the vote of those who elected them, for presidential candidates. Even in the notable contest of '76, between Hayes and Tilden, when a single vote would have turned the scale, and millions of money would have been gladly paid for it, no elector showed a disposition to betray his trust.

Now, supposing that the growth of Labor Reform sentiment during the next few years should so change the current of men's ideas that a vital alteration in the relations of capitalism to labor and the abrogation of the various forms of monopoly seemed as urgent as did the securing of power to elect the president, and the ascendancy which wealth has obtained in public affairs appeared as perilous as a presiden-

tial third term; supposing, in short, that the industrial situation assumed the foremost place and party politics became a
secondary consideration, would not the same determination
to assert the national will irrespective of formulas and
artificial restrictions, which has modified the constitution
without formal enactment, result in the development of a
supplementary or extra-constitutional system? Just what
shape it would take it is useless to speculate upon. It might be
a development of the labor bureau system or an outcome of
the proposed boards of arbitration. It might be unconnected
in any degree with the present administrative system, the
product of organization among the toilers gradually taking on
little by little the real governmental power, and leaving but
the semblance and shadow of authority in the hands of the
existing government.

Why is it that a politician chosen as presidential elector keeps
his pledge inviolate, while the same man elected to Congress
or the Senate trades his vote to a monopoly, or becomes a
member of a ring for the purpose of enriching himself at the
people's expense? Simply because he knows that in the
former case the condemnation of public opinion, which would
follow the exercise of his undoubted constitutional right of
absolute freedom of choice, would be so complete and crushing that it would utterly destroy him, while ordinary acts of
corruption are frequently condoned. The most profligate of
politicians would not dare to sell out his party in the matter
of electing a president, however huge the bribe that might be
offered him. If public opinion were as vigilant, as unanimous,
as unmistakably ready to visit swift and sure retribution upon the betrayer of labor's rights, whether he acted within strict
constitutional and legal limits or not, as it is in regard to the
violation of the presidential electors' pledge, how the entire
political situation, in its relations to the industrial system,
would be transformed!

No, you cannot make men moral by act of Parliament, nor
even of Congress; neither can you by paper constitutions prevent the national genius and the popular sense of right from

moulding institutions and finding expression in precedent and usage which modify or supersede the written law. But though the power of law, when confronted by a hostile or indifferent public opinion, may have been over-estimated by some classes of reformers, it is well not to run into the opposite extreme of undervaluing it. Law and public opinion act and react on each other. Every legal enactment in support of a great social reform, even though it merely proves the high-water-mark of a temporary wave of enthusiasm, gives an impetus to the cause. A recoil may take place, but the triumph once achieved is a stimulus to further exertion, and an inducement to perseverance until the end crowns the work. It may fail of the immediate object sought, but it helps in no small degree to educate and ripen public sentiment, even though it may not represent it.

It is precisely this educational influence of legislation which is needed at the present stage of the Labor Reform movement. Any measures now attainable are valuable rather as vantage ground in the contest which must be fought out, inch by inch, for the overthrow of capitalism, as new points of departure, as concessions of the principle for which we are contending, to be one day extended and amplified into the basis for a new social order, rather than for any immediate beneficial result to be expected.

To change the direction of the current is the all-important thing, trusting to the future to give it volume and impetus.

The times are ripe for change. Old things are passing away. The prejudices and dissensions which have long kept apart those who should be united are dying out. Party, and sectarian, and national differences, which have alienated the working classes from each other, are losing their force. The grand idea of the solidarity of labor is dawning upon the minds of the mass. Their thoughts are quickened by the closeness of contact and thoroughness of industrial organization, necessitated by the modern system of industry and commerce. Ideas spread literally with lightning rapidity. Wherever, throughout the broad world, an advance is made by the workers in the struggle for their rights, their brethren elsewhere catch the impulse and are stirred by the inspiration of victory. The Labor Reform movement in America owes much to the Irish Home Rule agitation. Whatever of moral support and material aid the Irish and their friends in America have contributed to the struggling peasantry in Ireland, has been more than repaid by the influence which that agitation has had on the cause at home. The watchword of "the land for the people" has been caught up and re-echoed on this side of the Atlantic, giving the movement the scope and comprehensiveness which it formerly lacked. In our turn we shall repeat history by making American social freedom the exemplar for the Old World nations, just as, in the early days of the Republic, its newly acquired political liberty was the beacon-light of the nations that sat in darkness.

Hitherto, the appeals of Labor Reformers have been mainly addressed to the intelligent self-interest of the working-classes. They have been exhorted to forego the opportunities of temporary personal advantage, which the competitive system offers to those of superior abilities, for the sake of securing the general good. Trade-unionism, in its cruder forms, substituted a class selfishness for the personal selfishness, which is the animating motive under unrestricted competition. Each trade sought to promote its own interests merely. In its later developments, the circle of sympathy and co-operative effort has gradually broadened, as the great truth of the common interest of all workers has become better appreciated. There is much progress still to make in this direction. Many of the selfish, debasing teachings of political economy must be unlearned. In tracing the moral and social development of man we note one unvarying rule—that, in proportion as men become enlightened, they realize that the well-being of the individual depends upon the well-being of the mass.

In a condition of savagery or semi-barbarism, life and property are not secure. Existence is a round of perpetual watchfulness. Every man needs to be continually on the alert and ready to defend himself. Tribal wars, individual

blood-feuds, raids, massacres, and ambuscades are the custom
ary incidents of life.   To be a stranger is to be an enemy.   The
continual sense of danger and the dread of being surprised and
taken at a disadvantage developed a keenness of observation,
a sharpness of sight and hearing, and a fertility of resource
unknown in civilized existence.   As nations have gradually
emerged from barbarism, violence has been repressed; acts
of open physical aggression upon the weak and helpless are no
longer tolerated.   Quarrels are settled by courts and laws, instead of by the sword.   The place of a nation in the scale of
civilization is judged mainly by the extent to which its laws
and institutions afford protection to life and property, and
provide a legal remedy for every acknowledged form of
wrong.   If a murder or a robbery is committed, the whole
community is anxious for the apprehension and punishment
of the criminal, even if the victim be a stranger, without
friends or influence.

Why?

Because every intelligent man knows that in this sphere, at
least, "an injury to one is the concern of all," that prompt-
itude and certainty in the prevention or punishment of crime
committed against others are the best guarantee for his own
safety.   Every one feels that laxity in the enforcement of law
menaces his personal interest.   In a highly civilized society,
feelings of humanity and pity may enter largely into the zeal
shown in bringing the perpetrators of crime to justice, but
the prevailing motive is an enlightened self-interest.

Supposing the attempt were made to impress a marauding
savage chieftain with the advantages of civilized laws against
robbery and murder.   His apparent self-interest would at once
be enlisted against the innovation.   " I am stronger and braver,
and have more followers than my neighbors.   I should be a
fool not to take their cattle and gold-dust when I can, and
kill them if they resist.   Laws against robbery and murder
would be a good thing for the weak and cowardly; not for
me."   This would be the train of reasoning that would
naturally suggest itself to the savage mind.

But, apart from morality altogether, no citizen of a civilized state, except the few utterly reckless and desperate, would deliberately wish to see all law abrogated and the right of the strongest established. The vast majority realize that if life and property were dependent upon the ability of the individual to defend them, no amount of personal superiority, in point of strength or activity, could ever give that degree of security that the law does., and that the privilege of committing aggressions at will upon their weaker neighbors would be no compensation for the continual apprehension and peril of a condition of social anarchy. It would need no argument to convince them of the waste and loss and general ruin which would follow such a reversion to barbarism.

Now, just as in those matters now within the purview of Government, this intelligent, far-sighted selfishness which underlies our present civilization has taken the place of the narrow, purblind selfishness of the savage which looks only at the immediate gratification of his animal propensities, so, in the industrial sphere, the idea of social co-operation will supersede competition. The imagined personal interests of many are enlisted on the side of the existing system. Tried by the standard of a higher enlightenment than is now general, they will be seen to be as thoroughly deceptive as the advantages of a social state in which might makes right. The advantage is real and tangible enough as compared with the position of the weaker, but that is all. As contrasted with the security and prosperity which all might enjoy if the social struggle in which every man's hand is against his neighbor were to give place to harmonious universal effort for the common good, they are delusive and unreal.

To how many thousands who have strained every nerve to become wealthy have riches proved a source of care and anxiety! How many who have plunged into the whirl of stock-gambling, or devoted themselves body and soul to mercantile speculations, have been driven to madness and suicide by the constant strain and worry, the alternations between hope and despair, the brooding over losses, the fierce, feverish excitement of the game! The brilliant financial successes envied by the world are frequently purchased at the price of shattered nerves, wrecked constitutions, and premature old age and decrepitude. When gained, a fortune can only be kept by ceaseless vigilance, and is often only a burden or a Nemesis to its possessor. The bankruptcy records show what an enormously large proportion of those who have money at their command yearly succumb to the stress of competition. All great cities are full of social wrecks and failures—men who began life with ample resources and brilliant prospects, but whose fate illustrates the familiar commonplaces of the moralist as to the uncertainty of riches and the ups and downs of life.

This phase of the subject is customarily presented as a sort of offset to the admitted evils of poverty and an inducement to the poor to be content with their lot. As well might the miserable lives and deaths of tyrants be quoted as a reason why the subjects of the Czar of Russia ought to be satisfied with the system which puts their lives and liberties at the mercy of a capricious despot. That slaveholders live in a continual fear of a servile insurrection, and frequently come to poverty owing to the idleness and unthrift begotten of the system, does not make it any more tolerable for the bondsman, though it does illustrate the workings of the principle of eternal justice. All oppression and injustice inevitably react upon the class which upholds them for their own apparent benefit. Instead of the anxieties and misfortunes attendant upon wealth or the pursuit of wealth being regarded as a compensation for the ills of poverty and a justification of existing inequalities, they afford an additional reason for working for the overthrow of social arrangements under which even the class who think they are benefited by competition are really the losers by it.

The poet Moore, in his series of trenchant political satires entitled "Fables for the Holy Alliance," tells, for the benefit of the despots of Europe, the story of a supposed attempt made by the Mahometan conqueror of Persia to suppress the religion of the Ghebers by extinguishing the sacred fire which was the object of their worship. After other means had failed it was proposed to keep the flames in check by the application of extinguishers, but in the end the extinguishers themselves, being made of combustible material, were ignited, and the flames blazed out more fiercely than ever. The application to the state of European affairs and the cherished methods of repression by standing armies, penal statutes, and the whole machinery of Imperialism, is obvious.

> For even soldiers sometimes think;
> Nay, colonels have been heard to reason;
> And reasoners, whether clad in pink,
> Or red, or blue, are on the brink
> (Nine cases out of ten) of treason.

The fable and its moral are equally applicable to the industrial situation to day. The " colonels " of the garrison of capitalism, leaders of those intellectual forces which have hitherto been depended upon to maintain the existing social order against attack, are beginning to reason ; and in some quarters the extinguishers of the press and the platform—the church and the college—are taking fire. Generous and unselfish spirits like William Morris and H. M. Hyndman, of England, have thrown off the traditions of social caste, and shaken themselves free from the entanglements of self-interest to make the people's cause their own. Labor Reform is not a class question. It appeals to the sympathies and the judgment of every reflecting man who has the welfare of humanity at heart, and apprehends that even-handed justice will surely in the end average every form of social and national wrongdoing. It is the cause of every man who believes in popular liberties and the permanency of Democratic institutions, now menaced by the growth of an oligarchy, of wealth, and weakened by the insidious and corrupting influence of capitalism.

Our politics, literature, and society need the regenerating influence of a great cause. The decline of oratory and poetry and art, the dearth of anything like real leadership in public affairs, the absence of sincerity, simplicity, and manliness, and the prevalence of cynicism and snobbery in the social life of the wealthy and educated class show the need of an up-heaval, which will purify and ennoble the national life by the generous impulses and loftier ideals of the conflict.

The world of society and culture is full of men and women, originally of good purposes and high motives, who have lost faith in themselves and in humanity. On entering life they had set their hearts on a " career." They resolved to achieve something beyond mere money-making. They had ideas above social frivolities and fooleries. It was the dream of their youth to make a name for themselves in literature or art, to become the advocates of some great reform, to do their share in the work of popular enlightenment, to rouse and thrill the apathetic masses by their powerful appeals in speech or writing. They have failed, and disappointment has made them sour and morbid. They have quickly discovered on entering their chosen path that the way to real accomplishment was rough and steep, the reward scant and uncertain ; and under the pressure, perhaps of necessity, perhaps of the influence of a sordid atmosphere, they have gradually sunk to the level of their surroundings. The high aims with which they set out have been forgotten in the struggle for temporary success and social position. The orator who was to have stirred the people by his fearless and forcible presentation of great truths has become the political hack or the quibbling lawyer. The would-be poet or philosopher is a journalist whose pen is at the service of the highest bidder. The aspiring young woman who hoped to do for the oppressed of her own sex what Harriet Beecher Stowe did for the negro has become the leader of a " society " clique. The ardent youths who, when at college, hoped to play leading parts on the stage of life, have developed into club-loungers and dilettanti, eaten up with ennui and discontent, railing at the barrenness and sordidness of the age, and the lack of opportunities for noble and heroic effort. The fashionable culture which gives polish of expres-sion and keen appreciation of literary form, which develops

the tastes and susceptibilities to a refinement bordering upon
effeminacy, which looks backward to past or passing systems
of thought, instead of forward to the future for its inspirations,
finds vent in such lackadaisical whimpering over its vanished
ideals as Matthew Arnold's lamentation.

> Ah, if it *be* past take away
>   At least the restlessness, the pain.
> Be man henceforth no more a prey
>   To these out-dated stings again !
> The nobleness of grief is gone.
> Ah, leave us not the fret alone!
> *   *   *   *   *   *   *
> Achilles ponders in his tent;
>   The kings of modern thought are dumb;
> Silent they are though not content,
>   And wait to see the future come.
> They have the grief men had of yore,
> But they contend and cry no more.

Just think of it ! In this last quarter of the nineteenth
century, when the world is convulsed with the most far-reaching and momentous question in all history—the right of the
people to the means of life ; when popular education and en-
franchisement have stirred the masses with a new impulse, and
men on all sides are questioning the justice of the system that
makes a fraction of society wealthy, while the great majority are doomed to hopeless poverty ; when the ruling forces
are confronted with a growing demand for a readjustment
of the laws which foster this inequality ; when, if ever, all that
is unselfish and thoughtful and heroic and high-minded has
the grandest of opportunities for noble and enduring work
for humanity, the so-called cultured and intellectual class are
bemoaning the emptiness and hollowness of modern life, and
remain sunk in ignominious apathy. Could anything show
more forcibly how the selfishness of capitalism has eaten out
the very heart of modern scholarship and refinement, and
stifled the natural promptings of duty and sympathy which
should rally them with generous enthusiasm to the side of
the struggling poor? 14

The stone which the builders rejected, the same shall become the head of the corner. The influence which shall breathe the breath of life into the dry bones of literature and scholarship must come from below ; from the, as yet, largely inarticulate aspirations, hopes, and strivings of the people after fuller and juster conditions, an ampler life, a more sympathetic, fraternal, and comprehensive interpretation of democracy.

Here and now is the heroic age ! The social atmosphere is surcharged with the electricity of the coming storm. In the issue now presented all for which the pioneers of freedom have fought and its martyrs suffered, converges and culminates. Last and crowning stage of the battle for human rights, what nobler, grander purpose could animate the lover of his kind? what loftier impulse could stir the heart, inspire the brain, nerve the hand, or touch, as with a live coal from the altar of liberty, the lips, than the resolve to do and dare in such a cause ?

Young man ! entering on the world's stage of action, full of high hopes and generous aspirations, and bent upon a career of usefulness which will enable you in dying to leave the world better and brighter for your having lived in it, can you withhold your aid from this movement ? You have, no doubt, often felt your heart thrilled with emotion on reading of the trials and triumphs of the patriots and reformers of bygone times. You in imagination have marched shoeless and ragged and half-starved through the snows of Valley Forge with the patriot army of the Revolution ; you have faced the British bayonets at Bunker Hill, and shared in the triumph at Yorktown. You have listened spell-bound to the eloquence of Patrick Henry, and stood in spirit among the signers of the Declaration of Independence. You have died on the scaffold with John Brown, and confronted with Lloyd Garrison the clamors and menaces of angry mobs, that the slave might be free. You have sprung to arms at the call of Abraham Lincoln, rolled back the tide of rebel victory at Gettysburg, marched with Sherman to the sea, and weltered amid the carnage of the Wilderness. "Ah, had I lived in such times," you have said to yourself, "I too would have been ready to strive, to suffer, to die for freedom. Then, indeed, the intensity of purpose, the joy of conflict and accomplishment, the grand scope of the aims to be achieved would have made life worth living, death worth dying."

Look around you. Seek not inspiration from the past, save as far as its traditions and examples may serve to nurture the firmness of moral fiber, the quenchless ardor and enthusiasm for freedom by which alone the progress of humanity is attained. If in the wrongs and shames of the living, struggling world to-day you find nothing to rouse you to action, if the appeals of the poor and the disinherited for justice strike no responsive chord in your heart, if any coarseness or crudeness, ignorance or perversity on their part repels you, if the supposed requirements of your position, the desire to stand well with "society" or the dread of conventional opinion holds you aloof, then rest assured that in no age and under no circumstances would you have risked means, or life or limb in the cause of the weak against the oppressor. He who does not instinctively take the part of the railroad striker in Chicago, the miner in Pennsylvania, the starving New York seamstress and the rack-rented Connaught peasant, without stopping to inquire whether every means by which redress has been sought has been invariably prudent or justifiable, would have been a time-server and a recreant at any critical stage of the eternal battle of right against might.

Confused issues and wrong-headed methods, the treachery of professed friends and the plausibility of defenses for existing evils, when and where have these been wanting in connection with any great reform movement? What noble cause has not been again and again wounded in the house of its friends, misrepresented by its enemies, outlawed by the respectability and learning and social aristocracy of the land? What worker for the elevation of mankind, however buoyed up to tireless effort by an unshaken trust in the final triumph of right, but must at times feel the reaction of despondency

and be disposed to ask " What good? "   The old, old problem of life, the sphinx-enigma, with destruction as the
penalty of failure to answer it aright!   Let the profounder
insight and firmer faith of the one American poet through
whom the fullest and highest meaning of Democracy has
found utterance give it solution :

O me ! O life—of the questions of these recurring,
Of the endless trains of the faithless, of cities filled with the foolish,
Of myself forever reproach ing myself (for who more foolish than I
    and who more faithless ?)
Of eyes that vainly crave the light—of the objects mean—of the strug-
    gle ever renewed ;
Of the poor results of all—of the plodding and sordid crowds I see
    around me,
Of the empty and useless years of the rest—with the rest me inter-
    twined ;
The question, O me ! so sad recurring—What good amid these, O me,
    O life?

ANSWER.

That you are here—that life exists and identity,
That the powerful play goes on and you will contribute a verse.

THE END.

APPENDIX 1

FOUR ARTICLES WRITTEN FOR 'THE PALLADIUM OF LABOR'

The Coming Struggle, 22 December 1883

Government, 3 January 1885

Education, 17 January 1885

What Might Be, 26 December 1885

THE COMING STRUGGLE

FREEDOM AND MONOPOLY LOCKING HORNS FOR THE DEATH GRAPPLE

Signs of Approaching Revolution

HOW THE MONOPOLISTS HAVE SHUT DOWN THE SAFETY VALVE

WAITING FOR THE EXPLOSION

A Change Coming – Peaceably We Hope – Forcibly We Fear

IT IS MORE THAN PROBABLE that within a very few years this continent will be the scene of one of the most tremendous, popular uprisings ever witnessed in any age or country. Had not the American people been a most law abiding and order-loving community, good natured in the extreme and given to tolerate abuses, instead of taking the trouble to redress them, the long-continued exactions and boundless insolence of the monopolists would long ago have precipitated the inevitable conflict. The forbearance of the nation has been strained almost to the very utmost, and the tension is being steadily increased. The reaction must come before long. Let us indicate a few of the signs of the times characterizing American and to a certain degree Canadian Society, which seem to foretell the coming revolution.

IN THE FIRST PLACE

the people are democratic by instinct, education and training. They have been brought up in the political creed that all were entitled to equal rights and opportunities. The constitution of the United States formulates this as the basic idea of the national government. All their traditions, history and associations embody it as a precious legacy handed down to them from the founders of the Republic. Well, they find by bitter experience that the insidious growth of the monopoly system has robbed the people of their natural rights. The time-honored maxim, 'all men are born free and equal,' is violated on every hand. The political system organized to protect the many in their rights has become a machine for enabling the few to rob them. The bond-holder goes free of taxation on his accumulations while the poor man is taxed on everything he eats and drinks and wears. The money-monopolist is free to manipulate the currency of the country while the ordinary citizen pays him exorbitant tribute. The railroads built with the money of the people have become the means by which a few insatiable capitalists have acquired such a mastery over the labor of every toiler as the lords of feudal times possessed over the vassals who crouched before them. And the public domain, the property of the whole people to which theoretically every man had an equal right, has been stolen by hordes of

LAND-GRABBING CORPORATIONS
or granted for a mere song to individual speculators, through the complicity of traitors sworn to defend the people's rights. America, once the land of promise to the oppressed and downtrodden European people, is such no longer. Her institutions theoretically the best ever framed for the government of mankind have been perverted to become the instruments of oppressions and injustice, because the people have been lacking in the eternal vigilance which is the price of liberty and have looked more to national greatness than to popular freedom.

REVOLUTIONS MOVE SLOWLY.
'But' it may be asked, 'if the people have borne these wrongs quietly for so long what reason is there to suppose that they will not continue to submit to them?' There are several reasons. Revolutions make headway but slowly in their first stages. It was centuries before the common people of France mustered courage to throw off the yoke of the throne and aristocracy. Look at the history of Russia, of Italy, of Ireland and see how the embers of discontent smoulder in men's hearts for generations before they burst out in the flame of revolt. Considering that monopoly has only had full swing in America for a few years it is not at all to be wondered at that agitation against its crimes is a thing of yesterday. Then again the people have in the main been fairly prosperous.

THE NATURAL RESOURCES

of America are so vast, her virgin soil so fruitful, opportunities so
numerous that despite the [spoliation] of monopoly enough remained to render the toiler much more comfortable than elsewhere. But
this condition of things is drawing to a close. Wages are no longer
high, because land is no longer cheap and accessible. The public
domain is well nigh exhausted, yet immigration continues. Every
year hundreds of thousands of immigrants attracted by the traditional reputation of the American Republic as a land where there is
room and work and bread for all, land upon this continent. They can
no longer find the opportunities which formerly abounded of making homes for themselves and acquiring in a few years a comfortable
independence. They crowd into the cities and by their competition
in the labor market cheapen the price of flesh and blood, and drag
the laboring class along with themselves down to industrial serfdom.
The unoccupied public lands were

THE SAFETY-VALVE

of American society. The safety-valve has for years been slowly but
surely closing. It will soon be shut tight. There will be no more land
obtainable excepting on the terms of the monopolists. Hitherto the
most active, enterprising and aspiring spirits have found great vent
for their activities in the Great West. But there is no longer a 'West'
in the sense in which good old Horace Greeley used the word. How
can a man 'grow up with the country' if it is owned by absented
capitalists, drained of its wealth by railroad monopolists, pre-empted
by land-grabbers and villainous speculators? The cities – the overgrown swarming cities – are becoming [congested] by the new arrivals from other lands as well as by the young men of native birth,
who flock to them owing to the locking up of the land by
speculators.

THE IRON LAW OF WAGES

begins to assert itself. The clutch of monopoly closes round the
masses insidiously from every side. The land-grabbers and the railway extortioner drive them into the great centres like cattle to a
slaughter pen. There they are robbed by the capitalistic task-master
who takes advantage of competition to buy his labor in the cheapest
market, plundered by the Shylocks who control the money-market
and keep up the prices of every necessity of life, squeezed by the

landlord who increases rents not in proportion to the value of his services but solely according to the demand, and victimized by a thousand forms of profit-mongering and exploitation. The end it is easy to foresee. The cities are always the centres of revolutionary activity. In the city ideas circulate rapidly. Men are brought into close and frequent contact with each other. They compare notes, exchange opinions and stimulate each other to activity by the enthusiasm begotten of sympathy in a common cause. At the beginning of the century the city population only amounted to 5 per cent of the total population of the United States. According to the last census it was about 22 per cent, or close upon one-quarter of the whole. This fact of itself is full of significance. The masses are rapidly learning the causes of the unfavorable conditions in which they find themselves. They are not like a stolid and apathetic peasant population.

THEY KNOW THEIR RIGHTS,

and they realize just how and by whom they have been robbed of them. In accordance with the tendency of the American character to exhaust all pacific and legal methods to obtain redress before proceeding to extremities they will first try peaceable agitation and legislation. But Labor Reform must come somehow and it is not at all likely that the monopolists will abandon their position without a struggle. It is not at all unlikely that the conflict will result as did the similar

STRUGGLE WITH THE SLAVE POWER

and that when the people resort to constitutional means to strangle monopoly and resume their rights, the monopolists may set law at defiance and strive to overthrow the republic. The rich men of the United States are notoriously hostile to democratic institutions. They would infinitely prefer a despotism under which they would feel secure in their ill-gotten gains and hope to rivet for ever their yoke on the necks of the people. But in one shape or other the conflict cannot be long delayed. Either democracy will kill monopoly or be killed by it. We in Canada have a vital interest in the coming struggle as socially and industrially we are already a part of the American system. The overthrow of capitalistic tyranny across the line means liberty for the toiler here. Our interests are the same as those of American labor. Our aims and aspirations are theirs, our tyrants are their tyrants, and whichever party triumphs in the struggle the result will be felt here for all coming time. Of all questions which appeal to the masses of this country the issue which I have endeavoured to outline is the most momentous in its consequences.

ENJOLRAS

GOVERNMENT!

Social Organization the True Function
of Administration

THE REAL RULERS

Are Not the Politicians but the
Monopolists

THE MONEY POWER

And the Machinery of Production
and Distribution Should Be
Controlled by the Whole
People

SIDE BY SIDE with the system of government, which has hitherto
had its function limited to the preservation of order and the maintenance of national power and dignity, has grown the greater and infinitely more important system of commercial and industrial organization, touching the lives and interests of the people at a thousand
points where government controls them at one. Of gradual and
[insidious] development at first it has latterly grown with wonderful
rapidity, owing to the strides of modern invention. It is no longer
kings, emperors, aristocracies or congresses that sway the destinies of
the nations. It may well be said that 'the kings reign but no longer
govern.' The real rulers are not the puppet princes and jumping jack
statesmen who strut their little hour upon the world's stage, but the
money kings, railroad presidents, and great international speculators
and adventurers who

CONTROL THE MONEY MARKET

and the highways of commerce. Where is the emperor or premier in
Europe that has the power of the Rothschilds? What are American
presidents and congresses but mere tools in the hands of Vanderbilt
and Gould? Every war, every peace, every commercial treaty is
dictated not by the men who do the stage business, and dazzle the
unthinking mob by their displays of regal splendour and court

ceremonials, but by a few shrewd, sharp, long-headed business men, who form the power behind the throne. All the diplomatic flummery and formalism, all the pomp and glitter of imperial state are so much empty sham, behind which the hand of the financier and the representative of huge corporate interests pulls the wires.

THE REAL GOVERNMENT

in our nineteenth century civilization is not the parliamentary or administrative bodies, in the name of which laws are promulgated. It is the industrial and commercial and social organization which governs, which regulates matters by its iron laws that need no popular assent and cannot – as matters now stand – be affected by the vote of those whom they press hardly. LAWS! What law, pray, that can be passed at Ottawa or Toronto has such vital, all-absorbing interest for Labor as the unwritten arbitrary law which says, 'you, wage-slave, have produced us, your master, so much wealth that we are in fact suffering from over-production. Therefore it is decreed that the factory is closed until further notice.' What 'law' duly assented to by the governor-general in full panoply of cocked hat, laced coat, knee breeches and sword is of one-tenth part the importance to the toiler as the silent, informal decrees of landlordism 'whereas the necessities of the public for accommodation have increased, therefore rents are henceforth increased twenty per cent.' Where is the law duly formulated on the statute book in good set terms and legal phraseology that affects the toiling masses like the machination of the speculators who put up the prices of coal and wheat and pork? What are the government taxes to the exactions continually

LEVIED ON INDUSTRY

by the usurer and the landlord and the profit monger and the capitalist?

Just now there is destitution and semi-starvation in the land because of the latest edict of the government – the real government of the monopolists, not the pretentious fraud that amuses itself with stage plays and solemn burlesque – which has decreed that Labor must stint and starve itself to 'restrict production' – which decrees that wages must be reduced and factories shut down and until the surplus stocks are worked off? Who voted for this measure? What political candidate stumped the country promising to support a general measure of 'restricting production' as a cure for the ills of

the body politic? Where, in short, does the idea of self-government
and popular freedom come in if measures of such
LIFE AND DEATH CONSEQUENCE
to the masses of the people can be carried out, not merely without
the people having a voice in them, but without any body even imagining that it is a matter upon which they have a right to be consulted? How utterly paltry and insignificant are the miserable party
issues over which politicians fight and voters spend their time and
breath compared with the questions of work and wages, and freedom to use the natural resources of the earth without being taxed to
maintain a host of drones and leeches! Yet we are told that such
measures as would secure to Labor its rights are 'unpractical.' The
real objection is that they are a great deal too practical for the exploiting classes who are quite willing that the people should amuse
themselves by playing at politics, over-turning and reconstructing
sham governments, while they retain in their hands the real power.

THE SOLUTION OF THE PROBLEM
lies in the extension of the powers and functions of government to
include the organization of industry. The people have in some countries political power, in others they are obtaining it. But what is the
good of it, if it is to be confronted and hemmed in on every side by
the non-political but organized power of monopolies, rings, corporations and the entire social machinery in the hands of landlordism
and capitalism? Where is the benefit to the toiler of a free ballot if
on all live practical bread-and-butter questions he is to be told
'hands off, this is not a political question. This must be left in the
hands of private enterprise. Mustn't interfere with the sacred
RIGHT OF FREE CONTRACT!'

The growth of popular sovereignty should be so dictated as to
breathe the breath of life into the decaying and hollow systems of
government and substitute for their formal parade and ceremonial, a
vital, active interest in matters now considered beyond the scope of
legislative interference. Let government representatives of the whole
people step in and instead of being controlled by the machinery of
capitalism, control it through all its ramifications. In place of the
monopolistic rule which really in the true sense of the word governs
the people by prescribing whether they shall work or not, and how

much they shall receive let us have representative popular recognized government conducted on business principles, doing the same thing not for the profit of a few, but with an eye to the benefit of all. Instead of the monopolist being 'free' to say 'you shall work on my terms or go idle, buy bread on my terms or starve, buy coal on my terms or freeze, rent homes on my terms or become a houseless vagrant,' the people should be

FREE TO ORGANIZE

all these departments of Labor and subsistence through their representatives. Until this freedom can be secured, liberty to the disinherited is a mockery and a delusion. This is the ideal government which Labor Reformers should keep steadily in view. It is only capable of gradual attainment, and may take generations to accomplish, but in the meantime, the legislation which tends to the increase of the sphere of government and the assumption by the state of the powers now in the hands of corporations should be welcomed as initial steps in the right direction.

ENJOLRAS

EDUCATION

Must Follow up and Secure the
Results of Agitation

SOCIAL REVOLUTION

Impossible Until the People are
Imbued with Labor Reform
Principles

MEN WHO ENVY CAPITALISTS

Are not Fit Material to Found a
Better Social State

THE CRYING, URGENT NEED of the Labor Reform movement is the education of the masses who are being drawn into sympathy with it. The work of organization is proceeding as fast as we could wish. Men and women are entering our ranks by tens of thousands. The popular mind everywhere is receptive to our teachings. The oppressions of capitalism are compelling those who never before thought of uniting to protect themselves from its encroachments, to join Labor organizations. The utter futility of strikes, as a means of settling the question of the remuneration of Labor, upon a permanent and equitable basis, is realized as it has never been before, and the workers are asking themselves what better weapons can be furnished from the armory of combination.

THE PHENOMENAL GROWTH
of the Order of the Knights of Labor is attracting many to its ranks by the sheer prestige of success. It is gathering in recruits on every side and the contagion of enthusiasm daily widens the circles of those who sympathize with the efforts to advance the cause of Labor Reform. There is abundance of zeal — we must take care that it is not zeal without knowledge.

Power and ignorance do not go well together. All that has really been done so far is to break ground to obtain a hearing, to get the

Reform that they are prepared to receive new ideas. Admitting a
man into a Labor organization no more makes a Labor Reformer of
him than enlisting a recruit into the army and putting a red coat on
his back and a rifle in his hand makes him a soldier. The instruction
in the one case – the drill and discipline in the other – are necessary
to produce the trained man who can be depended upon in an emergency. To thoroughly assimilate and indoctrinate with sound ideas
the numbers who are now pressing to join the standard of Labor Reform is the most imperative and essential work for some years to
come. The world is not yet ripe for
A SOCIAL REVOLUTION.

Were such a general upheaval as would utterly prostrate the power of
monopoly and put capital under our feet to come now, it would
come too soon, because it would find us unprepared. It is very difficult, in view of the outrages perpetrated by organized capital, the
murderous assaults by its hirelings upon workingmen – the brutal
and ferocious expressions of its subsidized press, the lavish ostentation and riotous waste of the millionaire, and the penury and starvation of the pale and haggard victims of their greed – it is difficult, I
say, in view of these wrongs and shames and outrages, to help sym-
pathizing with the anarchists and dynamiters of the John Most and
Justice Schwab type, who would solve the whole question by an
uprising of the people against their oppressors. If ever a revolution
was justifiable, the wage-slaves who have been robbed, not only of
their natural rights, but of those solemnly guaranteed them by the
constitution which purports to hold
ALL MEN 'FREE AND EQUAL,'
would be perfectly justified in reclaiming those rights by force. But
suppose they did so. Suppose that in the present condition of public
opinion the wage-workers throughout this continent rose as one
man, overcame the police, the military, the Pinkerton murderers,
hung every monopolist to the nearest tree or lamp-post, sent their
palaces up in smoke and confiscated their stolen goods to the public
use, what, so far as the condition of Labor is concerned, would be
the result? Why, simply that a few years later all the evils and abuses
which had provoked the outbreak would again be in full blast. We
should have a new set of millionaires and monopolists created out of
the dominant working class, by the operation of the same conditions

and influences which evolved the existing task masters, and the masses would be no better off than before. The people are not yet sufficiently educated to change the conditions and overthrow the system which breeds monopolists. If the monopolists as a class are worse men than their victims it is the fault of a system under which

THE BASER QUALITIES

of human nature conduce to prosperity while the nobler traits of humanity are often obstacles to success in life. The individuals who have climbed to the pinnacle of fortune over the heads of their fellows, careless of whom they crushed, bleeding to earth, may deserve all that a bloody revolution would bring upon them. But their fate would not of itself alter the conditions and other greedy and unscrupulous men would soon step on over prostrate humanity into their places.

With too many workingmen the millionaire is an object of envy. The only reason they have for hating the system, is because they do not happen to have drawn prizes in the lottery of life. — They desire nothing so much as to be monopolists themselves. 'I only wish I were

AS RICH AS VANDERBILT.'

'Ah, if somebody would die now and leave me a million dollars,' and such expressions which we hear every day from men who profess to be in favor of Labor Reform, show how deeply the virus of Mammon worship has tainted the community.

So long as the great bulk of the people wish and long to be privileged loafers — so long as envy of the fortunate condition of the millionaire rather than hatred of the infernal system which enabled him to become such, inspires the masses we cannot hope for any material gain by either a [peaceable] or a forcible revolution.

Now men are not individually to blame for wishing they were in Vanderbilt's shoes. It is the fault of wrong education — not school education merely, but the teaching of the press and the platform and the whole circle of influences which go towards the formation of opinion.

THE ACQUISITION OF WEALTH

and position at the expense of others has been held up before us all from boyhood as a perfectly natural and laudable ambition. There is all the more necessity therefore for true teachings on the subject, for

the inculcation of right sentiments regarding the matter to counteract the false education which sets up the millionaire as a man to be
admired and envied. We have to create a revolution in public opinion
before we can hope to revolutionize the system. — We have to
change not only men's formally expressed beliefs, but their aspirations and desires — to eradicate the deeprooted selfishness begotten
of competition and instill in its place a love for humanity and a
STRONG SENSE OF JUSTICE.

It is an education of the heart as much as the head that is needed.
There are countless prejudices to be overcome, the lessons taught by
centuries of false education and embodied in a misdirected public
opinion are to be unlearned, and the grand principles of human freedom and equality in the broadest sense — including the equal right
of every man to natural opportunities and resources and his own
earnings — to be inculcated. Not until this work now just begun is
accomplished, can the old order of things give place to the new.

ENJOLRAS

WHAT MIGHT BE.

If the World's Workers were Only Educated and Organized

SOCIAL REORGANIZATION

Universal Democracy and Co-operation — No Wars or Monopolies

A BEAUTIFUL IDEAL
Which Can Never be Realized While Labor is uneducated, Apathetic and Divided

AN AIM TO WORK FOR

By Doing Our Part in Spreading the Light

IT IS PRETTY GENERALLY UNDERSTOOD by this time among those who are interested in Labor Reform that it is a much wider and more comprehensive question than the mere matter of wages or hours — that it includes everything relating to the mental, moral and physical advancement of the worker, and implies a war to the death against every influence which tends to depress the condition of Labor. Yet there are still many whose sympathies are with us to a certain extent who do not realize to the full the ideal which ought steadily to be kept in view — amid temporary defeats and discouragements as the ultimate end and aim of the movement. Just let us think for a while what the effect upon government and society would be supposing the great majority of workingmen everywhere were thoroughly educated in the principles of Labor Reform, and determined at any sacrifice to carry them into effect. Let us picture to ourselves

THE SOCIAL CONDITION

that would result were our ideals realized by the resolute determination of the masses in all civilized lands to use their power for the good of the whole people, instead of letting the selfish few play

upon their prejudices and passions, and rule them for the benefit of
the upper class.

In the first place we should have a universal Democracy – kings
and queens, statesmen and aristocracies, and every form of restriction upon the power of the people in government would disappear. And with them would go all the useless ceremonials of government, all the pomp and parade of state affairs, all the fooleries and
frivolities of courts and parliaments and embassies. The host of titled
and untitled idlers, lords in waiting, ushers of the Black Rock [sic!],
and kindred functionaries who receive life pensions for imaginary
services would be turned out to hustle for an honest living.

THE ENORMOUS EXPENSE

attaching to personal government would be saved, and one source of
taxation cut off. More than this, however, the necessary and legitimate work of administration and legislation would be immensely
cheapened and simplified, by being put upon a business basis. The
governing body of the nation, parliament, congress or whatever it
might be called, would meet without any more nonsense or formality, than a county council and settle right down to the public business. Annual elections would bring the members into closer relations
with their constituents than at present, and any want of fidelity to
the public interest would be promptly punished. All wars between
civilized nations would of course cease. As it is always the working
class who are called on to do the fighting and bear the expense of
war, and the wealthy and aristocratic class who get all the benefit,
educated Labor would soon put an end to the military system. Such
international disputes as might arise would be settled by arbitration.
Standing armies would no longer be necessary, and the principal
cause of heavy taxes and national debts would be got rid of.

MONOPOLIES WOULD GO,

one and all of them. Railroads, telegraphs, steamship lines, insurance
and the issuing of currency would all be in the hands of the government. – Having no military establishment, no court tomfooleries or
red-tape formalities to occupy their attention, the administration
could little by little increase its sphere of action and take out of the
hands of private individuals the public trusts they have so badly
abused. There would be no more waste from unnecessary

competition and no more extortion from the public for the profit of
the Vanderbilts, Goulds and Stephens. These enterprises would not
be run to pay, but to accommodate the public as the Post Office is
now. The [employees] would receive good living wages, and both
industry and commerce would prosper by the change.

ON THE SAME PRINCIPLE

the gas supply, street railways, ferries, telephones and other local
enterprises would be run by the municipalities. — No individual
would be permitted to grow wealthy out of public undertakings.
Land monopoly would also cease. The right of the whole people in
the land would be recognized, and such a tax would be levied on the
occupancy of the soil as would make speculation impossible and render it improfitable [sic] for any one to hold more land than [he]
could actually use. The proper housing of the poor would be one of
the first questions to be considered.

There would be no abject poverty. It would be recognized as part
of the legitimate business of the state to see that every man who was
able and willing to work, should have employment at good wages.
The land tax would place the government in possession of an ample
revenue without any other taxes being necessary — with this parks,
public libraries, colleges, museums, picture galleries, magnificent
public buildings for every purpose of research and recreation could
be constructed.

PAUPERISM WOULD BE UNKNOWN.

Those who were by disease, accident or old age unable to work
would be pensioned not as a charity, but as a right — as their share
of the returns from the common inheritance — the earth. All industry would be co-operative. The interest of the workingmen and
women in the great enterprises of industry and commerce would be
recognized by law — and while organizing capacity, and brain work
received its just return, it would not be permitted as now, to treat
Labor as a mere commodity. And Labor would get the benefit of all
the wonderful discoveries and inventions, such as steam, electricity
and Labor saving machinery in a shortening of the hours of toil by
abolishing much of the useless work caused by the competition and
the waste of war. The really necessary Labor of the world, all men
being workers, could probably be done in three or four hours a day.

By this time, no doubt, the readers who have followed me so far
are ready to exclaim 'utopian!' 'visionary!' 'Altogether wild and
impracticable!' I know it. Look back a little and you will see that I
based the whole picture on the supposition that the great majority
of

THE WORLD'S WORKERS

were educated as to their true interests and resolute in carrying out
their purposes. Nobody can say that the state of things I have endeavoured to outline would not be to the best advantage of Labor —
that we should not gladly welcome such a condition of society were
it possible. Why then is it 'utopian?' — why is it the dream of a
visionary? If it would be for the benefit of the immense majority of
mankind, why cannot it be realized? Why? Simply because the
people who do the world's work, and physically at least have the
immense advantage over all opposing forces

ARE NOT EDUCATED,

— are not self-reliant — are not ready to make sacrifices. There you
have the whole thing in a nutshell. The picture is merely a faint presentation of what might be — what cannot be at present solely because of the blindness, ignorance and want of union among working-
men — but what I trust yet will be when the scales of error, of
misleading education and of temporary self-interest have fallen from
their eyes — so they can see the light.

ENJOLRAS

APPENDIX 2

LABOR REFORM SONGSTER

THE

LABOR REFORM

SONGSTER.

BY PHILLIPS THOMPSON.

––––––––––––

PHILADELPHIA :
JOURNAL OF THE KNIGHTS OF LABOR PRINT.
1892.

INTRODUCTION.

It has been said that a volume of poems, be it large or small, needs no preface, nor do I think that the Labor Reform Songs of Mr. Thompson need one. Yet, inasmuch as I have been asked to pen a few sentences by way of introduction, I gladly do so, and all the more readily that the songs are so timely, coming just when the industrial reform movement on this continent has reached the point when it needs songs, and just such songs as these: songs which will voice and interpret the thoughts which are rousing the masses of America to resistless action.

> Spoke well the Grecian when he said that poems
> Were the high laws that swayed a nation's mind—
> Voices that live on echoes—
> Brief and prophetic proems,
> Opening the great heart-book of human kind!

All movements which have had for their object the uplifting of humanity have been greatly helped by their poets. If it be true that the heart of a nation is dead when its songs are stilled, it is equally true that the vigor, the fervency of any great movement may be accurately measured by the earnestness of its poets and by the enthusiasm with which their songs are welcomed.

It would not be easy to exaggerate the help such a book of songs as this may be to the industrial reform movement. Sung in Assembly-rooms, in Alliances, at meetings of Unions and at public gatherings, they will reach thousands to whom arguments would at first be addressed in vain, and even veterans in the movement will listen to an argument in a better mood for having drank in some familiar truth in the setting of a well-remembered air. I repeat, it would not be easy to exaggerate the helpful influence of such songs as these to a cause like ours.

> One man with a dream at pleasure
> Shall go forth and conquer a crown;
> And one with a new song's measure
> Can trample a kingdom down.

Armed with such songs, we can sing the new gospel of human brotherhood into the hearts of the people.

A. W. WRIGHT,
Editor Journal of the Knights of Labor.

INDEX.

THE LABOR REFORM SONGSTER.

No. 1.

THE BITTER CRY.

From dawn to dark we toil; to earn wealth for oth - ers, The men who reap the spoil For-get we're their brothers, For Mam - mon each impulse of sym - pa - thy smothers, Oh, heed the bit - ter cry of the heart-bro - ken poor! The bit - ter cry, The bit - ter cry, Oh, heed the bit - ter cry of the heart-bro-ken poor.

'Mid Nature's lavish store
  We famish and shiver,
Some tempted evermore
  To cross the dark river,
And vainly we cry: " Is there none to deliver? "
  Oh heed the bitter cry of the down-trodden poor!

    CHORUS.—The bitter cry, etc.

You hold the bounties tight
  With which Heaven supplied us,
And when we ask our right
  You scorn and deride us.
The free air of Heaven is even denied us.
  Oh heed the bitter cry of the down-trodden poor!

    CHORUS.—The bitter cry, etc.

5

'Tis sounding through the earth
  To justice appealing;
Oppressors who from birth
  Have stifled all feeling
Will quake when the thunder of battle is pealing.
  Oh heed the bitter cry of the down-trodden poor!

      CHORUS.—The bitter cry, etc.

When millions hopeless pine
  In dread of starvation,
You lay a powder-mine
  In the heart of the nation
To blow to perdition your civilization.
  Oh heed the bitter cry of the down-trodden poor!

      CHORUS.—The bitter cry, etc.

                —*Phillips Thompson.*

No. 2.

THE MEN WHO WORK.

(Air—"Life on the Ocean Wave.")

Hurrah for the men who work,
  Whatever their trade may be;
Hurrah for the men who wield the pen,
  For those who plow the sea;
And for those who earn their bread
  By the sweat of an honest brow;
Hurrah for the men who dig and delve
  And they who reap and sow!

Hurrah for the sturdy arm,
  Hurrah for the steady will,
Hurrah for the worker's health and strength,
  Hurrah for the worker's skill!
Hurrah for the open heart,
  Hurrah for the noble aim,
Hurrah for the loving, quiet home,
  Hurrah for an honest name!

Hurrah for the men who strive,
 Hurrah for the men who save,
Who sit not down and drink till they drown,
 But struggle and breast the wave.
Hurrah for the men on the land
 And they who are on the sea ;
Hurrah for the men who are bold and brave,
 The good, the true and the free !

—*J. Richardson.*

No. 3. THE PENNSYLVANIA MINER.

Come, lis-ten, fel-low-working-men, my sto-ry, I'll re-late, How work-ers in the

coal-mines fare in Penn-syl-va-nia State; Come, hear a sad sur-viv-or, from be-

side his childrens' graves, And learn how free A-mer-i-cans are treat-ed now as slaves.

Chorus.

They robbed us of our pay, They starved us day by day, They

shot us down on the hill-side brown, And swore our lives a-way.

For years we toiled on patiently—they cut our wages down ;
We struck—they sent the Pinkertons to drive us from the town ;
We held a meeting near the mine, some hasty words were said,
A volley from the Pinkertons laid half-a-dozen dead.

 CHORUS.—They robbed us, etc.

I had a little family, the youngest scarce could creep ;
Next night the hireling ruffian band aroused us out of sleep ;
They battered in our cabin door—we pleaded all in vain—
They turned my wife and children out to perish in the rain.

 CHORUS.—They robbed us, etc.

They died of cold and famine there beneath the open sky,
While pitying neighbors stood around, but all as poor as I;
You never saw such misery—God grant you never may—
The sight is branded on my soul until my dying day.

CHORUS.—They robbed us, etc.

Half-crazed I wandered round the spot, and just beyond the town
I met a dastard Pinkerton and struck the villain down;
My brain was frenzied with the thought of children, friends and wife,
I set my heel upon his throat and trampled out his life.

CHORUS.—They robbed us, etc.

And now I roam an outlawed man, no house or friends have I,
For if the law can track me down I shall be doomed to die;
But very little should I care what may become of me,
If all the land would rise and swear such things no more shall be.

CHORUS.—They robbed us, etc.

—*Phillips Thompson.*

No. 4.   THE POWER OF THOUGHT.

(Air—"*Comin' through the Rye.*")

Not by cannon nor by saber,
    Not by flags unfurled,
Shall we win the rights of labor,
    Shall we free the world.
Thought is stronger far than weapons,
    Who shall stay its course?
It spreads in onward-circling waves
    And ever gathers force.

Hopes may fail us, clouds may lower,
    Comrades may betray,
Crushed beneath the heel of power
    Justice lies to-day.
But every strong and radiant soul,
    Whom once the truth makes free,
Shall send a deathless impulse forth
    To all eternity.

Words of insight, sympathetic,
  Flash from soul to soul,
Of the coming time prophetic,
  Freedom's distant goal.
Kindling with one aspiration,
  Hearts will feel their thrill,
And iron bands be ropes of sand
  Before the people's will.

Right shall rule whene'er we will it,
  All the rest is naught;
"Every bullet has its billet,"
  So has every thought.
When the people wish for freedom,
  None can say them nay,
'Tis slavery of the darkened mind
  Alone which stops the way.

                              —*Phillips Thompson.*

No. 5.   MARCHING TO FREEDOM.
          (Air—"Marching through Georgia.")

Rouse, ye sons of labor all, and rally in your might!
In the Eastern heavens see the dawning of the light,
Fling our banner to the breeze, make ready for the fight,
    Now we are marching to freedom.

CHORUS.

Hurrah! Hurrah! we'll sound the jubilee!
Hurrah! Hurrah! the world shall yet be free!
Sweeping all before us like the billows of the sea,
    As we go marching to freedom!

Long we sat disconsolate with hope of rescue fled,
Gloomy seemed our path before and dark the clouds overhead,
Now the shadows vanish and our doubts and fears are dead,
    Now we are marching to freedom!

CHORUS.—Hurrah! Hurrah! etc.

Frowning high before us see the money-despots' hold,
Built to shield the robbers with their piles of hoarded gold,
By the God above us! we'll no more be bought and sold!
    Now we are marching to freedom!
    Chorus.—Hurrah! Hurrah! etc.

Sound aloud our battle-cry! press onward to the fray!
Right and might are on our side, no more we will delay,
Victory must crown the fight, the world is ours to-day,
    Now we are marching to freedom!
    Chorus.—Hurrah! Hurrah! etc.

—Phillips Thompson.

No. 6.   THE FACTORY SLAVE.

(*Air*—"' *Way Down upon the Swanee River.*")

Toiling amid the smoke and clamor
    From morn till night,
Deafened by noise of wheel and hammer
    Far from the glad sunlight.
Piling up store of wealth for others
    While we grow poor,
Tell me, oh! suffering, toiling brothers,
    How long shall this endure?

Chorus.

All my life is full of sorrow,
    Welcome seems the grave;
Oh when will freedom's bright to-morrow
    Dawn on the factory slave?

Often in search of work we wander,
    Hungry we pine;
While wealth we earn our masters squander,
    Feasting in palace fine.
Hard to behold the pallid faces
    Of wife and child,
Stifled in foul and loathsome places,
    Thoughts fit to drive me wild.
    Chorus.—All my life, etc.

Hard is the lot of honest labor,
  Crushed and oppressed ;
Where each is taught to rob his neighbor,
  Greed steeling every breast.
Each has to freedom, air and earth right,
  Such Heaven gave ;
Rich men have robbed us of our birthright—
  Landless, a man's a slave.

     Chorus.—All my life, etc.

—Phillips Thompson.

No. 7.   THE GRAND LABOR CAUSE.

(*Air*—"*Red, White and Blue.*")

Oh union's the hope of the toiler,
  A pledge of the freedom we crave,
A certain defense from the spoiler,
  Who'd rob us from cradle to grave.
When workers stand shoulder to shoulder
  And firmly insist on just laws,
Each heart will grow stronger and bolder
  To fight for the grand labor cause !

     Chorus.

Three cheers for the grand labor cause !
Three cheers for the grand labor cause !
  Each heart will grow stronger and bolder
To fight for the grand labor cause !

When wealth seeks to rule through the nation
  And crush down the landless and poor,
The ballot's our only salvation
  From wrongs grown too great to endure.
A people united in spirit,
  Who heed neither scorn nor applause,
Will reap the reward that they merit
  In gaining the grand labor cause !

     Chorus.—Three cheers, etc.

Then send round the watchword of union,
    No more shall dissensions betray,
When banded in closest communion
    We move on the tyrants' array.
Bright hopes for the future we'll cherish,
    Free soil, equal rights and just laws,
Like a dog may the miscreant perish
    Who's false to the grand labor cause !

CHORUS.—Three cheers, etc.

—Phillips Thompson.

No. 8.   LONG, LONG AGO.

Where is the free-dom which once we pos-sessed, Long, long a-go,
Long, long a-go? Here in this glo-ri-ous land of the West,
Long, long a-go, Long a-go. Where is the man-hood that
once was our pride? Where is the prom-ise on which we re-lied?
Was it for this that our an-ces-tors died, Long, long a-go, long a-go?

Once men stood equal and scorned to be slaves,
    Long, long ago ; long, long ago.
Hurling their tyrants to infamous graves,
    Long, long ago ; long ago.
Now we are trodden and spurned by the few,
Vassals and serfs to the plutocrat crew,
Fled is the spirit our ancestors knew,
    Long, long ago ; long ago.

Stealthy like wolves have the foul harpy band,
    Long, long ago; long, long ago.
Reft us of liberty, money and land,
    Long, long ago; long ago.
Land-thief and bond-thief have rushed to the spoil,
Fastened their clutch on our dear native soil,
Robbed us of even the freedom to toil,
    Long, long ago ; long ago.

Spirit of freedom ! who once deigned to dower,
    Long, long ago ; long, long ago.
Heroes of old with invincible power,
    Long, long ago ; long ago.
Thrill every heart with the pulse of the free,
Rouse up the nation that yet we may be
Worthy of sires who were guided by thee,
    Long, long ago ; long ago.

—Phillips Thompson.

No. 9.   IN THE REIGN OF JUSTICE.

(Air—"In the Sweet By and By.")

There's a glorious future in store
    When the toil-worn shall rise from the dust,
Then the poor shall be trampled no more
    And mankind to each other be just.

CHORUS.

In the sweet by and by,
When the spirit of justice shall reign,
By and by.
In the sweet by and by,
When the spirit of justice shall reign.

Then the world with new life shall be blessed,
    Oppression shall vanish away,
None shall toil at another's behest
    In the light of that glorious day.

CHORUS.—In the sweet, etc.

In this weltering chaos of night,
  Though the struggle be bitter and long,
Let us still turn our eyes to the light
  And gain strength for the battle with wrong.

CHORUS.—In the sweet, etc.

In the fullness of time it will come
  And our labors the way will prepare,
Though our hearts may be cold in the tomb
  Yet our spirits that rapture will share.

CHORUS.—In the sweet, etc.

—Phillips Thompson.

No. 10.   SPREAD THE LIGHT.
         (*Air—"Hold the Fort."*)

Fellow-toilers, pass the watchword!
  Would you know your powers?
Spread the light! and we shall conquer,
  Then the world is ours.

CHORUS.

  Spread the light! the world is waiting
    For the cheering ray,
  Fraught with promise of the glories
    Of the coming day.

In the conflict of the ages,
  In this thrilling time,
Knowledge is the road to freedom,
  Ignorance is crime.

CHORUS.—Spread the light, etc.

Wolves and vampires in the darkness
  Prey on flesh and blood,
From the radiance of the sunlight
  Flee the hellish brood.

CHORUS.—Spread the light, etc.

Light alone can save the nations,
  Long the spoilers' prey,
Bound and blinded in their prison
  Waiting for the day.

     CHORUS.—Spread the light, etc.

Men who know their rights as freemen
  Ne'er to tyrants cower,
Slaves will rise and burst their fetters
  When they feel their power.

     CHORUS.—Spread the light, etc.

                              —*Phillips Thompson.*

No. 11.   THIRTY CENTS A DAY!
            (*Air—"The Faded Coat of Blue."*)

In a dim-lighted chamber a dying maiden lay,
The tide of her pulses was ebbing fast away ;
In the flush of her youth she was worn with toil and care,
And starvation showed its traces on the features once so fair.

                CHORUS.

No more the work-bell calls the weary one.
Rest, tired wage-slave, in your grave unknown ;
Your feet will no more tread life's thorny, rugged way,
They have murdered you by inches upon thirty cents a day !

From earliest childhood she'd toiled to win her bread;
In hunger and rags, oft she wished that she were dead ;
She knew naught of life's joys or the pleasures wealth can bring,
Or the glory of the woodland in the merry days of spring.

     CHORUS.—No more the work-bell, etc.

By the rich she was tempted to eat the bread of shame,
But her mother dear had taught her to value her good name ;
'Mid want and starvation she waved temptation by,
As she would not sell her honor she in poverty must die.

     CHORUS.—No more the work-bell, etc.

She cried in her fever: " I pray you let me go,
For my work is yet to finish, I cannot leave it so ;
The foreman will curse me and dock my scanty pay,
I am starving amid plenty upon thirty cents a day ! "

CHORUS.—No more the work-bell, etc.

Too late, Christian ladies ! You cannot save her now.
She breathes out her life—see the death-damp on her brow ;
Full soon she'll be sleeping beneath the churchyard clay,
While you smile on those who killed her with their thirty cents a day !

CHORUS.—No more the work-bell, etc.

—Phillips Thompson.

No. 12.   MARCH ! MARCH ! MARCH !
(Air—"Tramp ! Tramp ! Tramp !")

In the crowded scenes of toil, in the workshop and the mine,
    There are those who sigh the weary hours away ;
Not a single ray of hope on their wretched lot to shine,
    Or the promise of a brighter, better day.

CHORUS.

March ! March ! March ! the ranks are forming,
    Cheer up, friends, the time has come,
For the toilers of our land now begin to understand
    Their just rights to comfort, liberty and home.

Where the earth is fresh and fair, in the seats of power and pride,
    Sit the favored few who live by labor's pains ;
Not a wish is unfulfilled, not a luxury denied,
    Though they scorn the toil of which they reap the gains.

CHORUS.—March ! March ! March ! etc.

Shall the many evermore be the vassals of the few,
    And the landlord and the usurer rob the poor ?
If your power you only felt, if your rights you only knew,
    Not another day's oppression you'd endure.

CHORUS.—March ! March ! March ! etc.

So unite in all your strength and make ready for the fight,
 Standing boldly by the cause with heart and hand,
To defy the tyrant foe who has robbed us of our right,
 And assert a freeman's title to the land.

    CHORUS —March ! March ! March ! etc.

—Phillips Thompson.

No. 13.   ONE MORE BATTLE TO FIGHT.

(*Air—"One More River to Cross."*)

The car of progress rolls along,
 One more battle to fight;
The voice of the people is growing strong,
 One more battle to fight.

CHORUS.

One more battle,
 One more battle for freedom;
One more battle,
 One more battle to fight.

Too long have the poor been bought and sold,
 One more battle to fight;
And men bowed down to the shrine of gold,
 One more battle to fight.

    CHORUS.—One more battle, etc.

Too long have the many like me and you,
 One more battle to fight;
Enriched with our labor the wealthy few,
 One more battle to fight.

    CHORUS.—One more battle, etc.

The signal sounds from shore to shore,
 One more battle to fight;
To manhood rise ! Be slaves no more !
 One more battle to fight.

    CHORUS.—One more battle, etc.

We'll teach the world a wiser plan,
  One more battle to fight;
When the little rag-baby becomes a man,
  One more battle to fight.

        CHORUS.—One more battle, etc.

No more shall loafers own the soil,
  One more battle to fight;
Nor bond-thieves fatten on poor men's toil,
  One more battle to fight.

        CHORUS.—One more battle, etc.

Oppression shall perish and freedom reign,
  One more battle to fight;
The people shall come to their own again,
  One more battle to fight.

        CHORUS.—One more battle, etc.

                              —*Phillips Thompson.*

No. 14.   RALLY TO THE POLLS.
              (*Air—"Battle Cry of Freedom."*)

We'll rally to the polls, boys, rally once again,
  Fighting the battle of the people!
If we want to win our rights we must show that we are men,
  Fighting the battle of the people!

                CHORUS.

    Farmer and toiler, join hand in hand;
      Down with the Shylocks, rescue the land!
    As we rally to the polls, boys, rally once again,
      Fighting the battle of the people!

We are coming from the farm and the workshop and the mine,
  Fighting the battle of the people!
The masses are aroused and are falling into line,
  Fighting the battle of the people!

        CHORUS.—Farmer and toiler, etc.

We are bound to make an end of the plutocratic crew,
  Fighting the battle of the people!
And we'll use the freeman's vote as true freemen ought to do,
  Fighting the battle of the people!

     CHORUS.—Farmer and toiler, etc.

We are summoned to the work by the nation's tears and prayers,
  Fighting the battle of the people!
And we'll free her from the clutch of the robber millionaires,
  Fighting the battle of the people!

     CHORUS.—Farmer and toiler, etc.

                      —Phillips Thompson.

No. 15.   ROUSE AND RALLY.

Our patriot sires in days of old Threw off the Briton's sway
Americans were free and bold; Where are their sons to-day?
Our wrongs are greater thousand fold Than were our fathers' then;
Repeat last two lines as refrain.
Then rouse, and rally, by hill and valley, And claim our rights as men.

    Despotic power, oppressive laws,
      Our fathers brave defied,
    And baffled in their country's cause
      The lion in his pride.
    And shall we cower before the wolf,
      The usurer in his den?
    No! Rouse and rally, by hill and valley,
      And claim your rights as men.

The money-kings now rule the land
　　While men of freedom dream,
They crush the poor with iron hand
　　And boast their power supreme.
But liberty will yet revive
　　To bless the land again,
So rouse and rally, by hill and valley,
　　And claim your rights as men.

The broad and fertile plains which stretch
　　Their leagues of golden grain
Enrich some greedy, thievish wretch
　　Who profits by our pain.
Let each true heart resent the wrong
　　With voice and vote and pen,
And rouse and rally, by hill and valley,
　　And claim your rights as men.

　　　　　　　　　　　　—*Phillips Thompson.*

No. 16.   THE MARCH OF THE WORKERS.

(*Air—"John Brown."*)

What is this the sound and rumor? What is this that all men hear,
Like the wind in hollow valleys when the storm is drawing near,
Like the rolling on of ocean in the eventide of fear?
　　　'Tis the people marching on!

CHORUS.

Hark the rolling of the thunder!
Lo the sun! and lo thereunder
Riseth wrath and hope and wonder,
　　And the host comes marching on!

Forth they come from grief and torment, on they wend toward health
　　and mirth;
All the wide world is their dwelling, every corner of the earth;
Buy them, sell them for thy service! Try the bargain what 'tis worth,
　　For the days are marching on!

CHORUS.—Hark the rolling of the thunder, etc.

These are they who build thy houses, weave thy raiment, win thy wheat,
Smooth the rugged, fill the barren, turn the bitter into sweet,
All for thee this day—and ever. What reward for them is meet?
    Till the host comes marching on!

      CHORUS.—Hark the rolling of the thunder, etc.

Many a hundred years passed over have they labored deaf and blind,
Never tidings reached their sorrow, never hope their toil might find;
Now at last they've heard and hear it, and the cry comes down the wind,
    And their feet are marching on!

      CHORUS.—Hark the rolling of the thunder, etc.

Oh ye rich men, hear and tremble, for with words the sound is rife:
"Once for you and death we labored; changed henceforward is the strife.
We are men and we shall battle for the world of men and life,
    And our host is marching on!"

      CHORUS.—Hark the rolling of the thunder, etc.

"On we march, then, we, the workers, and the rumor that ye hear
Is the blended sound of battle and deliverance drawing near,
For the hope of every creature is the banner that we bear,
    And the world is marching on!"

      CHORUS.—Hark the rolling of the thunder, etc.
                        —*William Morris.*

No. 17.   STAND FOR THE RIGHT.
(Air—"Pull for the Shore, Sailor.")

    Hope for the future, toiler, help is at hand;
    Hear ye the battle-cry that rings through the land!
    Dark was your pathway, toiler, through the weary night,
    Put your trust in union and stand for the right!

              CHORUS.

    'Stand for the right, toiler, stand for the right;
    Out of the gloomy midnight into the light!
    Each for the other striving giant wrongs to fight,
    Throw away your selfish aims and stand for the right!

See how the vile oppressor thrives by your pain,
Singly your liberties you strive for in vain ;
Would ye regain your birthright ? firmly unite ;
Battle with monopoly and stand for the right !

    CHORUS.—Stand for the right, etc.

Think of your brothers, toiler, downcast and poor ;
Help them to war against the ills they endure ;
Joined in a common cause there's none can scorn your might,
Rally at the ballot-box and stand for the right !

    CHORUS.—Stand for the right, etc.

Wrongs done to humblest worker, robbed and oppressed,
Surely will soon or late recoil on the rest;
Union's your only safeguard, join to spread the light,
Banded in one brotherhood and stand for the right !

    CHORUS.—Stand for the right, etc.

—Phillips Thompson.

No. 18.　　　AWAKE! BE FREE!
(*Air—"America."*)

Our country, great and grand,
Is known in every land
   As freedom's home.
Yet through man's greed and lust,
Through laws the most unjust,
And from the giant trust,
   Great evils come.

Our liberties are gone,
Justice no more is done
   To faithful toil.
But want and woeful need
From Mammon's reign proceed,
Which hurtful tumults breed
   And freedom spoil.

How long shall we be slaves
And bow to sordid knaves
  Who rob the poor?
Let every man awake
And freedom's weapon take,
The yoke of bondage break,
  And serve no more.

Great God of Liberty!
Through truth that maketh free,
  Make free the land.
Give us to see the light,
Lead us to follow right,
And show that right is might,
  By Thine own hand.

Our country then shall be
A home for brave and free
  And noble men.
No landlord then shall reign
To clutch the toiler's gain,
Our flag without a stain
  Shall wave again.

—H. W. Fuison.

No. 19.   THERE ARE NINETY AND NINE.
(Air—"There Were Ninety and Nine.")

There are ninety and nine who live and die
  In poverty, want and cold,
That one may revel in luxury
  And be wrapped in its silken fold.
The ninety and nine in hovels bare,
The one in a palace with riches rare.

They toil in the fields, the ninety and nine,
  For the fruits of their mother earth;
They delve in the depths of the dusky mine
  And bring its hid treasures forth.
But the wealth released by their sturdy blows
To the hands of the one forever flows.

In the sweat of their brows the desert blooms,
    And the forest before them falls ;
They have builded the walls of humble homes
    And cities with lofty halls.
But the one owns cities and farms and lands,
And the ninety and nine have empty hands.

But the night so dreary and dark and long
    At length will the morning bring,
And over the hills the victors' song
    Of the ninety and nine shall ring,
And echo afar, from zone to zone :
" Rejoice for labor has gained its own ! "

—Selected.

No. 20. THE POOR VOTER ON ELECTION DAY.

(*Air—"Partant pour la Syrie."*)

The proud-est now is but my peer, The high-est not more high; To-day, of all the wea-ry year, A king of men am I; To-day a-like are great and small, the name-less and un-known, My pal-ace is the peo-ple's hall, The bal-lot box my throne, My pal-ace is the peo-ple's hall, The bal-lot box my throne.

Who serves to-day upon the list
    Beside the served shall stand ;
Alike the brown and wrinkled fist,
    The glove and dainty hand !

The rich is level with the poor,
　　The weak is strong to-day;
And sleekest broadcloth counts no more
　　Than homespun frock of gray.

To-day let pomp and vain pretense
　　My stubborn right abide;
I set a plain man's common sense
　　Against a pedant's pride.
To-day shall simple manhood try
　　The strength of gold and land;
The wide world has not wealth to buy
　　The power in my right hand!

While there's a grief to seek redress
　　Or balance to adjust,
Where weighs our living manhood less
　　Than Mammon's vilest dust.
While there's a right to need my vote,
　　A wrong to sweep away,
Up! clouted knee and ragged coat!
　　A man's a man to-day!

　　　　　　　　　—John G. Whittier.

No. 21.　　　　COMING BY AND BY.

(*Air—"Coming By and By."*)

A better day is coming, a morning promised long,
When girded right, with holy might, will overthrow the wrong;
When man shall rise and take his rights, not vainly plead and sigh,
And win the cause of righteous laws and justice by and by.

CHORUS.

Coming by and by, coming by and by!
The better day is coming, the morning draweth nigh,
Coming by and by, coming by and by!
The welcome dawn will hasten on, 'tis coming by and by!

To grind the faces of the poor the rich no more shall dare,
For age and youth will love the truth and spread it everywhere;
No more from want and sorrow will come the hopeless cry,
And strife will cease and perfect peace will flourish by and by.

    CHORUS.—Coming by and by, etc.

O for that welcome dawning, when happiness and peace
Shall bless the land from East to West and suffering shall cease;
This glorious consummation the mourner's tears shall dry,
Then every voice will loud rejoice, it's coming by and by.

    CHORUS.—Coming by and by, etc.

—Selected and Adapted.

No. 22.   THE CALL TO ACTION.

Men who by la - bor have fattened the sor-did ones, Lift up your heads from the dust where you bow,

Know that your birth-rights,tho' heaven-ac-cord-ed ones, Van-ish for ev - er, un - less res - cued now.

Hear ye the trumpet sound, Wake from your sleep profound, Hurling your strength on the insolent foe;

Shake off each ser-vile chain, Stand for your rights again, Vic-to-ry waits but your res - o - lute blow.

How have the arrogant robbers rewarded you?
What can ye show for your toil-broken lives?
Basely the men ye enrich have defrauded you,
    Crushing the hearts of your children and wives.
    Will ye supinely bear
    Wrongs in your dumb despair,
Toiling on abjectly, shackled and blind?
    Choose ye the nobler part,
    Nerving each fainting heart,
Bravely to fight in the cause of mankind.

Rise to the height of sublime aspiration,
　Born of the teachings of martyr and sage;
When the fullness of time brings the great consummation,
　Its light will glow radiant on history's page.
　　Down through the ages each,
　　Passes by thought and speech,
Lending an impulse to leaven the whole;
　　Thought is eternal force,
　　Holding its steady course,
Nothing can vanquish the strength of the soul.

—Phillips Thompson.

No. 23.　THE SONG OF THE PROLETAIRE.

Base op - pres - sors! cease your slumbers, Lis - ten　to　a peo - ple's cry; Hark! u-

Allegro.

ni - ted, countless num - bers, Swell the　peal of ag - o - ny.　Lo, from la - bor's

sons and daughters, In the depths of mis - er - y, Like the sound of many waters Comes the cry: " We

ritard.

will be free," Comes the　cry: " We will be free," Comes the　cry: " We will be　free."

Tyrants quail! dawn is breaking,
　Dawn of freedom's glorious day;
Mammon on his throne is quaking,
　Iron bands are giving way.
Statecraft, kingcraft, black oppression
　Cannot bear our scrutiny,
For we've learned the startling lesson
　That if we will, we can be free!
　That if we will, we can be free!
　That if we will, we can be free!

By our own, our children's charta,
　By the fire within our veins,
By each truth-attesting martyr,
　By our tears, our groans and pains,
By our rights by nature given,
　By the voice of liberty,
We proclaim before high Heaven
　That we will, we must be free !
　That we will, we must be free !
　That we will, we must be free !

Winds and waves, the tidings carry ;
　Electra, in your fiery car,
Winged with lightning, do not tarry,
　Bear the news to lands afar.
Bid them sound the thrilling story,
　Louder than the thunder's glee,
That a people ripe for glory
　Are determined to be free !
　Are determined to be free !
　Are determined to be free!

—Tom O'Reilly.

No. 24.　THE MEN OF AULD LANG SYNE.

(Air—"Auld Lang Syne.")

Should old reformers be forgot
　Whose names resplendent shine,
Who stood for right and faltered not
　In the days of auld lang syne.

CHORUS.—In auld lang syne, my dear,
　　In auld lang syne,
　　They lit the spark amid the dark,
　　In the days of auld lang syne.

Brave pioneers in freedom's cause,
　With impulses divine,
Withstood the power of tyrants' laws
　In the days of auld lang syne.

CHORUS.—In auld lang syne, my dear, etc.

They lit the flame of reason's lamp
    And bid its radiance shine,
No despot's wrath the zeal could damp
    Of the men of auld lang syne.

CHORUS.—In auld lang syne, my dear, etc.

In dungeon deep, on gallows tree,
    In battle's foremost line,
They gave their lives for liberty
    In the days of auld lang syne.

CHORUS.—In auld lang syne, my dear, etc.

Then let the dust where heroes sleep
    Be freedom's holiest shrine,
And green the memories will keep
    Of the men of auld lang syne.

CHORUS.—In auld lang syne, my dear, etc.
                                —*Phillips Thompson.*

No. 25.   A MAN'S A MAN FOR A' THAT.

Is there for hon-est pov-er-ty, That hangs his head, and a' that? The cow-ard slave we pass him by, We daur be puir for a' that, For a' that, and a' that our toils ob-scure, and a' that; The rank is but the guin-ea's stamp, The man's the goud for a' that.

What though on hamely fare we dine,
    Wear hodden-gray an' a' that,
Gie fools their silks and knaves their wine—
    A man's a man for a' that,

For a' that and a' that,
   Their tinsel show and a' that;
The honest man, though ne'er sae puir,
   Is king o' men for a' that.

A king can make a belted knight,
   A marquis, duke and a' that;
But an honest man's aboon his might,
   Gude faith, he maunna fa' that!
For a' that and a' that,
   Their dignities and a' that;
The pith o' sense and pride o' worth
   Are higher ranks than a' that.

Then let us pray that come it may,
   As come it will for a' that,
That sense and worth, o'er a' the earth,
   May bear the gree and a' that.
For a' that and a' that—
   It's comin' yet for a' that,
When man to man, the warld o'er,
   Shall brithers be for a' that.   *—Robert Burns.*

No. 26.   WHEN LABOR HAS COME TO ITS OWN.
(Air—"When Johnny Comes Marching Home.")

When labor has come to its own again,
      Hurrah! Hurrah!
We'll live in a real Republic then,
      Hurrah! Hurrah!
Then none shall rule by wealth or birth,
And each shall have his share of earth,
   For we'll all be free when labor has come to its own.

The millionaires will hunt their holes,
      Hurrah! Hurrah!
And drop their cash to save their souls,
      Hurrah! Hurrah!
For we'll clear out Wall Street's robber den,
And burn each bond and mortgage then,
   For we'll all be free when labor has come to its own.

We'll pile them up so that all may see,
  Hurrah! Hurrah!
As high as the Statue of Liberty,
  Hurrah! Hurrah!
And we'll make Jay Gould the torch apply,
To flare the light over sea and sky,
 That shall tell the world that labor has come to its own.

Then all must ply some useful trade,
  Hurrah! Hurrah!
And none their rights will dare invade,
  Hurrah! Hurrah!
And those who honest toil would shirk,
Shall have no bread if they will not work,
 We'll have no more drones when labor has come to its own.

Grim poverty will be unknown,
  Hurrah! Hurrah!
And plenty through the land be strown,
  Hurrah! Hurrah!
Then, farmers and laborers, all combine
And bring the stragglers into line,
 Let us haste the day when labor shall come to its own.
       —*Phillips Thompson.*

No. 27.   LABOR'S HARVEST HOME.
   (Air—"Jesus, We Thy Lambs Would Be.")

  Rouse the sleepers through the land,
  Harvest time is now at hand,
  Fields are white with ripened grain,
  And plenty smiles on hill and plain.

CHORUS.—When the reaping time shall come
   And labor shout the harvest home,
  When the reaping time shall come
   And labor shout the harvest home.

  Those whose toil has given birth
  To the products of the earth
  Claim the right the fruit to keep,
  Nor where they sowed let others reap.

CHORUS.—When the reaping time shall come, etc.

Ye who bar the reapers' way,
Is it sword or sickle—say?
Ere the famished throng can pass
Must they mow you down like grass?

CHORUS.—When the reaping time shall come, etc.

Down with the idler, robber, knave!
Freedom for the toiling slave!
Nevermore shall stealth or sloth
Enjoy the field's luxuriant growth.

CHORUS.—When the reaping time shall come, etc.

Fruit of bitter, toilsome years,
Sown in struggle, pain and tears,
We shall garner when the world
Sees from its place oppression hurled.

CHORUS.—When the reaping time shall come, etc.

—*Phillips Thompson.*

No. 28. UNION ALL ALONG THE LINE

(*Air—"Just Before the Battle, Mother."*)

The crisis darkly looms before us,
    Our chains are being tighter drawn,
The dollar rules the great Republic
    And rights of men are laughed to scorn.

CHORUS.—If our rights we would recover
        We must at the polls combine,
    Our only prospect for the future
        Is union all along the line.

For long we've put our trust in parties
    Whose promises are subtle snares,
They buy and sell the poor like cattle
    To pander to the millionaires.

CHORUS.—If our rights we would recover, etc.

Make a stand against oppression,
    Nor at the feet of Mammon cower,
And let the ballot be our weapon
    To make the tyrant feel our power.

CHORUS.—If our rights we would recover, etc.

Do not heed the party shouters,
　　Striving ever to mislead;
Think rather of your wives and children,
　　The victims of the usurer's greed.

Chorus.—If our rights we would recover, etc.

—Phillips Thompson.

No. 29.　SONG OF THE "LOWER CLASSES."

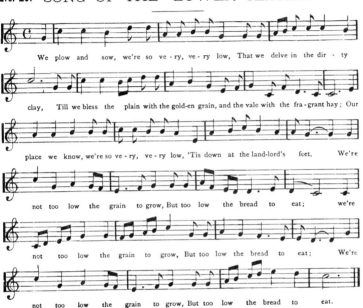

We plow and sow, we're so ve-ry, ve-ry low, That we delve in the dir-ty clay, Till we bless the plain with the gold-en grain, and the vale with the fra-grant hay; Our place we know, we're so ve-ry, ve-ry low, 'Tis down at the land-lord's feet. We're not too low the grain to grow, But too low the bread to eat; we're not too low the grain to grow, But too low the bread to eat; We're not too low the grain to grow, But too low the bread to eat.

Down, down we go, we're so very, very low,
　　To the hell of the deep-sunk mines;
But we gather the proudest gems that glow
　　When the brow of a despot shines;
And whene'er he lacks, upon our backs
　　Fresh loads he deigns to lay;
We're far too low to vote the tax, } *Repeat.*
　　But not too low to pay. }

We're low, we're low—mere rabble we know;
    But at our plastic power
The world at the lordling's feet will glow
    Into palace and church and tower;
Then prostrate fall in the rich man's hall
    And cringe at the rich man's door;
We're not too low to build the wall, } *Repeat.*
    But too low to tread the floor.

We're low, we're low—we're very, very low;
    Yet from our fingers glide
The silken flow and the robes that glow
    Round the limbs of the sons of pride;
And what we get, and what we give,
    We know, and we know our share;
We're not too low the cloth to weave, } *Repeat.*
    But too low the cloth to wear.

                    —*Ernest Jones.*

THE SOCIAL HISTORY OF CANADA
General Editor: Michael Bliss